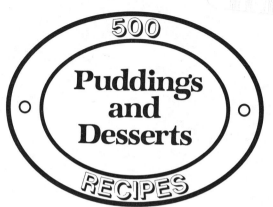

500

Puddings
and
Desserts

RECIPES

500
Puddings and Desserts
RECIPES

Edited by
Norma MacMillan

Notes

All measurements in this book are given in Metric,
Imperial and American. Follow one set only because
they are not interchangeable.

Standard spoon measurements are used in all recipes
1 tablespoon = one 15 ml spoon
1 teaspoon = one 5 ml spoon
All spoon measurements are level.

Ovens and grills (broilers) should be preheated to
the specified temperature or heat setting.

**This edition first published 1981 by
Octopus Books Limited
59 Grosvenor Street
London W1**

© 1981 Octopus Books Limited

ISBN 0 7064 1513 2

Printed in the United States of America

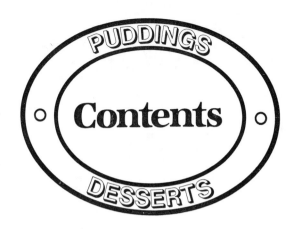

Contents

PUDDINGS

Baked Puddings

DESSERTS

Mincemeat and Apple Roll

Metric/Imperial
350 g/12 oz cooking apples, peeled,
    cored and chopped
75 g/3 oz soft brown sugar
225 g/8 oz mincemeat
225 g/8 oz self-raising flour
pinch of salt
100 g/4 oz shredded suet
120 ml/4 fl oz milk

American
3 cups peeled, cored and chopped
    tart apples
½ cup light brown sugar
⅔ cup mincemeat
2 cups self-rising flour
pinch of salt
½ cup shredded suet
½ cup milk

Mix together the apples, all but 2 tablespoons of the sugar and the mincemeat.

Sift the flour and salt into a bowl. Mix in the suet, then bind to a soft dough with the milk. Roll out the dough to a 30 cm/12 inch square. Spread the apple mixture over the square to within 1 cm/½ inch of the edges. Moisten the edges and roll up fairly tightly, folding in the edges as you go. Place the roll in a greased 25 cm/10 inch sandwich tin (layer cake pan), curving it around to fit. Brush with a little milk and sprinkle with the reserved sugar.

Bake in a preheated moderately hot oven (200°C/400°F, Gas Mark 6) for 25 to 30 minutes or until risen and golden brown. Serve hot with custard sauce (see page 213) or cream.

Serves 4–6

Ricotta Cheese Pudding

Metric/Imperial
dry white breadcrumbs
3 egg yolks
100 g/4 oz sugar
225 g/8 oz ricotta or curd
  cheese
50 g/2 oz ground almonds
2 tablespoons chopped mixed peel
3 tablespoons sultanas
2 teaspoons grated lemon rind
sifted icing sugar

American
dry white breadcrumbs
3 egg yolks
½ cup sugar
1 cup ricotta or small-curd cottage
  cheese
½ cup ground almonds
2 tablespoons chopped candied peel
3 tablespoons seedless white raisins
2 teaspoons grated lemon rind
sifted confectioners' sugar

Coat the bottom and side of a greased 15 cm/6 inch loose-bottomed round cake pan (springform pan) with the breadcrumbs.

Beat the egg yolks with the sugar until pale and fluffy. Mix in the cheese, almonds, peel, sultanas (raisins) and lemon rind. Turn into the pan and smooth the top.

Bake in a preheated moderate oven (180°C/350°F, Gas Mark 4) for about 30 minutes or until firm to the touch.

Leave to cool, then turn out the pudding and sprinkle with icing (confectioners') sugar.
Serves 8

Apricot Noodle Pudding

Metric/Imperial
225 g/8 oz egg noodles
100 g/4 oz soft brown sugar
1 teaspoon ground cinnamon
pinch of grated nutmeg
225 g/8 oz apricots, stoned and
  chopped
40 g/1½ oz butter, melted
3 eggs, separated

American
½ lb egg noodles
⅔ cup light brown sugar
1 teaspoon ground cinnamon
pinch of grated nutmeg
½ lb apricots, pitted and
  chopped
3 tablespoons butter, melted
3 eggs, separated

Cook the noodles in boiling water until tender. Drain well, rinse under cold running water and drain again. Tip the noodles into a mixing bowl and add the sugar, cinnamon, nutmeg, apricots and butter. Lightly beat the egg yolks and stir into the noodle mixture.

Beat the egg whites until stiff and fold into the noodle mixture. Turn into a greased baking dish, cover and bake in a preheated moderate oven (180°C/350°F, Gas Mark 4) for 45 minutes.
Serves 4

Lemon Apple Meringue

Metric/Imperial
750 g/1 ½ lb cooking apples, peeled,
  cored and sliced
3 tablespoons lemon juice
225 g/8 oz caster sugar
25 g/1 oz butter
2 eggs, separated

American
1 ½ lb tart apples, peeled, cored and
  sliced
3 tablespoons lemon juice
1 cup sugar
2 tablespoons butter
2 eggs, separated

Put the apples in a saucepan with the lemon juice, 100 g/4 oz (½ cup) of the sugar and the butter. Cover and cook gently until the apples are pulpy. Remove from the heat and beat in the egg yolks. Pour into a baking dish.

Beat the egg whites until stiff. Add 2 tablespoons of the remaining sugar and continue beating for 1 minute. Fold in the rest of the sugar.

Pile the meringue on top of the apple mixture to cover completely. Bake in a preheated moderate oven (180°C/350°F, Gas Mark 4) for 10 to 15 minutes or until the meringue is firm to the touch and light golden brown.
Serves 4–6

Country Apple Cobbler

Metric/Imperial
1 kg/2 lb cooking apples, peeled,
  cored and sliced
sugar to taste
225 g/8 oz self-raising flour
pinch of salt
75 g/3 oz butter
1 tablespoon caster sugar
2 eggs
½ teaspoon ground cinnamon
2 tablespoons golden syrup

American
2 lb tart apples, peeled, cored and
  sliced
sugar to taste
2 cups self-rising flour
pinch of salt
6 tablespoons butter
1 tablespoon sugar
2 eggs
½ teaspoon ground cinnamon
2 tablespoons light corn syrup

Put the apples in a greased 20 cm/8 inch pie dish and sprinkle with sugar to taste. Add enough water just to cover. Bake in a preheated moderately hot oven (200°C/400°F, Gas Mark 6) for 10 minutes or until the apples are tender.

Meanwhile, sift the flour and salt into a mixing bowl. Stir in the sugar. Rub in the butter until the mixture resembles breadcrumbs. Add the eggs and mix to a soft dough. Break off pieces of the dough and form into scone (biscuit) shapes. Place these on top of the apples. Sprinkle with the cinnamon and drizzle over the syrup.

Return to the oven and bake for 20 minutes until risen and golden.
Serves 6

Peach Cobbler

Metric/Imperial	American
3 tablespoons tapioca	3 tablespoons tapioca
120 ml/4 fl oz milk	½ cup milk
50 g/2 oz sugar	¼ cup sugar
15 g/½ oz butter	1 tablespoon butter
6 peaches, peeled, stoned and sliced	6 peaches, peeled, pitted and sliced
4–6 tablespoons brown sugar	4–6 tablespoons brown sugar
Topping:	**Topping:**
50 g/2 oz butter	4 tablespoons butter
25 g/1 oz sugar	2 tablespoons sugar
1 egg	1 egg
100 g/4 oz plain flour	1 cup all-purpose flour
½ teaspoon cream of tartar	½ teaspoon cream of tartar
pinch of bicarbonate of soda	pinch of baking soda
pinch of salt	pinch of salt
5–6 tablespoons milk	5–6 tablespoons milk

Put the tapioca, milk and sugar in a saucepan and bring to the boil. Simmer for 15 minutes or until the tapioca is tender and the milk has been absorbed. Remove from the heat, stir in the butter and cool.

Spread the tapioca over the bottom of a baking dish and cover with the peach slices. Sprinkle with the brown sugar.

For the topping, cream the butter with the sugar until pale and fluffy. Beat in the egg. Sift in the flour, cream of tartar, soda and salt and mix well, then bind to a soft dough with the milk. Roll out the dough and cut into 6 cm/2½ inch rounds. Arrange the rounds on top of the peaches, slightly overlapping them.

Bake in a preheated moderate oven (180°C/350°F, Gas Mark 4) for 10 to 15 minutes or until the topping is lightly browned and risen. Serve warm.
Serves 6–8

Almond Soufflé Pudding

Metric/Imperial	American
3 eggs, separated	3 eggs, separated
100 g/4 oz caster sugar	½ cup sugar
75 g/3 oz ground almonds	¾ cup ground almonds

Beat the egg yolks and sugar together until pale and thick. Fold in the ground almonds. Beat the egg whites until stiff and fold in. Spoon into a greased 900 ml/1½ pint (1 quart capacity) baking dish.

Bake in a preheated moderate oven (180°C/350°F, Gas Mark 4) for 45 minutes. Serve immediately.
Serves 4

Chocolate Semolina Pudding

Metric/Imperial
600 ml/1 pint milk
2 tablespoons cocoa powder
4 tablespoons sugar
4 tablespoons semolina
½ teaspoon vanilla essence
50 g/2 oz butter
2 eggs, beaten

American
2½ cups milk
2 tablespoons unsweetened cocoa
¼ cup sugar
¼ cup semolina
½ teaspoon vanilla extract
4 tablespoons butter
2 eggs, beaten

Mix a little of the milk with the cocoa and sugar to a smooth paste. Put the rest of the milk in a saucepan and heat until almost boiling. Add the cocoa mixture and the semolina and simmer, stirring well, for 2 minutes.

Remove from the heat and stir in the vanilla, butter and eggs. Pour into a greased baking dish and bake in a preheated moderate oven (180°C/350°F, Gas Mark 4) for 30 minutes.
Serves 4

Variation:
Rich Semolina Pudding: Omit the cocoa powder (unsweetened cocoa) and replace the vanilla with 1 tablespoon grated orange rind. Omit the butter and use only the egg yolks. Add 50 g/2 oz sultanas (⅓ cup seedless white raisins). Bake as above.

Rice Kugel

Metric/Imperial
225 g/8 oz short grain
   rice
50 g/2 oz butter, melted
100 g/4 oz brown sugar
100 g/4 oz sultanas
1 teaspoon ground cinnamon
½ teaspoon ground mixed spice
½ teaspoon grated lemon rind
2 eggs, beaten

American
1 cup plus 2 tablespoons pudding
   rice
4 tablespoons butter, melted
⅔ cup brown sugar
⅔ cup seedless white raisins
1 teaspoon ground cinnamon
½ teaspoon ground allspice
½ teaspoon grated lemon rind
2 eggs, beaten

Cook the rice in boiling salted water until just tender. Drain, if necessary, and rinse in cold water. Mix the rice with the remaining ingredients and pour into a greased 1.2 litre/2 pint (1 quart capacity) baking dish.

Bake in a preheated moderate oven (180°C/350°F, Gas Mark 4) for 1 hour.
Serves 6

Queen of Puddings

Metric/Imperial	American
75 g/3 oz jam	1/4 cup jam
50 g/2 oz fresh breadcrumbs	1 cup fresh breadcrumbs
450 ml/3/4 pint milk	2 cups milk
2 eggs, separated	2 eggs, separated
75 g/3 oz caster sugar	6 tablespoons sugar

Spread 2 tablespoons of the jam on the bottom of a baking dish. Sprinkle over the crumbs.

Heat the milk in a saucepan until it is hot but not boiling. Beat the egg yolks and 2 tablespoons of the sugar together, then gradually stir in the hot milk. Strain this custard over the crumbs in the dish.

Place the dish in a roasting pan containing hot water and bake in a preheated cool oven (150°C/300°F, Gas Mark 2) for about 1 hour until set.

Spread the remaining jam over the custard. Beat the egg whites until stiff and beat in the remaining sugar. Pile on top of the custard.

Return to the oven and increase the temperature to moderately hot (190°C/375°F, Gas Mark 5). Bake for 15 minutes. Serve hot.

Serves 4

Variation:

After spreading the remaining jam over the baked custard, add 2 to 3 tablespoons of diced fresh or canned fruit. Pile the egg whites on top and add another 1 to 2 tablespoons fruit. Bake as above.

Lemon Delicious Pudding

Metric/Imperial	American
3 eggs, separated	3 eggs, separated
100 g/4½ oz sugar	½ cup plus 1 tablespoon sugar
300 ml/½ pint milk	1¼ cups milk
1 tablespoon self-raising flour	1 tablespoon self-rising flour
grated rind and juice of 2 lemons	grated rind and juice of 2 lemons
pinch of salt	pinch of salt

Beat the egg yolks and 100 g/4 oz (½ cup) of the sugar together until thick and light. Gradually beat in the milk, flour, lemon rind and juice and salt.

Beat the egg whites until stiff. Add the rest of the sugar and continue beating for 1 minute. Fold the egg whites into the lemon mixture.

Spoon into a greased baking dish and place in a roasting pan containing hot water. Bake in a preheated moderate oven (160°C/325°F, Gas Mark 3) for 1 hour or until set.

Serves 4

Hazelnut and Chestnut Meringue

Metric/Imperial
500 g/1 lb chestnuts, shelled and
   skinned
500 g/1 lb caster sugar
2 tablespoons rum
150 ml/¼ pint double cream
5 egg whites
100 g/4 oz hazelnuts, finely
   chopped
50 g/2 oz hazelnuts, coarsely
   chopped
chocolate leaves to decorate

American
1 lb chestnuts, shelled and
   skinned
2 cups sugar
2 tablespoons rum
⅔ cup heavy cream
5 egg whites
1 cup finely chopped
   hazelnuts
½ cup coarsely chopped
   hazelnuts
chocolate leaves to decorate

Put the chestnuts in a saucepan, cover with water and bring to the boil. Simmer until tender, then drain and mash. While still hot, stir in 175 g/6 oz (¾ cup) of the sugar and the rum. Cool.

Whip the cream until thick and fold into the chestnut mixture.

Draw a 20 cm/8 inch circle on a sheet of non-stick paper and place it on a baking sheet. Beat the egg whites until stiff, then beat in 150 g/5 oz (⅔ cup) of the remaining sugar. Fold in the rest of the sugar with the finely chopped hazelnuts. Spread about two-thirds of the meringue in the circle on the paper to form the base of the basket, then pipe the remaining meringue around the edge in rosettes.

Dry out the meringue in a preheated very cool oven (120°C/250°F, Gas Mark ½) for 1½ to 2 hours or until firm and just beginning to colour. Cool, then remove from the paper.

Fold the coarsely chopped hazelnuts into the chestnut mixture and pile in the meringue basket. Serve decorated with chocolate leaves.
Serves 6–8

Crème Brûlée

Metric/Imperial
6 egg yolks
75 g/3 oz caster sugar
600 ml/1 pint double cream
1 teaspoon vanilla essence

American
6 egg yolks
6 tablespoons sugar
2½ cups heavy cream
1 teaspoon vanilla extract

Beat together the egg yolks and 2 tablespoons of the sugar. Heat the cream to scalding point, then gradually beat it into the egg yolk mixture. Stir in the vanilla. Pour the mixture into four ovenproof pots.

Place the pots in a roasting pan containing hot water and bake in a preheated moderate oven (160°C/325°F, Gas Mark 3) for 25 to 30 minutes. Cool.

Sprinkle the remaining sugar over the custard and grill (broil) until the sugar has caramelized. Chill before serving.
Serves 4

Meringue Baskets with Jellied Fruit

Metric/Imperial
6 egg whites
pinch of cream of tartar
350 g/12 oz caster sugar
1 tablespoon cornflour, sifted
1 × 425 g/15 oz can tropical fruit salad
1 packet raspberry or strawberry jelly

American
6 egg whites
pinch of cream of tartar
1½ cups sugar
1 tablespoon cornstarch, sifted
1 × 15 oz can tropical fruit salad
1 package raspberry- or strawberry-flavored gelatin

Beat the egg whites with the cream of tartar until stiff. Add 6 tablespoons of the sugar and continue beating for 1 minute. Fold in the remaining sugar and the cornflour (cornstarch).

Put half the meringue mixture into a forcing bag fitted with a plain star nozzle. Pipe 24 rounds 7.5 cm/3 inches in diameter on baking sheets lined with non-stick silicone paper.

Put the rest of the meringue mixture into the forcing bag and pipe rosettes around the edge of each round to make baskets. Dry out in a preheated cool oven (140°C/275°F, Gas Mark 1) for 2 hours or until firm and crisp. Cool.

Drain the fruit salad, reserving the syrup. Make the syrup up to 450 ml/ ¾ pint (2 cups) with water and dissolve the jelly (gelatin) in this liquid. Stir in the fruit salad and chill until set. Fill the meringue baskets with the jellied fruit.
Serves 12

Cherry Custard Pudding

Metric/Imperial
350 g/12 oz fresh cherries, stoned
50 g/2 oz butter
50 g/2 oz caster sugar
grated rind and juice of 1 large lemon
2 eggs, separated
300 ml/½ pint milk
50 g/2 oz self-raising flour, sifted
½ teaspoon ground cinnamon

American
3 cups fresh cherries, pitted
4 tablespoons butter
¼ cup sugar
grated rind and juice of 1 large lemon
2 eggs, separated
1¼ cups milk
½ cup self-rising flour, sifted
½ teaspoon ground cinnamon

Put the cherries in a baking dish. Cream together the butter, sugar and lemon rind until pale and fluffy. Beat in the egg yolks, then the milk, lemon juice, flour and cinnamon. The mixture should have a loose texture.

Beat the egg whites until stiff and fold into the lemon mixture. Spoon on top of the cherries. Place the dish in a roasting pan containing hot water and bake in a preheated moderate oven (180°C/350°F, Gas Mark 4) for 40 to 45 minutes or until the top is set and golden.
Serves 4

Pear Batter Pudding

Metric/Imperial
200 g/7 oz plain flour
pinch of salt
3 eggs, beaten
250 ml/8 fl oz warm milk
2 large pears, peeled, cored and
  sliced
sugar

American
1¼ cups all-purpose flour
pinch of salt
3 eggs, beaten
1 cup warm milk
2 large pears, peeled, cored and
  sliced
sugar

Sift the flour and salt into a bowl. Make a well in the centre and add the eggs. Mix thoroughly, then gradually stir in the milk.

Divide the batter between four greased 10 cm/4 inch diameter straight-sided baking dishes. Lay the pear slices on top. Bake in a preheated hot oven (220°C/425°F, Gas Mark 7) for about 15 minutes or until well risen and firm. Sprinkle with sugar and serve hot.
Serves 4

Variation:
Plum Batter Pudding: Make the batter with 100 g/4 oz (1 cup) flour, pinch of salt, 1 egg and 300 ml/½ pint (1¼ cups) milk. Melt 25 g/1 oz (2 tablespoons) butter in a baking dish and arrange 225 g/8 oz plums, halved and stoned (pitted) on top. Pour over the batter and bake as above for 30 minutes.

Fluffy Meringue Apples

Metric/Imperial	American
275 g/10 oz caster sugar	1¼ cups sugar
150 ml/¼ pint water	⅔ cup water
3 large cooking apples, peeled, halved and cored	3 large tart apples, peeled, halved and cored
2 eggs, separated	2 eggs, separated
2 × 75 g/3 oz packets cream cheese	2 × 3 oz packages cream cheese
25 g/1 oz flaked almonds	¼ cup slivered almonds

Dissolve 100 g/4 oz (½ cup) of the sugar in the water. Bring to the boil and simmer for 1 minute. Add the apple halves and poach until tender.

Remove the apple halves from the syrup and arrange them, hollow sides up, in a baking dish. Pour a little syrup into each apple hollow.

Beat together the egg yolks and 50 g/2 oz (¼ cup) of the remaining sugar. Gradually beat in the cream cheese. Pour over the apples.

Beat the egg whites until stiff. Add 50 g/2 oz (¼ cup) of the remaining sugar and continue beating for 1 minute. Fold in the rest of the sugar. Pile the meringue on the apples, covering them completely. Sprinkle over the almonds.

Bake in a preheated moderate oven (180°C/350°F, Gas Mark 4) for 35 minutes or until the meringue is crisp and light golden brown.

Serves 4–6

Coffee Apple Pudding

Metric/Imperial	American
2 large cooking apples, peeled, cored and chopped	2 large tart apples, peeled, cored and chopped
175 g/6 oz self-raising flour	1½ cups self-rising flour
½ teaspoon ground cinnamon	½ teaspoon ground cinnamon
75 g/3 oz butter	6 tablespoons butter
100 g/4 oz caster sugar	½ cup sugar
2 eggs	2 eggs
1 tablespoon coffee essence	1 tablespoon coffee flavoring

Put the apples in a saucepan with just enough water to cover the bottom of the pan. Cook gently until the apples have pulped.

Sift together the flour and cinnamon. Cream the butter with the sugar until light and fluffy. Beat in the eggs and coffee essence (flavoring), then fold in the flour followed by the apple pulp. Pour into a greased 1.2 litre/2 pint (1 quart capacity) baking dish.

Bake in a preheated moderate oven (180°C/350°F, Gas Mark 4) for 45 minutes or until firm to the touch and golden brown.

Serves 4–6

Apple Brown Betty

Metric/Imperial
500 g/1 lb cooking apples, peeled,
   cored and sliced
2 tablespoons water
about 100 g/4 oz soft brown sugar
100 g/4 oz fresh breadcrumbs
½ teaspoon ground cinnamon
2 tablespoons shredded suet

American
1 lb tart apples, peeled, cored and
   sliced
2 tablespoons water
about ⅔ cup light brown sugar
2 cups fresh breadcrumbs
½ teaspoon ground cinnamon
2 tablespoons shredded suet

Put the apples and water in a saucepan and poach gently until the apples are tender. Sweeten to taste with the sugar, reserving 2 tablespoons.

Mix together the breadcrumbs, cinnamon and the reserved sugar.

Spread half the apples in a greased baking dish and cover with half the crumb mixture. Add the remaining apples and crumb mixture and sprinkle with the suet.

Cover with greased greaseproof (wax) paper or foil and bake in a preheated moderate oven (180°C/350°F, Gas Mark 4) for 30 to 40 minutes. Serve hot with cream or ice cream.

Serves 4

Chocolate Crumble

Metric/Imperial
3 tablespoons cornflour
3 tablespoons chocolate powder
3 tablespoons finely grated orange
   rind
450 ml/¾ pint milk
2 tablespoons orange juice
100 g/4 oz sugar
175 g/6 oz rolled oats
75 g/3 oz butter, softened

American
3 tablespoons cornstarch
3 tablespoons sweetened cocoa
3 tablespoons finely grated orange
   rind
2 cups milk
2 tablespoons orange juice
½ cup sugar
1 cup rolled oats
6 tablespoons butter, softened

Mix the cornflour (cornstarch), chocolate (cocoa) and orange rind to a paste with a little of the milk. Bring the remaining milk to the boil, then gradually stir in the cornflour (cornstarch) mixture with the orange juice. Simmer, stirring, until very thick. Stir in 50 g/2 oz (¼ cup) of the sugar until dissolved, then pour into a baking dish.

Mix the oats, butter and remaining sugar together until crumbly. Spread over the chocolate mixture and bake in a preheated moderate oven (180°C/350°F, Gas Mark 4) for 10 to 15 minutes or until the top is crisp. Cool, then chill well before serving.

Serves 4

Rich Baked Custard

Metric/Imperial	American
6 eggs	6 eggs
600 ml/1 pint milk	2½ cups milk
3 tablespoons caster sugar	3 tablespoons sugar
½ teaspoon vanilla essence	½ teaspoon vanilla extract

Beat the eggs in a bowl. Heat the milk until scalding, then gradually stir into the eggs. Add the sugar and vanilla and strain into a buttered 1 litre/1¾ pint (1 quart capacity) baking dish.

Bake in a preheated cool oven (150°C/300°F, Gas Mark 2) for 1½ hours or until a knife inserted into the centre comes out clean. Cool, then chill.

Serves 4

Variations:

Masked Custard: Carefully turn out the custard onto a serving plate. Cover with whipped cream completely, then decorate with brandy-soaked cherries and chopped toasted almonds.

Light Orange Custard: Mix 2 egg yolks with the grated rind of 1 orange and 25 g/1 oz (2 tablespoons) sugar. Make the juice of the orange up to 300 ml/ ½ pint (1¼ cups) with milk and add to the egg yolk mixture. Beat the 2 egg whites until frothy but not stiff and fold into the orange mixture. Pour into a baking dish and bake in a preheated moderate oven (180°C/350°F, Gas Mark 4), for 1 hour. Serve warm or cold.

Pineapple Soufflé Pudding

Metric/Imperial	American
50 g/2 oz butter	4 tablespoons butter
50 g/2 oz caster sugar	¼ cup sugar
grated rind and juice of 1 lemon	grated rind and juice of 1 lemon
2 eggs, separated	2 eggs, separated
50 g/2 oz self-raising flour	½ cup self-rising flour
175 ml/6 fl oz canned pineapple juice	¾ cup canned pineapple juice

Cream the butter, sugar and lemon rind until pale and fluffy. Beat in the egg yolks. Sift in the flour and fold in. Stir in the pineapple and lemon juices.

Beat the egg whites until stiff and fold into the pineapple mixture. The mixture may look curdled at this stage, but don't worry.

Spoon into a baking dish and place the dish in a roasting pan containing hot water. Bake in a preheated moderate oven (180°C/350°F, Gas Mark 4) for about 40 minutes. The pudding separates during cooking into a sauce layer on the bottom with a light soufflé mixture on top. Serve hot.

Serves 4–6

Rhubarb Pudding

Metric/Imperial
100 g/4 oz self-raising flour
pinch of salt
50 g/2 oz butter
100 g/4 oz sugar
150 ml/¼ pint milk
500 g/1 lb rhubarb, cut into 2.5 cm/
  1 inch pieces
sugar for sprinkling

American
1 cup self-rising flour
pinch of salt
4 tablespoons butter
½ cup sugar
⅔ cup milk
1 lb rhubarb, cut into 1 inch
  pieces
sugar for sprinkling

Sift the flour and salt into a bowl. Rub in the butter until the mixture resembles breadcrumbs. Stir in the sugar, then add the milk to make a thick batter. Fold in the rhubarb.

Pour into a greased 1 litre/1¾ pint (1 quart capacity) baking dish and bake in a preheated moderately hot oven (200°C/400°F, Gas Mark 6) for 30 to 40 minutes.

Sprinkle with sugar before serving.
Serves 4

Variations:

Apple Pudding: Substitute chopped apples for the rhubarb, or half apples and half blackberries.

Rhubarb and Date Pudding: Make a sticky batter with 175 g/6 oz self-raising flour (1½ cups self-rising flour), pinch of salt, 75 g/3 oz (6 tablespoons) butter, 100 g/4 oz (½ cup) sugar, 1 egg and about 6 tablespoons milk. Fold in 225 g/8 oz (about 1½ cups) chopped rhubarb and 100 g/4 oz (¾ cup) chopped dates. Pour into a greased 1.2 litre/2 pint (1 quart capacity) baking dish and place in a roasting pan containing hot water. Bake in a preheated moderate oven (180°C/350°F, Gas Mark 4) for about 1¼ hours.
Serves 4–6

Apple Dumplings with Walnut Sauce

Metric/Imperial
shortcrust pastry made with 350 g/
    12 oz flour
4 large cooking apples, cored
6 tablespoons mincemeat
1 egg, lightly beaten
Sauce:
50 g/2 oz butter
50 g/2 oz brown sugar
1½ tablespoons double cream
50 g/2 oz walnuts, chopped

American
pie pastry made with 3 cups
    flour
4 large tart apples, cored
6 tablespoons mincemeat
1 egg, lightly beaten
Sauce:
4 tablespoons butter
⅓ cup brown sugar
1½ tablespoons heavy cream
½ cup chopped walnuts

Divide the dough into four portions. Roll out each portion to a round large enough to enclose an apple. Place the apples in the centre of the dough rounds and fill the cavities with mincemeat. Wrap the dough around the apples. Moisten the edges with the egg and press to seal.

Place the dumplings on a baking sheet and brush with egg. Bake in a preheated moderately hot oven (200°C/400°F, Gas Mark 6) for 35 minutes.

Meanwhile, for the sauce, melt the butter in a saucepan and stir in the sugar until dissolved. Add the cream and walnuts and heat through gently.

Serve the dumplings hot, with the sauce.
Serves 4

Superman Special

Metric/Imperial
600 ml/1 pint milk
2 tablespoons caster sugar
50 g/2 oz butter
100 g/4 oz cake crumbs
2 eggs, beaten
½ teaspoon vanilla essence
4 tablespoons sultanas

American
2½ cups milk
2 tablespoons sugar
4 tablespoons butter
2 cups cake crumbs
2 eggs, beaten
½ teaspoon vanilla extract
¼ cup seedless white raisins

Put the milk in a saucepan with the sugar and butter and bring to just below boiling point, stirring. Heat for 5 minutes, then stir in the cake crumbs.

Remove from the heat and add the remaining ingredients. Mix well. Pour into a greased baking dish and place in a roasting pan containing hot water. Bake in a preheated moderate oven (180°C/350°F, Gas Mark 4) for 45 minutes. Serve hot or cold.
Serves 4

Bread Pudding

Metric/Imperial	American
100 g/4 oz white bread	6 large slices white bread
40 g/1½ oz sugar	3 tablespoons sugar
50 g/2 oz mixed dried fruit	⅓ cup mixed dried fruit
1 egg	1 egg
40 g/1½ oz butter, melted	3 tablespoons butter, melted
15 g/½ oz chopped mixed peel	2 tablespoons chopped candied peel
½ teaspoon ground mixed spice	½ teaspoon ground allspice
½ teaspoon ground cinnamon	½ teaspoon ground cinnamon
½ teaspoon grated orange rind	½ teaspoon grated orange rind
orange sauce to serve (see page 214)	orange sauce to serve (see page 214)

Soak the bread in cold water, then wring dry. Mash the bread with a fork. Add the remaining ingredients and mix well. Turn into a greased baking dish and bake in a preheated moderately hot oven (200°C/400°F, Gas Mark 6) for 45 minutes. Serve with orange sauce.

Serves 4

Apple Crumb Pudding

Metric/Imperial	American
50 g/2 oz butter	4 tablespoons butter
50 g/2 oz brown sugar	⅓ cup brown sugar
1 tablespoon golden syrup	1 tablespoon light corn syrup
1 teaspoon ground mixed spice	1 teaspoon apple pie spice
225 g/8 oz fresh breadcrumbs	4 cups fresh breadcrumbs
grated rind and juice of 1 lemon	grated rind and juice of 1 lemon
2–3 large cooking apples, peeled, cored and sliced	2–3 large tart apples, peeled, cored and sliced
50 g/2 oz sugar	¼ cup sugar
50 g/2 oz raisins	⅓ cup raisins

Cream the butter with the brown sugar and syrup, then beat in the spice, breadcrumbs and lemon rind. Spread half this mixture over the bottom of a greased baking dish.

Mix together the apples, sugar, raisins and lemon juice and pile in the baking dish. Cover with the rest of the crumb mixture.

Cover the dish and bake in a preheated moderate oven (180°C/350°F, Gas Mark 4) for 1¼ hours.

Uncover the dish and continue baking for 15 minutes or until the top of the pudding is browned.

Serves 4

Apple Charlotte

Metric/Imperial
½ large sandwich loaf, crusts
  removed and thickly sliced
200 g/7 oz unsalted butter
6 tablespoons oil
1.5 kg/3½ lb cooking apples, peeled,
  cored and sliced
juice of 1 lemon
¼ teaspoon ground cinnamon
100 g/4 oz sugar
6 tablespoons apricot jam

American
½ large loaf of white bread, crusts
  removed and thickly sliced
⅞ cup sweet butter
6 tablespoons oil
3½ lb tart apples, peeled, cored and
  sliced
juice of 1 lemon
¼ teaspoon ground cinnamon
½ cup sugar
6 tablespoons apricot jam

Cut out six to eight heart-shaped croûtes with a biscuit (cookie) cutter from
some of the bread slices. Cut the remaining slices into fingers about 1 cm/
½ inch wide and slightly longer than the depth of a 1.8 litre/3 pint (2 quart
capacity) charlotte mould.

Melt 175 g/6 oz (¾ cup) of the butter with the oil in a frying pan. Add the
bread hearts and fingers and fry until golden. Arrange the hearts,
overlapping, in the bottom of the greased charlotte mould and stand most of
the fingers around the side, again overlapping.

Melt the remaining butter in a saucepan. Add the apples, lemon juice and
cinnamon. Cover and cook gently until the apples are pulpy. Stir in the sugar
and jam until well mixed.

Spoon the apple mixture into the mould and cover with the remaining bread
fingers. Bake in a preheated moderately hot oven (190°C/375°F, Gas Mark
5) for 10 to 15 minutes.

Cool slightly, then turn out the charlotte onto a heated serving plate. Serve
hot or chilled.
Serves 4–6

Bread and Butter Pudding

Metric/Imperial
4 thin slices of bread, buttered
50 g/2 oz currants
50 g/2 oz sultanas
50 g/2 oz caster sugar
450 ml/¾ pint milk
3 eggs, beaten
few drops of vanilla essence
grated nutmeg

American
4 thin slices of bread, buttered
⅓ cup currants
⅓ cup seedless white raisins
¼ cup sugar
2 cups milk
3 eggs, beaten
few drops of vanilla extract
grated nutmeg

Cut the bread slices into triangles. Arrange alternate layers of bread triangles, dried fruit and 25 g/1 oz (2 tablespoons) of the sugar in a greased baking dish. Put the remaining sugar in a saucepan with the milk and heat, stirring to dissolve the sugar. Remove from the heat and beat in the eggs and vanilla. Strain into the dish and leave to soak for 30 minutes.

Sprinkle a little nutmeg over the top, then bake in a preheated moderate oven (180°C/350°F, Gas Mark 4) for 45 to 50 minutes or until set and golden.
Serves 4

Orange Marmalade Pudding

Metric/Imperial
100 g/4 oz unsalted butter
100 g/4 oz caster sugar
grated rind and juice of 1 orange
2 eggs, beaten
75 g/3 oz self-raising flour
50 g/2 oz fresh breadcrumbs
100 g/4 oz glacé cherries, chopped
50 g/2 oz candied angelica, chopped
3 tablespoons orange jelly
   marmalade
1 orange, peeled and thinly sliced

American
8 tablespoons (1 stick) sweet butter
½ cup sugar
grated rind and juice of 1 orange
2 eggs, beaten
¾ cup self-rising flour
1 cup fresh breadcrumbs
½ cup chopped candied cherries
¼ cup chopped candied angelica
3 tablespoons orange jelly
   marmalade
1 orange, peeled and thinly sliced

Cream the butter with the sugar and orange rind until light and fluffy. Beat in the eggs. Sift in the flour, add the breadcrumbs and fold all together thoroughly. Stir in the orange juice, cherries and angelica.

Spread the marmalade over the bottom and sides of a 1 kg/2 lb loaf pan and cover with the orange slices, overlapping slightly. Pour in the batter.

Place the loaf pan in a roasting pan containing hot water and bake in a preheated moderately hot oven (200°C/400°F, Gas Mark 6) for 45 minutes.

Turn out to serve, with custard sauce (see page 213) or whipped cream.
Serves 6

Fudge Pudding

Metric/Imperial	American
100 g/4 oz self-raising flour	1 cup self-rising flour
50 g/2 oz caster sugar	¼ cup sugar
2 tablespoons cocoa powder	2 tablespoons unsweetened cocoa
50 g/2 oz blanched almonds, chopped	¼ cup chopped blanched almonds
50 g/2 oz butter, melted	4 tablespoons butter, melted
150 ml/¼ pint milk	⅔ cup milk
¼ teaspoon vanilla essence	¼ teaspoon vanilla extract
Sauce:	**Sauce:**
150 g/5 oz soft brown sugar	⅞ cup light brown sugar
2 tablespoons cocoa powder	2 tablespoons unsweetened cocoa
200 ml/⅓ pint boiling water	1 cup boiling water

Sift the flour into a bowl and stir in the sugar, cocoa and almonds. Make a well in the centre and add the butter, milk and vanilla. Mix well together. Pour into a greased baking dish.

Beat together the sauce ingredients, then pour over the mixture in the baking dish. Bake in a preheated moderate oven (180°C/350°F, Gas Mark 4) for 40 to 45 minutes.

Serves 4

Baked Rice Pudding

Metric/Imperial	American
75 g/3 oz short grain rice	½ cup pudding rice
50 g/2 oz sugar	¼ cup sugar
1.2 litres/2 pints milk	5 cups milk
25 g/1 oz butter	2 tablespoons butter

Put the rice, sugar and milk in a baking dish and dot with the butter. Bake in a preheated cool oven (150°C/300°F, Gas Mark 2) for about 2½ hours. Stir once or twice during the first hour.

Serves 4

Variations:

Caramel-Topped Rice Pudding: Sprinkle a layer of brown sugar over the baked rice pudding and continue baking until it has melted and caramelized.

Deluxe Rice Pudding: Put 50 g/2 oz (⅓ cup) rice in a baking dish with 1 to 2 tablespoons sugar, 600 ml/1 pint (2½ cups) milk, 150 ml/¼ pint single cream (⅔ cup light cream), 2 to 3 tablespoons sultanas (seedless white raisins) and 1 to 2 tablespoons halved glacé (candied) cherries. Bake as above.

Plum and Orange Cobbler

Metric/Imperial
500 g/1 lb Victoria plums, halved and
  stoned
juice of 2 oranges
1 orange, peeled and segmented
3 tablespoons honey
Topping:
225 g/8 oz wholemeal flour
1 teaspoon ground mixed spice
2 teaspoons baking powder
½ teaspoon salt
25 g/1 oz butter
25 g/1 oz soft brown sugar
grated rind of 1 orange
150 ml/¼ pint natural yogurt or milk
milk or beaten egg to glaze

American
1 lb El Dorado or Santa Rosa plums,
  halved and pitted
juice of 2 oranges
1 orange, peeled and segmented
3 tablespoons honey
Topping:
2 cups wholewheat flour
1 teaspoon apple pie spice
2 teaspoons baking powder
½ teaspoon salt
2 tablespoons butter
2½ tablespoons light brown sugar
grated rind of 1 orange
⅔ cup unflavored yogurt or milk
milk or beaten egg to glaze

Put the plums in a baking dish and stir in the orange juice, orange segments and honey.

For the topping, put the flour, spice, baking powder and salt in a bowl. Rub in the butter until the mixture resembles breadcrumbs. Stir in the sugar and orange rind, then bind to a soft dough with the yogurt or milk.

Roll out the dough to about 1 cm/½ inch thick and cut into 8 or 10 rounds using a 4 cm/1½ inch cutter. Arrange the dough rounds around the edge of the baking dish, overlapping them slightly. Brush with milk or beaten egg.

Bake in a preheated hot oven (220°C/425°F, Gas Mark 7) for about 15 minutes or until the topping is risen and browned.
Serves 4

Chocolate Biscuit Mould

Metric/Imperial
175 g/6 oz plain chocolate
450 ml/¾ pint milk
75 g/3 oz digestive biscuits, crushed
1 egg, separated
50 g/2 oz nuts, chopped

American
1 cup semi-sweet chocolate chips
2 cups milk
¾ cup crushed graham crackers
1 egg, separated
½ cup chopped nuts

Melt the chocolate in a heatproof bowl over a pan of hot water or in a double boiler. Gradually stir in the milk, then mix in the crushed biscuits (crackers). Add the egg yolk and cook gently, stirring, until the mixture thickens. Cool.

Beat the egg white until stiff and fold into the chocolate mixture. Spoon into a greased 600 ml/1 pint (2½ cup capacity) mould and place in a roasting pan containing hot water. Bake in a preheated moderately hot oven (190°C/ 375°F, Gas Mark 5) for 45 minutes. Turn out and serve sprinkled with the nuts.
Serves 4

Apple Pan Dowdy

Metric/Imperial
3 large cooking apples, peeled,
  cored and sliced
1–2 tablespoons brown sugar
1–2 tablespoons golden syrup
¼ teaspoon grated nutmeg
½ teaspoon ground cinnamon
Batter:
100 g/4 oz self-raising flour
pinch of salt
75 g/3 oz sugar
1 egg
4 tablespoons milk
50 g/2 oz butter, melted

American
3 large tart apples, peeled, cored
  and sliced
1–2 tablespoons brown sugar
1–2 tablespoons light corn syrup
¼ teaspoon grated nutmeg
½ teaspoon ground cinnamon
Batter:
1 cup self-rising flour
pinch of salt
6 tablespoons sugar
1 egg
¼ cup milk
4 tablespoons butter, melted

Put the apples in a greased baking dish and sprinkle over the brown sugar, syrup and spices. Cover the dish and bake in a preheated moderate oven (180°C/350°F, Gas Mark 4) for 15 to 20 minutes or until nearly soft.

Meanwhile, sift the flour and salt into a mixing bowl. Add 50 g/2 oz (¼ cup) of the sugar with the remaining batter ingredients and mix to a thick batter. Spoon the batter over the apples and sprinkle with the remaining sugar. Continue baking for 30 to 35 minutes.

Turn out the pudding, upside-down, onto a serving dish and serve with cream or ice cream.
Serves 4

Carrot Pudding

Metric/Imperial
50 g/2 oz butter
50 g/2 oz sugar
2 eggs, separated
50 g/2 oz potato flour
1 teaspoon ground cinnamon
225 g/8 oz carrots, grated
1 tablespoon chopped walnuts
4 tablespoons wine
grated rind and juice of 1 lemon
25 g/1 oz dates, stoned and chopped
pinch of salt

American
4 tablespoons butter
¼ cup sugar
2 eggs, separated
½ cup potato starch
1 teaspoon ground cinnamon
2 cups grated carrots
1 tablespoon chopped walnuts
¼ cup wine
grated rind and juice of 1 lemon
3 tablespoons chopped pitted dates
pinch of salt

Cream together the butter and sugar. Beat in the egg yolks. Fold in the potato flour (starch), cinnamon, carrots, walnuts, wine, lemon rind and juice and dates. Beat the egg whites with the salt until stiff and fold into the carrot mixture. Spoon into a greased baking dish.

Bake in a preheated moderate oven (180°C/350°F, Gas Mark 4) for 45 minutes.
Serves 4–5

Plum and Almond Whirls

Metric/Imperial
225 g/8 oz self-raising flour
pinch of salt
100 g/4 oz shredded suet
about 150 ml/¼ pint milk
175 g/6 oz plum jam
25 g/1 oz soft brown sugar
25 g/1 oz flaked almonds

American
2 cups self-rising flour
pinch of salt
½ cup shredded suet
about ⅔ cup milk
½ cup plum jam
2½ tablespoons light brown sugar
¼ cup slivered almonds

Sift the flour and salt into a mixing bowl. Stir in the suet and add enough milk to bind to a soft dough. Turn onto a floured surface and knead lightly. Roll out to a 30 cm/12 inch square.

Spread the jam over the square to within 1 cm/½ inch of the edges. Dampen the edges and roll up tightly, folding in the edges as you go. Cut the roll into 10 or 12 slices and place these, cut sides up, in a greased baking pan.

Bake in a preheated moderately hot oven (200°C/400°F, Gas Mark 6) for 15 minutes. Sprinkle over the brown sugar and almonds and bake for a further 10 minutes.
Serves 4–6

Caramel Custard

Metric/Imperial
Caramel:
100 g/4 oz sugar
2 tablespoons water
Custard:
100 g/4 oz sugar
150 ml/¼ pint water
grated rind of 1 lemon
150 ml/¼ pint milk
6 egg yolks
1 egg

American
Caramel:
½ cup sugar
2 tablespoons water
Custard:
½ cup sugar
⅔ cup water
grated rind of 1 lemon
⅔ cup milk
6 egg yolks
1 egg

To make the caramel, dissolve the sugar in the water, then bring to the boil and boil until the syrup turns golden. Pour the syrup into four dampened, warmed dariole moulds or custard cups.

For the custard, dissolve the sugar in the water. Add the lemon rind. Bring to the boil and boil until the syrup reaches the thread stage (a little cooled syrup will form a thread when drawn between finger and thumb). Cool.

Mix together the milk, egg yolks and egg and gradually beat in the cooled syrup. Strain into the moulds.

Place the moulds in a roasting pan containing hot water and bake in a preheated moderate oven (180°C/350°F, Gas Mark 4) for about 30 minutes or until set.

Allow the custards to cool, then chill for at least 2 hours before turning out.
Serves 4

Variation:
Orange Caramel Custard: Make the caramel and use to line the moulds as above. For the custard, beat 3 eggs with 40 g/1½ oz (3 tablespoons) sugar until pale and fluffy. Beat in 300 ml/½ pint (1¼ cups) orange juice and the finely grated rind of 1 orange. Strain into the moulds and bake as above, for about 1 hour.

Rhubarb Coconut Puff

Metric/Imperial	American
500 g/1 lb rhubarb, sliced	1 lb rhubarb, sliced
sugar to taste	sugar to taste
75 g/3 oz butter	6 tablespoons butter
50 g/2 oz caster sugar	¼ cup sugar
1 egg	1 egg
100 g/4 oz desiccated coconut	1 cup shredded coconut
25 g/1 oz flaked almonds	¼ cup slivered almonds

Put the rhubarb in a saucepan with enough water just to cover the bottom of the pan and sugar to taste and poach until tender.

Cream the butter and sugar together until pale and fluffy. Beat in the egg, then stir in the coconut.

Turn the rhubarb into a greased baking dish and top with the coconut mixture. Level the top. Sprinkle over the almonds.

Bake in a preheated moderately hot oven (190°C/375°F, Gas Mark 5) for 20 minutes or until the top is light golden brown. Serve with whipped cream.
Serves 6

Black Pear Pudding

Metric/Imperial	American
4 pears, peeled, cored and sliced	4 pears, peeled, cored and sliced
100 g/4 oz blackberries	1 cup blackberries
grated rind and juice of 1 lemon	grated rind and juice of 1 lemon
75 g/3 oz soft brown sugar	½ cup light brown sugar
50 g/2 oz butter	4 tablespoons butter
1 egg, beaten	1 egg, beaten
100 g/4 oz wholemeal flour	1 cup wholewheat flour
1 teaspoon ground cinnamon	1 teaspoon ground cinnamon
2 teaspoons baking powder	2 teaspoons baking powder
1 tablespoon milk	1 tablespoon milk

Put the pears and blackberries in a 900 ml/1½ pint (1 quart capacity) baking dish. Sprinkle over the lemon rind and juice and 2 tablespoons of the sugar.

Cream the butter with the remaining sugar until fluffy. Beat in the egg, then mix in the flour, cinnamon, baking powder and milk. Add a little more milk if necessary to give a soft dropping consistency. Spread the batter over the fruit to give a level surface.

Bake in a preheated moderate oven (180°C/350°F, Gas Mark 4) for 45 minutes or until the topping is risen and browned.
Serves 4

Hot Berry Snow

Metric/Imperial
500 g/1 lb mixed red berries
    (strawberries, raspberries,
    redcurrants)
1 tablespoon honey
150 ml/¼ pint natural yogurt
2 eggs, separated
1 tablespoon plain flour
25 g/1 oz ground almonds
2 tablespoons soft brown sugar

American
1 lb mixed red berries
    (strawberries, raspberries,
    redcurrants)
1 tablespoon honey
⅔ cup unflavored yogurt
2 eggs, separated
1 tablespoon all-purpose flour
¼ cup ground almonds
2 tablespoons light brown sugar

Put the berries in a baking dish and spoon over the honey.

Beat together the yogurt, egg yolks, flour and almonds. Beat the egg whites until stiff and fold into the yogurt mixture. Spoon over the berries and sprinkle with the sugar.

Bake in a preheated moderately hot oven (200°C/400°F, Gas Mark 6) for 15 to 20 minutes or until the topping is risen and golden brown.

Serves 4

Norwegian Cream

Metric/Imperial
175 g/6 oz apricot jam
3 eggs
1 tablespoon sugar
few drops of vanilla essence
450 ml/¾ pint milk, warmed
75 g/3 oz plain chocolate, pared into
    curls
300 ml/½ pint double cream

American
½ cup apricot jam
3 eggs
1 tablespoon sugar
few drops of vanilla extract
2 cups milk, warmed
3 squares semi-sweet chocolate,
    pared into curls
1¼ cups heavy cream

Spread the jam over the bottom of a 1.2 litre/2 pint (1 quart capacity) baking dish.

Mix together 2 whole eggs, the yolk of the third egg, the sugar and vanilla. Stir in the milk, then strain the mixture into the dish on top of the jam. Cover the dish with foil and place it in a roasting pan containing hot water. Bake in a preheated moderate oven (160°C/325°F, Gas Mark 3) for 1¾ hours or until set. Cool.

Cover the surface of the custard with about half of the chocolate curls.

Whip the cream until thick. Beat the remaining egg white until stiff and fold into the cream. Pile on top of the chocolate and decorate with the remaining chocolate.

Serves 6

Mexican Chocolate Caramel Custard

Metric/Imperial	American
225 g/8 oz sugar	1 cup sugar
25 g/1 oz plain chocolate	1 square semi-sweet chocolate
250 ml/8 fl oz strong black coffee	1 cup strong black coffee
600 ml/1 pint milk	2½ cups milk
pinch of salt	pinch of salt
1 teaspoon rum	1 teaspoon rum
3 eggs	3 eggs
6 egg yolks	6 egg yolks

Put 100 g/4 oz (½ cup) of the sugar in a heavy pan and cook gently until melted. Bring to the boil and boil until the syrup turns golden. Divide the syrup between six dariole moulds or custard cups and turn the moulds until they are evenly coated.

Put the chocolate and coffee in the blender and grind until smooth. Pour into a saucepan and add the milk, remaining sugar, the salt and rum. Cook, stirring, for 2 to 3 minutes, then allow to cool.

Beat the eggs and egg yolks together and mix in the chocolate mixture. Strain into the moulds. Place the moulds in a roasting pan containing hot water. Cover the moulds with greased greaseproof (wax) paper or foil and bake in a preheated moderate oven (180°C/350°F, Gas Mark 4) for about 45 minutes or until a knife inserted into the centre of the custards comes out clean. Cool, then chill.

Turn out the custards to serve.
Serves 6

Variations:
Nut Caramel Custard: Toast 50 g/2 oz (½ cup) chestnuts, almonds or walnuts and grind the nuts. Omit the chocolate and coffee and increase the milk to 900 ml/1½ pints (3¾ cups), if liked. Add the nuts to the custard after straining.

Pineapple Caramel Custard: Cook 100 g/4 oz (1 cup) chopped fresh pineapple in a little water with sugar to taste until tender. Put into the caramel-coated moulds before adding the custard. Omit the chocolate and coffee and increase the milk to 900 ml/1½ pints (3¾ cups). Use dry sherry instead of rum, if liked.

Catalan Crème Caramel

Metric/Imperial
600 ml/1 pint milk
1 cinnamon stick
grated rind of 1 lemon
6 egg yolks
3 tablespoons cornflour
100 g/4 oz sugar

American
2½ cups milk
1 cinnamon stick
grated rind of 1 lemon
6 egg yolks
3 tablespoons cornstarch
½ cup sugar

Put 450 ml/¾ pint (2 cups) of the milk in a saucepan with the cinnamon stick and lemon rind. Bring to the boil and simmer for 5 minutes.

Beat the egg yolks with 5 tablespoons of the remaining milk. Dissolve the cornflour (cornstarch) in the rest of the milk.

Strain the hot milk into a clean saucepan. Add all but 2 tablespoons of the sugar, the egg yolk mixture and the cornflour (cornstarch). Stir over a very gentle heat until the custard thickens. Pour it into shallow flameproof serving dishes and cool.

When the custard has set, sprinkle over the reserved sugar. Place under a hot grill (broiler) and caramelize the sugar. Chill before serving.
Serves 4

Caramel Queen of Puddings

Metric/Imperial
75 g/3 oz golden syrup
15 g/½ oz butter
300 ml/½ pint milk
50 g/2 oz fresh breadcrumbs
2 eggs, separated
few drops of vanilla essence
50 g/2 oz caster sugar

American
¼ cup light corn syrup
1 tablespoon butter
1¼ cups milk
1 cup fresh breadcrumbs
2 eggs, separated
few drops of vanilla extract
¼ cup sugar

Melt the syrup and butter in a saucepan and cook gently until a deep golden brown. Stir in the milk and bring to the boil, stirring. Remove from the heat and stir in the breadcrumbs. Cool.

Beat in the egg yolks and vanilla. Pour into a greased baking dish and bake in a preheated moderate oven (160°C/325°F, Gas Mark 3) for 30 minutes.

Beat the egg whites until stiff. Add 2 tablespoons of the sugar and continue beating for 1 minute. Fold in the rest of the sugar. Pile the meringue on top of the pudding to cover it completely, then return to a cool oven (140°C/275°F, Gas Mark 1) and bake for a further 30 minutes.
Serves 4

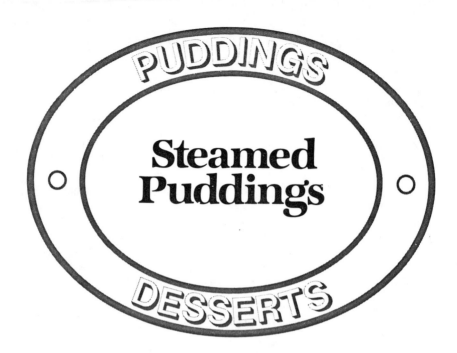

Chocolate Cap Pudding

Metric/Imperial
100 g/4 oz butter
100 g/4 oz caster sugar
2 eggs
175 g/6 oz self-raising flour
pinch of salt
1 tablespoon coffee essence
1 tablespoon cooking chocolate
　drops
100 g/4 oz cooking chocolate

American
8 tablespoons (1 stick) butter
½ cup sugar
2 eggs
1½ cups self-rising flour
pinch of salt
1 tablespoon coffee flavoring
1 tablespoon chocolate
　flavoring
⅔ cup semi-sweet chocolate chips

Cream the butter and sugar together until light and fluffy. Beat in the eggs. Sift over the flour and salt and fold in with the coffee essence (flavoring) and chocolate drops (flavoring). Pour into a greased 1.2 litre/2 pint (1 quart capacity) pudding basin (steaming mold), cover with greased greaseproof (wax) paper or foil and tie on securely. Steam for 2 hours.

　Melt the chocolate in a heatproof bowl over a pan of hot water, or in a double boiler. Turn out the pudding onto a heated plate and pour over the melted chocolate.
Serves 6–8

Steamed Lemon Pudding

Metric/Imperial
100 g/4 oz butter
grated rind and juice of 2 lemons
175 g/6 oz sugar
2 eggs
100 g/4 oz self-raising flour

American
8 tablespoons (1 stick) butter
grated rind and juice of 2 lemons
¾ cup sugar
2 eggs
1 cup self-rising flour

Cream the butter with the lemon rind and 100 g/4 oz (½ cup) of the sugar until pale and fluffy. Beat in the eggs. Sift in the flour and fold in thoroughly.

Mix the remaining sugar with the lemon juice and pour into a greased 1.5 litre/2½ pint (1½ quart capacity) pudding basin (steaming mold). Spoon the batter on top.

Cover with greased greaseproof (wax) paper or foil, tie on securely and steam for 1½ hours.
Serves 4–6

Christmas Pudding

Metric/Imperial
100 g/4 oz currants
225 g/8 oz raisins
225 g/8 oz sultanas
100 g/4 oz chopped mixed peel
4–5 tablespoons brandy
grated rind and juice of 1 small lemon
175 g/6 oz butter
225 g/8 oz brown sugar
2 eggs
225 g/8 oz fresh breadcrumbs
1 tablespoon ground mixed spice
1 teaspoon grated nutmeg

American
⅔ cup currants
1⅓ cups raisins
1⅓ cups seedless white raisins
⅔ cup chopped mixed candied peel
4–5 tablespoons brandy
grated rind and juice of 1 small lemon
12 tablespoons (1½ sticks) butter
1⅓ cups brown sugar
2 eggs
4 cups fresh breadcrumbs
1 tablespoon apple pie spice
1 teaspoon grated nutmeg

Put the dried fruit and peel in a bowl, pour over the brandy, lemon rind and juice and leave to soak overnight.

Cream the butter with the sugar until fluffy. Beat in the eggs, then mix in the breadcrumbs, spices and fruit mixture. Pour into a greased 2.5 litre/4½ pint (2½ quart capacity) pudding basin (steaming mold). Cover with greased greaseproof (wax) paper or foil and tie on securely. Steam for 8 hours.

Cover with fresh greaseproof (wax) paper or foil and store in a cool, dry place. On the day of serving, steam for a further 2 hours.
Serves at least 8

Date and Honey Pudding

Metric/Imperial
65 g/2½ oz butter
40 g/1½ oz sugar
1 tablespoon honey
1 egg
100 g/4 oz self-raising flour
1 tablespoon water
25 g/1 oz dates, stoned and chopped
honey sauce to serve (see page 217)

American
5 tablespoons butter
3 tablespoons sugar
1 tablespoon honey
1 egg
1 cup self-rising flour
1 tablespoon water
3 tablespoons chopped pitted dates
honey sauce to serve (see page 217)

Cream together the butter, sugar and honey. Beat in the egg. Sift in the flour and fold in thoroughly. Add the water if necessary to give a stiff dropping consistency. Fold in the dates.

Spoon into a greased pudding basin (steaming mold) and cover with greased greaseproof (wax) paper or foil. Tie on securely.

Steam for 1½ hours. Serve with honey sauce.

Serves 4

Steamed Jam Pudding

Metric/Imperial
100 g/4 oz self-raising flour
50 g/2 oz shredded suet
50 g/2 oz caster sugar
1 egg, beaten
2 tablespoons milk
6 tablespoons apricot jam, sieved

American
1 cup self-rising flour
¼ cup shredded suet
¼ cup sugar
1 egg, beaten
2 tablespoons milk
6 tablespoons apricot jam, strained

Sift the flour into a bowl and mix in the suet and sugar. Make a well in the centre, add the egg and milk and combine thoroughly.

Put half the jam in the bottom of a 600 ml/1 pint (2½ cup capacity) pudding basin (steaming mold) and pour in the suet mixture. Cover with greased greaseproof (wax) paper or foil and tie on securely. Steam for 1½ hours.

Turn the pudding out of the basin (mold) onto a serving plate and pour over the remaining jam.

Serves 4

Steamed Coconut Pudding

Metric/Imperial
50 g/2 oz desiccated coconut
150 ml/¼ pint milk
100 g/4 oz golden syrup
100 g/4 oz butter
100 g/4 oz caster sugar
2 eggs
175 g/6 oz self-raising flour

American
½ cup shredded coconut
⅔ cup milk
⅓ cup light corn syrup
8 tablespoons (1 stick) butter
½ cup sugar
2 eggs
1 ½ cups self-rising flour

Put the coconut and milk in a bowl and leave to soak. Pour the syrup into the bottom of a greased 1.2 litre/2 pint (1 quart capacity) pudding basin (steaming mold).

Cream the butter and sugar together until light and fluffy. Beat in the eggs. Sift in the flour and fold in, then stir in the coconut milk. Pour into the basin (mold), cover with greased greaseproof (wax) paper or foil and tie on securely. Steam for 2½ hours.
Serves 6

Chocolate and Banana Pudding

Metric/Imperial
100 g/4 oz self-raising flour
15 g/½ oz cocoa powder
100 g/4 oz butter
100 g/4 oz caster sugar
2 eggs, beaten
2 ripe bananas, sliced
chocolate sauce to serve (see page 215)

American
1 cup self-rising flour
2 tablespoons unsweetened cocoa
8 tablespoons (1 stick) butter
½ cup sugar
2 eggs, beaten
2 ripe bananas, sliced
chocolate sauce to serve (see page 215)

Sift the flour and cocoa into a bowl. Cream the butter with the sugar until light and fluffy. Beat in the eggs, then fold in the flour mixture and the bananas. Pour into a greased 900 ml/1½ pint (1 quart capacity) pudding basin (steaming mold), cover with greased greaseproof (wax) paper and foil and tie on securely. Steam for 2 hours.

Serve with chocolate sauce.
Serves 6

Steamed Sultana (Raisin) Pudding

Metric/Imperial
225 g/8 oz butter
225 g/8 oz caster sugar
2 eggs, beaten
100 g/4 oz self-raising flour, sifted
1 teaspoon ground mixed spice
350 g/12 oz sultanas
2 tablespoons chopped walnuts
120 ml/4 fl oz milk

American
16 tablespoons (2 sticks) butter
1 cup sugar
2 eggs, beaten
1 cup self-rising flour, sifted
1 teaspoon apple pie spice
2 cups seedless white raisins
2 tablespoons chopped walnuts
½ cup milk

Cream the butter with the sugar until pale and fluffy. Beat in the eggs, then fold in the flour, spice, sultanas (raisins) and walnuts. Bind with the milk.

Turn into a greased pudding basin (steaming mold) and cover with greased greaseproof (wax) paper or foil. Tie on securely. Steam for 2½ hours.
Serves 4

Steamed Fruit Pudding

Metric/Imperial
1 teaspoon bicarbonate of soda
6 tablespoons cold water
100 g/4 oz butter
300 ml/½ pint hot water
225 g/8 oz sultanas
225 g/8 oz raisins
100 g/4 oz currants
50 g/2 oz glacé cherries, chopped
50 g/2 oz chopped mixed peel
225 g/8 oz plain flour
150 g/5 oz brown sugar
1 teaspoon ground mixed spice
4–5 tablespoons brandy

American
1 teaspoon baking soda
6 tablespoons cold water
8 tablespoons (1 stick) butter
1¼ cups hot water
1⅓ cups seedless white raisins
1⅓ cups raisins
⅔ cup currants
⅓ cup chopped candied cherries
⅓ cup chopped mixed candied peel
2 cups all-purpose flour
⅞ cup brown sugar
1 teaspoon apple pie spice
4–5 tablespoons brandy

Dissolve the soda in the cold water. Melt the butter in the hot water. Put all the ingredients in a bowl and mix well. Leave overnight: the mixture will thicken.

The next day, tip the mixture into a greased 1.8 litre/3 pint (2 quart capacity) pudding basin (steaming mold), cover with greased greaseproof (wax) paper or foil and tie on securely. Steam for 4 hours.
Serves 6

Vanilla Sponge Pudding

Metric/Imperial
100 g/4 oz butter
100 g/4 oz sugar
2 eggs
175 g/6 oz self-raising flour
few drops of vanilla essence
3 tablespoons milk

American
8 tablespoons (1 stick) butter
½ cup sugar
2 eggs
1½ cups self-rising flour
few drops of vanilla extract
3 tablespoons milk

Cream together the butter and sugar until pale and fluffy. Beat in the eggs. Sift in the flour and fold in thoroughly. Add the vanilla and milk and mix well.

Pour into a greased 900 ml/1½ pint (1 quart capacity) pudding basin (steaming mold) and cover with greased greaseproof (wax) paper or foil. Tie on securely. Steam for 1¼ to 1½ hours.

Serve hot with jam or a fruit sauce.

Serves 4–6

Variations:

Chocolate Sponge Pudding: Substitute 2 tablespoons chocolate (sweet cocoa) powder for the same amount of flour and omit the vanilla. Serve with chocolate sauce (see page 215).

Fudge Sponge Pudding: Use 150 g/5 oz (10 tablespoons) butter and 150 g/5 oz (¾ cup + 2 tablespoons) brown sugar instead of the quantities given above, and reduce the milk to 2 tablespoons. Add 1 tablespoon golden (light corn) syrup. Coat the inside of the basin (mold) with a generous layer of butter and brown sugar.

Blackberry and Apple Sponge Pudding: Beat 100 g/4 oz (8 tablespoons) butter with 100 g/4 oz (½ cup) sugar, then beat in 2 eggs and a few drops of vanilla essence (extract). Fold in 175 g/6 oz (1½ cups) sifted self-raising flour. Cook 500 g/1 lb cooking apples, peeled, cored and sliced, until tender. Mix the apples with 225 g/8 oz blackberries, the juice of ½ lemon and 100 g/4 oz (½ cup) sugar. Put 4 tablespoons of the fruit mixture in the bottom of a greased large pudding basin (steaming mold) and pour in the sponge mixture. Cover and steam for 1½ hours. Heat the remaining fruit mixture and serve as a sauce with the pudding.

Serves 4

Suet Pastry

Metric/Imperial
225 g/8 oz self-raising flour
pinch of salt
100 g/4 oz shredded suet
water

American
2 cups self-rising flour
pinch of salt
½ cup shredded suet
water

Sift the flour and salt into a bowl and stir in the suet. Bind to a soft dough with water.

Jam Roly-Poly

Metric/Imperial
100 g/4 oz quantity suet pastry (see
    above – half quantity)
4 tablespoons jam

American
1 cup quantity suet pastry (see
    above – half quantity)
¼ cup jam

Roll out the dough to an oblong about 5 mm/¼ inch thick. Spread over the jam, then roll up. Pinch and seal the edges together well. Wrap loosely in foil.
    Steam for 1½ to 2 hours.
Serves 3–4

Apricot Diplomat

Metric/Imperial
1 × 425 g/15 oz can apricot halves
2–3 trifle sponge cakes, crumbled
3 eggs
50 g/2 oz sugar
450 ml/¾ pint warm milk

American
1 × 15 oz can apricot halves
2 slices of pound cake, crumbled
3 eggs
¼ cup sugar
2 cups warm milk

Drain the apricot halves, reserving the syrup. Arrange half the apricot halves on the bottom of a greased 900 ml/1½ pint (1 quart capacity) pudding basin (steaming mold). Cover with the cake crumbs.
    Beat together the eggs and sugar, then stir in the milk and 3 to 4 tablespoons of the apricot syrup. Pour into the basin (mold). Cover with greased greaseproof (wax) paper or foil and steam for about 1¼ hours, by which time the pudding should be nearly set. Arrange the remaining apricot halves on top and continue steaming for 15 to 20 minutes. Serve hot or cold.
Serves 4

Variations:
Use crushed pineapple or passion fruit instead of apricots.

Ginger Pudding

Metric/Imperial
50 g/2 oz butter
2 tablespoons golden syrup
1 teaspoon ground ginger
½ teaspoon bicarbonate of soda
6 tablespoons lukewarm milk
100 g/4 oz self-raising flour
pinch of salt

American
4 tablespoons butter
2 tablespoons light corn syrup
1 teaspoon ground ginger
½ teaspoon baking soda
6 tablespoons lukewarm milk
1 cup self-rising flour
pinch of salt

Beat the butter, syrup and ginger together until fluffy. Dissolve the soda in the milk, then beat into the ginger mixture. Sift in the flour and salt and mix well. Spoon into a greased pudding basin (steaming mold), cover with greased greaseproof (wax) paper or foil and tie on securely. Steam for 1½ to 2 hours.
Serves 4

Brigade Pudding

Metric/Imperial
225 g/8 oz self-raising flour
pinch of salt
100 g/4 oz shredded suet
2 tablespoons golden syrup
225 g/8 oz mincemeat
3 large cooking apples, peeled,
    cored and grated

American
2 cups self-rising flour
pinch of salt
½ cup shredded suet
2 tablespoons light corn syrup
⅔ cup mincemeat
3 large tart apples, peeled, cored
    and grated

Sift the flour and salt into a mixing bowl. Stir in the suet, then bind to a soft dough with water. Roll out the dough thinly and cut into four rounds: one the size of the bottom of a 1.5 litre/2½ pint (1½ quart capacity) pudding basin (steaming mold), the next a little bigger, the third a little bigger than the second and the last as big as the top of the basin (mold).

Put the syrup in the greased basin (mold) and add the first round of dough. Mix the mincemeat with the apples and spread one-third of this mixture on the dough. Add the next dough round and cover with another third of the mincemeat mixture. Continue in this way, ending with the largest dough round.

Cover with greased greaseproof (wax) paper or foil, tie on securely and steam for 2½ hours.
Serves 6

Guards' Pudding

Metric/Imperial	American
175 g/6 oz fresh breadcrumbs	3 cups fresh breadcrumbs
75 g/3 oz sugar	6 tablespoons sugar
75 g/3 oz butter, melted	6 tablespoons butter, melted
2 eggs, beaten	2 eggs, beaten
4 tablespoons raspberry jam	¼ cup raspberry jam
¼ teaspoon bicarbonate of soda	¼ teaspoon baking soda
1 teaspoon hot water	1 teaspoon hot water

Mix together the breadcrumbs, sugar, butter, eggs and jam. Dissolve the soda in the water and stir into the breadcrumb mixture. Pour into a greased pudding basin (steaming mold) and cover with greased greaseproof (wax) paper or foil. Tie on securely, then steam for 2 hours.

Serves 4

Apple and Blackberry Hat

Metric/Imperial	American
225 g/8 oz quantity suet pastry (see page 38)	2 cup quantity suet pastry (see page 38)
500 g/1 lb cooking apples, peeled, cored and sliced	1 lb tart apples, peeled, cored and sliced
225 g/8 oz blackberries	½ lb blackberries
50 g/2 oz sugar	¼ cup sugar

Roll out two-thirds of the dough to about 5 mm/¼ inch thick and use to line a greased 1.2 litre/2 pint (1 quart capacity) pudding basin (steaming mold). Fill with the apples and blackberries, layering the fruits and sprinkling the layers with the sugar.

Roll out the remaining dough and place on top. Pinch the edges together to seal.

Cover with greased greaseproof (wax) paper or foil and tie on securely. Steam for 3 hours.

Serves 4

Variations:

Fill the suet crust with peeled, cored and sliced pears and chopped walnuts and sprinkle with brown sugar mixed with a pinch of ground coriander.

Fill the suet crust with halved and stoned (pitted) apricots or plums and sprinkle with sugar to taste.

Fill the suet crust with mixed dried fruits (prunes, apricots, raisins, etc.) which have been soaked overnight and drained.

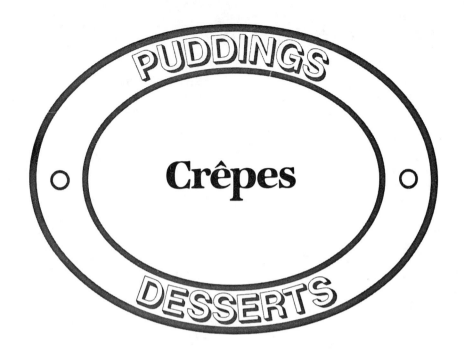

Basic Crêpe Batter

Metric/Imperial
100 g/4 oz plain flour
pinch of salt
1–2 eggs, beaten
300 ml/½ pint milk
oil for frying

American
1 cup all-purpose flour
pinch of salt
1–2 eggs, beaten
1¼ cups milk
oil for frying

Sift the flour and salt into a bowl. Make a well in the centre and add the egg (or eggs) and about one-third of the milk. Beat together, then gradually beat in the remaining milk to make a smooth batter. The batter should be thin.

Lightly oil an 18 cm/8 inch crêpe or frying pan (skillet) and heat it. Pour in about 2 tablespoons of the batter (just enough to cover the bottom of the pan in a thin layer). Cook gently until the bottom of the crêpe is golden, then turn it over, or toss, and cook the other side. Slide the crêpe onto a plate and keep warm. Cook the remaining crêpes in the same way, and stack them on the plate interleaved with greaseproof (wax) paper.
Makes about 8

Variation:
Rich Crêpe Batter: Sift 1 tablespoon icing (confectioners') sugar with the flour and salt, use 1 egg, 1 egg yolk, and add 1 tablespoon brandy, if liked.
Makes 12

Chestnut Crêpes

Metric/Imperial
1 tablespoon strong black coffee
2 tablespoons rum or brandy
1 × 225 g/8 oz can sweetened
  chestnut purée
300 ml/½ pint double cream
12 crêpes, made with rich batter (see
  page 41)
icing sugar

American
1 tablespoon strong black coffee
2 tablespoons rum or brandy
1 × ½ lb can sweetened chestnut
  purée
1¼ cups heavy cream
12 crêpes, made with rich batter (see
  page 41)
confectioners' sugar

Mix together the coffee, rum or brandy and chestnut purée. Whip the cream until thick and fold half of it into the chestnut mixture. Divide between the crêpes and roll them up.

Arrange the rolls on a serving platter and cover with the remaining cream. Sprinkle with a little icing (confectioners') sugar and serve.
Serves 4–6

Apricot Crêpe Cake

Metric/Imperial
8 crêpes (see page 41)
1 tablespoon flaked almonds
Filling:
1 × 425 g/15 oz can apricot halves
2 teaspoons arrowroot
3 tablespoons orange jelly
  marmalade

American
8 crêpes (see page 41)
1 tablespoon slivered almonds
Filling:
1 × 15 oz can apricot halves
2 teaspoons arrowroot
3 tablespoons orange jelly
  marmalade

Drain the apricot halves, reserving the syrup, and cut each half into four slices. Dissolve the arrowroot in 1 tablespoon of the syrup and put the remaining syrup in a saucepan with the marmalade. Heat until the marmalade has melted, then stir in the arrowroot and bring to the boil. Simmer, stirring, until thickened and clear. Stir in the apricot slices.

Place one crêpe on an ovenproof plate and spread over a little of the apricot mixture. Continue making layers in this way and scatter the almonds on top. Heat through in a preheated moderate oven (180°C/350°F, Gas Mark 4) for about 15 minutes.

Serve warm, cut into wedges.
Serves 6

Crêpes Soufflés à l'Orange

Metric/Imperial
6 crêpes (see page 41)
4–5 tablespoons orange liqueur
Filling:
25 g/1 oz butter
25 g/1 oz plain flour
40 g/1½ oz sugar
7 tablespoons milk
2 eggs, separated
6 tablespoons orange liqueur
Sauce:
juice of 2 oranges
juice of 1 lemon
grated rind of 1 orange
sugar to taste

American
6 crêpes (see page 41)
4–5 tablespoons orange liqueur
Filling:
2 tablespoons butter
¼ cup all-purpose flour
3 tablespoons sugar
7 tablespoons milk
2 eggs, separated
6 tablespoons orange liqueur
Sauce:
juice of 2 oranges
juice of 1 lemon
grated rind of 1 orange
sugar to taste

For the filling, melt the butter in a saucepan and stir in the flour and sugar. Gradually stir in the milk and cook for 1 minute. Remove from the heat and beat in the egg yolks and liqueur. Beat the egg whites until stiff and fold in.

Divide the filling between the crêpes and fold each in half. Arrange, in one layer, in a greased baking dish and bake in a preheated moderately hot oven (200°C/400°F, Gas Mark 6) for 8 to 10 minutes or until well risen.

Meanwhile, put all the sauce ingredients in a saucepan and bring to the boil. Simmer for about 3 minutes.

Arrange the crêpes on a heated serving platter and pour over the warmed liqueur. Set alight and serve flaming. Pour over the sauce just before serving.
Serves 3

Quick Jammy Crêpes

Metric/Imperial
1 packet dessert topping mix
  milk
1 tablespoon strawberry jam
8 crêpes (see page 41)

American
1 package dessert topping mix
  milk
1 tablespoon strawberry jam
8 crêpes (see page 41)

Make up the dessert topping with the milk according to packet directions. Stir in the jam. Divide the filling between the crêpes, roll up and serve.
Serves 4

Variation:
Omit the jam from the filling and spread the crêpes first with 225 g/8 oz (⅔ cup) mincemeat. Serve sprinkled with sugar.

Crêpes Suzette

Metric/Imperial
100 g/4 oz sugar
finely grated rind and juice of 2
  oranges
8 crêpes (see page 41)
2 tablespoons brandy
2 tablespoons orange liqueur

American
½ cup sugar
finely grated rind and juice of 2
  oranges
8 crêpes (see page 41)
2 tablespoons brandy
2 tablespoons orange liqueur

Melt the sugar gently in a large frying pan or chafing dish. When it is pale golden, stir in the orange rind and juice.

Dip each crêpe into the orange mixture, then fold it into quarters and add to the pan. Stir in the brandy and liqueur and heat through for 1 to 2 minutes. Set alight, if you wish, and serve flaming.

Serves 4

St Clement's Crêpes

Metric/Imperial
100 g/4 oz butter
50 g/2 oz icing sugar, sifted
3 oranges
grated rind and juice of ½ lemon
8 crêpes (see page 41)

American
8 tablespoons (1 stick) butter
½ cup confectioners' sugar, sifted
3 oranges
grated rind and juice of ½ lemon
8 crêpes (see page 41)

Melt the butter in a frying pan or chafing dish. Stir in the icing (confectioners') sugar, the grated rind and juice of one of the oranges, and the lemon rind and juice. Heat gently until the sauce simmers.

Peel the remaining oranges and chop the flesh. Divide the orange flesh between the crêpes and fold them into triangles. Place in the sauce and heat through gently. Serve hot, in the pan or chafing dish.

Serves 4

Chocolate Banana Crêpes

Metric/Imperial
40 g/1½ oz butter
50 g/2 oz soft brown sugar
2 tablespoons cocoa powder
1 tablespoon golden syrup
2 bananas, sliced
8 crêpes (see page 41)
icing sugar

American
3 tablespoons butter
⅓ cup light brown sugar
2 tablespoons unsweetened cocoa
1 tablespoon light corn syrup
2 bananas, sliced
8 crêpes (see page 41)
confectioners' sugar

Melt the butter with the sugar in a saucepan. Stir in the cocoa and syrup, then fold in the bananas. Divide this mixture between the crêpes and fold them into triangles. Arrange in a baking dish and reheat in a preheated moderate oven (180°C/350°F, Gas Mark 4) for 5 to 10 minutes.

Serve sprinkled with icing (confectioners') sugar.

Serves 4

Pear and Almond Crêpes

Metric/Imperial
100 g/4 oz butter
50 g/2 oz icing sugar
50 g/2 oz ground almonds
few drops of almond essence
grated rind of 1 lemon
1 × 425 g/15 oz can pears, drained
   and diced
8 crêpes (see page 41)

American
8 tablespoons (1 stick) butter
½ cup confectioners' sugar
½ cup ground almonds
few drops of almond extract
grated rind of 1 lemon
1 × 15 oz can pears, drained and
   diced
8 crêpes (see page 41)

Cream the butter with the sugar until pale and fluffy. Beat in the almonds, almond essence (extract) and lemon rind, then fold in the pears.

Divide the filling between the crêpes and roll them up. Arrange in an oven-proof serving dish and reheat in a preheated moderate oven (180°C/350°F, Gas Mark 4) for 15 minutes.

Serves 4

Wholemeal Honey Crêpes

Metric/Imperial
50 g/2 oz fine wholemeal flour
50 g/2 oz soya flour
1 egg
milk
25 g/1 oz butter, melted
butter for frying
50 g/2 oz mixed nuts, finely chopped
4 tablespoons dark honey

American
½ cup fine wholewheat flour
½ cup soy flour
1 egg
milk
2 tablespoons butter, melted
butter for frying
½ cup finely chopped mixed nuts
¼ cup dark honey

Sift the flours into a bowl and beat in the egg and enough milk to make a batter the consistency of thick cream. Stir in the melted butter. Chill for 1 hour.

Melt a little butter in a crêpe or frying pan and pour in just enough batter to cover the bottom in a thin layer. When the crêpe is golden brown on the underside, turn it over and cook the other side.

Slide the crêpe out of the pan and keep warm while you cook the remaining crêpes in the same way.

Divide the nuts and honey between the crêpes and roll them up. Serve hot.
Serves 4

Banana Cream Crêpes

Metric/Imperial
3 large bananas
grated rind and juice of ½ lemon
40 g/1½ oz sugar
150 ml/¼ pint double cream
8 crêpes (see page 41)
icing sugar

American
3 large bananas
grated rind and juice of ½ lemon
3 tablespoons sugar
⅔ cup heavy cream
8 crêpes (see page 41)
confectioners' sugar

Mash the bananas with the lemon rind and juice and the sugar. Whip the cream until thick and fold into the banana mixture.

Divide the banana filling between the crêpes and fold into triangles. Arrange on a warmed serving plate and sprinkle with icing (confectioners') sugar.
Serves 4

Orange Cream Cheese Crêpes

Metric/Imperial
2 × 75 g/3 oz packets cream cheese
2 tablespoons top of milk
3 tablespoons clear honey
50 g/2 oz sultanas
grated rind and juice of 2 oranges
1 tablespoon arrowroot
8 crêpes (see page 41)
2 tablespoons soft brown sugar
twisted orange slices to decorate

American
2 × 3 oz packages cream cheese
2 tablespoons half-and-half
3 tablespoons clear honey
⅓ cup seedless white raisins
grated rind and juice of 2 oranges
1 tablespoon arrowroot
8 crêpes (see page 41)
2 tablespoons light brown sugar
twisted orange slices to decorate

Mix together the cream cheese, top of milk (half-and-half), 2 tablespoons of the honey, the sultanas (raisins) and half of the grated orange rind.

Make up the orange juice to 300 ml/½ pint (1¼ cups) with water and pour into a saucepan. Add the remaining honey and orange rind and the arrowroot. Bring to the boil, stirring, and simmer until clear and thickened.

Divide the cream cheese mixture between the crêpes and roll them up. Arrange on a heated serving plate and pour over a little of the sauce. Sprinkle over the brown sugar. Decorate with twisted orange slices and serve with the remaining sauce.
Serves 4

Orange and Gooseberry Crêpes

Metric/Imperial
500 g/1 lb fresh or frozen and thawed
  gooseberries
grated rind and juice of 1 orange
75–100 g/3–4 oz sugar
8 crêpes (see page 41)
sifted icing sugar

American
1 lb fresh or frozen and thawed
  gooseberries
grated rind and juice of 1 orange
6–8 tablespoons sugar
8 crêpes (see page 41)
sifted confectioners' sugar

Put the gooseberries in a saucepan with the orange rind and juice and cook gently until the gooseberries are tender but still hold their shape. Stir in sugar to taste.

Divide the filling between the crêpes and fold into quarters. Sprinkle with icing (confectioners') sugar and serve hot.
Serves 4

Saucer Crêpes

Metric/Imperial
50 g/2 oz butter
50 g/2 oz caster sugar
2 eggs, beaten
75 g/3 oz plain flour, sifted
150 ml/¼ pint milk
2 tablespoons water
jam or lemon juice and sugar to
  serve

American
4 tablespoons butter
¼ cup sugar
2 eggs, beaten
¾ cup all-purpose flour, sifted
⅔ cup milk
2 tablespoons water
jam or lemon juice and sugar to
  serve

Cream the butter with the sugar until pale and fluffy. Beat in the eggs, followed by the flour, milk and water to make a thin batter.

Divide the batter between greased ovenproof saucers and bake in a preheated hot oven (220°C/425°F, Gas Mark 7) for 15 minutes. Serve hot with jam, or lemon juice and sugar.
Makes 8–12

Apple Crêpe Cake

Metric/Imperial
50 g/2 oz unsalted butter
3 apples, peeled, cored and thinly
  sliced
150 ml/¼ pint Calvados, warmed
  (optional)
cream to serve
Batter:
1 egg
3 egg yolks
50 g/2 oz sugar
150 g/5 oz plain flour
25 g/1 oz butter, melted
2 tablespoons oil
150 ml/¼ pint milk

American
4 tablespoons sweet butter
3 apples, peeled, cored and thinly
  sliced
⅔ cup applejack, warmed
  (optional)
cream to serve
Batter:
1 egg
3 egg yolks
¼ cup sugar
1¼ cups all-purpose flour
2 tablespoons butter, melted
2 tablespoons oil
¾ cup milk

First make the batter. Beat the eggs, egg yolks and sugar together until pale and fluffy. Sift in the flour and fold in, then beat in the melted butter and oil followed by the milk.

Melt 25 g/1 oz (2 tablespoons) of the butter in a frying pan (skillet), add the apples and cook gently until just soft.

Melt the remaining butter in a cast iron frying pan (skillet). Pour in enough of the batter to make a 5 mm/¼ inch layer and cook gently for 30 seconds. Spread the apples over the top and cover with the rest of the batter. Transfer the pan to a preheated moderate oven (180°C/350°F, Gas Mark 4) and cook for 5 minutes or until well risen and firm.

Turn the cake over carefully and replace in the pan. Cook for a few more minutes or until lightly browned.

Pour over the Calvados (applejack), if using, and set alight. Serve flaming, with cream.

Serves 4

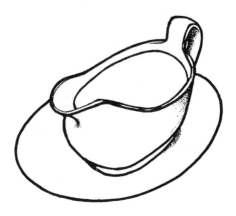

Apple Crêpes with Berry Sauce

Metric/Imperial
150 g/5 oz plain flour
1 teaspoon baking powder
½ teaspoon salt
50 g/2 oz sugar
1 egg, beaten
250 ml/8 fl oz milk
50 g/2 oz butter, melted
2–3 apples, peeled, cored and finely
  chopped
¼ teaspoon ground cinnamon
butter for frying
Sauce:
1 × 425 g/15 oz can blackberries or
  other berries
100 g/4 oz sugar
4 cooking apples, peeled, cored and
  chopped

American
1¼ cups all-purpose flour
1 teaspoon baking powder
½ teaspoon salt
¼ cup sugar
1 egg, beaten
1 cup milk
4 tablespoons butter, melted
2–3 apples, peeled, cored and finely
  chopped
¼ teaspoon ground cinnamon
butter for frying
Sauce:
1 × 15 oz can loganberries or other
  berries
½ cup sugar
4 tart apples, peeled, cored and
  chopped

First make the batter. Sift the flour, baking powder and salt into a bowl and stir in the sugar. Mix together the egg, milk and melted butter and add to the dry ingredients. Beat well, then stir in the apples and cinnamon.

For the sauce, drain the berries, reserving the syrup. Put 150 ml/¼ pint (⅔ cup) of the syrup in a saucepan with the sugar and stir until the sugar has dissolved. Add the apples and cook until soft. Stir in the berries and simmer for 5 minutes. Blend or sieve (strain) the mixture to a smooth purée and return to the pan. Reheat gently and keep hot.

Melt butter in a frying pan (skillet). Drop the batter into the pan in tablespoons, keeping them well spaced apart, and cook until the undersides are golden brown. Turn over to cook the other sides. Serve the crêpes hot with the berry sauce.

Serves 4

Apple and Mincemeat Crêpes

Metric/Imperial
225 g/8 oz apple purée
4 tablespoons mincemeat
8 crêpes (see page 41)
2 tablespoons brown sugar
2 teaspoons ground cinnamon

American
1 cup apple sauce
¼ cup mincemeat
8 crêpes (see page 41)
2 tablespoons brown sugar
2 teaspoons ground cinnamon

Mix together the apple purée (sauce) and mincemeat and divide between the crêpes. Roll them up and arrange in a flameproof serving dish.

Mix together the sugar and cinnamon and sprinkle over the crêpes. Brown under a hot grill (broiler).

Serves 4

Apple and Plum Crêpestack

Metric/Imperial
25 g/1 oz butter
750 g/1 ½ lb cooking apples, peeled, cored and sliced
1 tablespoon water
50 g/2 oz sugar
25 g/1 oz flaked almonds, toasted
8 crêpes (see page 41)
plum jam

American
2 tablespoons butter
1 ½ lb tart apples, peeled, cored and sliced
1 tablespoon water
¼ cup sugar
¼ cup slivered almonds, toasted
8 crêpes (see page 41)
plum jam

Melt the butter in a saucepan. Add the apples and water, cover the pan and cook gently until the apples are tender. Stir in the sugar and most of the almonds.

Spread the crêpes with the jam, then layer with the apple mixture on an ovenproof plate. Cover with foil and reheat in a preheated moderate oven (180°C/350°F, Gas Mark 4) for 5 to 10 minutes. Sprinkle with the rest of the almonds before serving.

Serves 4

Brandy Soufflé

Metric/Imperial	**American**
about 12 sponge fingers	about 12 ladyfingers
6 tablespoons brandy	6 tablespoons brandy
100 g/4 oz glacé cherries, chopped	½ cup chopped candied cherries
25 g/1 oz butter	2 tablespoons butter
25 g/1 oz plain flour	¼ cup all-purpose flour
150 ml/¼ pint milk	⅔ cup milk
150 ml/¼ pint single cream	⅔ cup light cream
50 g/2 oz caster sugar	¼ cup sugar
3 egg yolks	3 egg yolks
4 egg whites	4 egg whites

Use the sponge (lady) fingers to line the bottom of a soufflé dish. Sprinkle them with 3 tablespoons of the brandy, then cover with the cherries.

Melt the butter in a saucepan. Stir in the flour and cook for 1 minute, then gradually stir in the milk and cream. Bring to the boil, stirring, and simmer until thickened. Remove from the heat and stir in the sugar, egg yolks and the remaining brandy. Cool.

Beat the egg whites until stiff and fold into the brandy mixture. Spoon into the soufflé dish and bake in a preheated moderately hot oven (190°C/375°F, Gas Mark 5) for 40 minutes. Serve immediately.
Serves 4–6

Port Wine Soufflé

Metric/Imperial
1 tablespoon gelatine
5 tablespoons hot water
2 eggs, separated
50 g/2 oz sugar
200 ml/⅓ pint milk, heated
5 tablespoons port wine
red food colouring (optional)
150 ml/¼ pint double cream

American
1 envelope unflavored gelatin
5 tablespoons hot water
2 eggs, separated
¼ cup sugar
1 cup milk, heated
5 tablespoons port wine
red food coloring (optional)
⅔ cup heavy cream

Tie a doubled piece of greaseproof (wax) paper around a 15 cm/6 inch soufflé dish so that it stands about 5 cm/2 inches above the rim. Lightly grease the paper collar.

Dissolve the gelatine in the hot water and allow to cool. Beat the egg yolks and sugar together until pale and fluffy, then gradually beat in the hot milk. Cool, then stir in the gelatine. Add the port wine and some food colouring, if necessary, to give a pale pink colour. Chill until on the point of setting.

Whip the cream until thick. Fold most of the cream into the port wine mixture. Beat the egg whites until stiff and fold in. Spoon into the soufflé dish and chill until set.

Just before serving, carefully remove the paper collar and decorate the top of the soufflé with the reserved whipped cream.

Serves 4–6

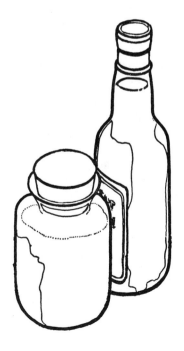

Soufflé Omelet

Metric/Imperial
75 g/3 oz caster sugar
3 eggs, separated
¼ teaspoon vanilla, almond, lemon or
    other essence or 1 tablespoon
    liqueur
3 egg whites
pinch of salt

American
6 tablespoons sugar
3 eggs, separated
¼ teaspoon vanilla, almond, lemon or
    other extract or 1 tablespoon
    liqueur
3 egg whites
pinch of salt

Beat together 50 g/2 oz (¼ cup) of the sugar and the egg yolks until creamy. Stir in the chosen flavouring.

Beat the six egg whites with the salt until stiff. Stir in 1 tablespoon of the yolk mixture, then carefully fold in the remainder.

Spoon the omelet mixture into a greased baking dish, piling it high and making some slashes in the sides to help the centre to cook. Bake in a preheated moderate oven (180°C/350°F, Gas Mark 4) for 15 to 20 minutes or until puffed up and set.

Sprinkle the remaining sugar over the top and brown under a very hot grill (broiler).
Serves 6

Variations:

Apricot Soufflé Omelet: Beat 2 egg yolks with 1 tablespoon sugar and 2 teaspoons water. Beat 2 egg whites until stiff and fold into the yolk mixture. Melt 1 tablespoon butter in a 15 to 18 cm/6 to 7 inch omelet pan, add the omelet mixture and cook until golden brown underneath. Transfer the pan to a hot grill (broiler) and lightly brown the top of the omelet. Cover half of the omelet with hot cooked or canned apricots and fold over the other half. Sprinkle with sugar and serve.
Serves 1–2

Strawberry Soufflé Omelet: Use 4 eggs, separated. Beat the egg yolks with 1 tablespoon sugar and 1 tablespoon double (heavy) cream. Beat the egg whites until stiff and fold in. Melt 25 g/1 oz (2 tablespoons) butter in an omelet pan and cook as for the apricot soufflé omelet above. Spread the top of the omelet with 2 tablespoons strawberry jam and cover half with 100 g/4 oz strawberries. Fold over the omelet and sprinkle with icing (confectioners') sugar.
Serves 2

Apple Soufflé Omelet: Use 4 eggs, separated. Beat the egg yolks with 2 tablespoons sugar and ½ teaspoon ground cinnamon. Beat the egg whites until stiff and fold in. Melt 25 g/1 oz (2 tablespoons) butter in an omelet pan and cook as for apricot soufflé omelet above. Spread the omelet with 120 ml/ 4 fl oz (½ cup) hot thick apple purée (sauce) and fold it in half.
Serves 2

Soufflé Omelet Alaska

Metric/Imperial
225 g/8 oz raspberries or sliced
    strawberries
2 tablespoons kirsch
50 g/2 oz caster sugar
1 × 18 cm/7 inch baked sponge cake
3 eggs, separated
1 tablespoon water
small block of ice cream

American
½ lb raspberries or sliced
    strawberries
2 tablespoons kirsch
¼ cup sugar
1 × 7 inch baked white cake layer
3 eggs, separated
1 tablespoon water
small block of ice cream

Sprinkle the fruit with the kirsch and 2 tablespoons of the sugar. Place the cake on an ovenproof plate and pile the fruit on top.

Beat the egg yolks, water and remaining sugar together. Beat the egg whites until stiff and fold into the yolk mixture.

Place the ice cream on top of the fruit and cover with the egg mixture. Bake in a preheated hot oven (220°C/425°F, Gas Mark 7) for about 3 minutes or until the topping is set and lightly browned.
Serves 6

Cream Cheese Cherry Soufflé

Metric/Imperial
25 g/1 oz cornflour
200 ml/⅓ pint milk
grated rind and juice of 1 lemon
½ × 225 g/8 oz packet cream cheese
50 g/2 oz sugar
4 eggs, separated
1 × 425 g/15 oz can black cherries,
    drained
25 g/1 oz icing sugar, sifted

American
¼ cup cornstarch
⅞ cup milk
grated rind and juice of 1 lemon
½ × ½ lb package cream cheese
¼ cup sugar
4 eggs, separated
1 × 15 oz can bing cherries,
    drained
¼ cup confectioners' sugar, sifted

Put the cornflour (cornstarch) and milk in a saucepan and bring to the boil, stirring until thickened. Remove from the heat and stir in the lemon rind and juice, cream cheese, sugar and egg yolks. Beat the egg whites until stiff and fold into the cream cheese mixture.

Place the cherries in a greased 1.2 litre/2 pint (1 quart capacity) soufflé dish and top with the cream cheese mixture. Bake in a preheated moderately hot oven (190°C/375°F, Gas Mark 5) for 30 to 35 minutes. Serve immediately, sprinkled with the icing (confectioners') sugar.
Serves 4–6

Iced Raspberry Soufflé

Metric/Imperial
500 g/1 lb raspberries
4 egg whites
225 g/8 oz caster sugar
300 ml/½ pint double cream
To decorate:
whipped cream
raspberries

American
1 lb raspberries
4 egg whites
1 cup sugar
1¼ cups heavy cream
To decorate:
whipped cream
raspberries

Purée the raspberries in a blender or sieve (strainer). Beat the egg whites until stiff, then gradually beat in the sugar. Beat in the raspberry purée. Whip the cream until thick and fold into the raspberry mixture.

Spoon into a freezerproof soufflé dish and freeze until solid.

One hour before serving, transfer the soufflé to the refrigerator to soften. Serve decorated with whipped cream and raspberries.

Serves 6–8

Cold Crème de Menthe Soufflé

Metric/Imperial
3 eggs, separated
100 g/4 oz caster sugar
150 ml/¼ pint water
2 tablespoons crème de menthe
    liqueur
2 teaspoons gelatine
300 ml/½ pint natural yogurt
crushed ratafia biscuits to decorate

American
3 eggs, separated
½ cup sugar
⅔ cup water
2 tablespoons crème de menthe
    liqueur
1 envelope unflavored gelatin
1¼ cups unflavored yogurt
crushed ratafia cookies to decorate

Beat together the egg yolks, sugar, 6 tablespoons of the water and the crème de menthe liqueur until thick. Dissolve the gelatine in the remaining water over heat and add to the mixture. Leave until on the point of setting.

Fold the yogurt into the crème de menthe mixture. Beat the egg whites until stiff and fold in.

Tie a doubled piece of greaseproof (wax) paper around a 600 ml/1 pint (2½ cup capacity) soufflé dish so that it stands about 5 cm/2 inches above the rim. Lightly grease the paper collar. Spoon the soufflé mixture into the dish and chill until set.

Just before serving, remove the paper collar and press crushed ratafias onto the sides of the soufflé.

Serves 5–6

Strawberry Soufflé

Metric/Imperial	**American**
500 g/1 lb strawberries, hulled and sliced	1 lb strawberries, hulled and sliced
2 tablespoons brandy	2 tablespoons brandy
4 teaspoons gelatine	1½ envelopes unflavored gelatin
150 ml/¼ pint hot water	⅔ cup hot water
100 g/4 oz caster sugar	½ cup sugar
juice of 1 lemon	juice of 1 lemon
300 ml/½ pint double cream	1¼ cups heavy cream
2 egg whites	2 egg whites

Put most of the strawberries in a bowl (reserve a few slices for the decoration) and sprinkle with the brandy. Leave to marinate for 1 hour.

Meanwhile, prepare the soufflé dish. Tie a doubled piece of greaseproof (wax) paper around a 600 ml/1 pint (2½ cup capacity) soufflé dish so that it stands about 5 cm/2 inches above the rim. Lightly grease the paper collar.

Dissolve the gelatine in the hot water; cool. Stir the sugar and lemon juice into the strawberries, then add the dissolved gelatine. Chill until the mixture is beginning to set.

Whip the cream until thick. Beat the egg whites until stiff. Fold the egg whites and most of the cream into the strawberry mixture. Spoon into the soufflé dish and chill until set.

Just before serving, remove the paper collar and decorate the top of the soufflé with the remaining whipped cream and the reserved strawberry slices.
Serves 4–6

Cold Apricot and Apple Soufflé

Metric/Imperial	American
750 g/1½ lb cooking apples, peeled, cored and sliced	1½ lb tart apples, peeled, cored and sliced
6 apricots, halved and stoned	6 apricots, halved and pitted
150 ml/¼ pint water	⅔ cup water
6 eggs, separated	6 eggs, separated
275 g/10 oz caster sugar	1¼ cups sugar
2 tablespoons lemon juice	2 tablespoons lemon juice
5 teaspoons gelatine	2 envelopes unflavored gelatin
2 tablespoons apricot liqueur	2 tablespoons apricot liqueur
150 ml/¼ pint whipping cream	⅔ cup whipping cream
halved grapes to decorate	halved grapes to decorate

Tie a doubled piece of greaseproof (wax) paper around a 1.5 litre/2½ pint (1½ quart capacity) soufflé dish so that it stands about 5 cm/2 inches above the rim. Grease the paper collar.

Put the apples, apricots and 6 tablespoons of the water in a saucepan and cook gently until soft. Purée in a blender or sieve (strainer).

Beat the egg yolks, sugar and lemon juice until the mixture is very thick and creamy. Dissolve the gelatine in the remaining water over heat and add to the egg yolk mixture with the fruit purée and apricot liqueur. Whip the cream until thick and fold into the mixture. Beat the egg whites until stiff and fold in.

Spoon the mixture into the soufflé dish and chill until set.

Carefully remove the paper collar and decorate the soufflé with the grapes.
Serves 6–8

Variation:

Cold Peach and Apple Soufflé: Use 2 large cooking (tart) apples and cook with water as above. Purée with 4 peaches, peeled, stoned (pitted) and sliced. Proceed as above, using orange liqueur instead of apricot liqueur and increasing the cream to 450 ml/¾ pint (2 cups).

Grapefruit Soufflé

Metric/Imperial	American
finely grated rind of 2 large grapefruit	finely grated rind of 2 large grapefruit
25 g/1 oz butter	2 tablespoons butter
25 g/1 oz plain flour	¼ cup all-purpose flour
juice of 1 large grapefruit	juice of 1 large grapefruit
1 grapefruit, peeled and segmented	1 grapefruit, peeled and segmented
50 g/2 oz sugar	¼ cup sugar
4 egg yolks	4 egg yolks
5 egg whites	5 egg whites

Put the grapefruit rind and butter in a saucepan and melt the butter. Stir in the flour, then the grapefruit juice and bring to the boil. Simmer, stirring, until thick and smooth. Stir in the grapefruit segments and sugar and cook for 1 minute, then cool slightly.

Beat the egg yolks into the grapefruit mixture. Beat the egg whites until stiff and fold in. Spoon into a 1.5 litre/2½ pint (1½ quart capacity) soufflé dish.

Bake in a preheated moderate oven (180°C/350°F, Gas Mark 4) for 45 minutes or until well risen and golden brown. Serve immediately.
Serves 4

Harlequin Soufflé

Metric/Imperial	American
175 g/6 oz mixed dried fruit	1 cup mixed dried fruit
450 ml/¾ pint water	2 cups water
grated rind and juice of 1 lemon	grated rind and juice of 1 lemon
25 g/1 oz soft brown sugar	2½ tablespoons light brown sugar
4 egg whites	4 egg whites

Put the dried fruit in a bowl, pour over the water and lemon rind and juice and leave to soak overnight.

The next day, tip the fruit mixture into a saucepan and bring to the boil. Cover and simmer for 30 minutes or until the fruit is tender. Drain, reserving the liquid.

Remove any stones (pits) from the fruit. Make up the liquid to 150 ml/¼ pint (⅔ cup) with water if necessary. Put the fruit and liquid in the blender and blend to a purée. Stir in the sugar and cool.

Beat the egg whites until stiff and fold into the fruit mixture. Spoon into a 1.5 litre/2½ pint (1½ quart capacity) soufflé dish. Bake in a preheated moderately hot oven (200°C/400°F, Gas Mark 6) for 20 minutes or until the soufflé has risen and the top is lightly browned. Serve immediately.
Serves 4

Cold Lemon Soufflé

Metric/Imperial	American
finely grated rind of 2 lemons	finely grated rind of 2 lemons
4 tablespoons lemon juice	¼ cup lemon juice
3 eggs, separated	3 eggs, separated
75 g/3 oz caster sugar	6 tablespoons sugar
1 tablespoon gelatine	1 envelope unflavored gelatin
4 tablespoons hot water	¼ cup hot water
300 ml/½ pint double cream	1¼ cups heavy cream
To decorate:	**To decorate:**
crushed ratafia biscuits	crushed ratafia cookies
whipped cream	whipped cream

Put the lemon rind and juice, egg yolks and sugar into a bowl and beat until thick and pale. Dissolve the gelatine in the water. Stir into the lemon mixture and leave until on the point of setting.

Meanwhile, prepare the soufflé dish. Tie a doubled piece of greaseproof (wax) paper around a 600 ml/1 pint (2½ cup capacity) soufflé dish so that it stands about 5 cm/2 inches above the rim. Lightly grease the paper collar.

Whip the cream until thick, then fold into the lemon mixture. Beat the egg whites until stiff and fold in. Spoon into the soufflé dish and chill until set.

Just before serving, carefully remove the paper collar and press the crushed ratafias onto the side of the soufflé. Decorate the top with piped whipped cream.
Serves 6

Variation:
Cold Grapefruit Soufflé: Use the finely grated rind and juice of 1 large grapefruit instead of lemon rind and juice. Use only 2 eggs. Increase the sugar to 100 g/4 oz (½ cup). Decorate with grapefruit segments.

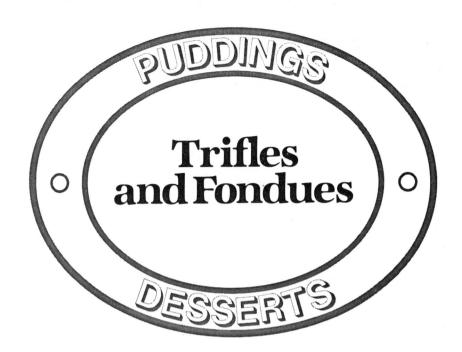

Fruit Meringue Trifle

Metric/Imperial
8 meringue shells, broken into large
   pieces
1½ lb mixed peaches, pears and
   apricots, peeled if necessary,
   stoned and sliced
175 ml/6 fl oz white wine
300 ml/½ pint double cream
sugar to taste
To decorate:
whipped cream
peach, pear and apricot slices

American
8 meringue shells, broken into large
   pieces
1½ lb mixed peaches, pears and
   apricots, peeled if necessary,
   pitted and sliced
¾ cup white wine
1¼ cups heavy cream
sugar to taste
To decorate:
whipped cream
peach, pear and apricot slices

Put half the meringue pieces on the bottom of a glass serving bowl. Cover with half the fruit and sprinkle with 1 tablespoon of the wine.

Whip the cream until thick. Gradually beat in all but 1 tablespoon of the remaining wine and sweeten the mixture to taste. Pour over the fruit in the bowl. Cover with the rest of the fruit and sprinkle with the remaining 1 tablespoon of wine. Top with the remaining meringue pieces.

Decorate with whipped cream and fruit slices. Serve within 1 hour of making so the meringue does not become soggy.
Serves 6–8

Cranberry Trifle

Metric/Imperial
1 Swiss roll, thinly sliced
1 × 382 g/13½ oz jar cranberry jelly
4 tablespoons sherry
600 ml/1 pint cold custard sauce (see page 213)
300 ml/½ pint double cream
fresh orange slices
toasted flaked almonds

American
1 jelly roll, thinly sliced
1 × ¾ lb can cranberry jelly
¼ cup sherry
2½ cups cold custard sauce (see page 213)
1¼ cups heavy cream
fresh orange slices
toasted slivered almonds

Arrange the cake slices around the bottom and sides of a glass bowl. Spread over the cranberry jelly and sprinkle with the sherry. Pour over the custard sauce and chill until serving time.

Whip the cream until thick and use to decorate the top of the trifle with the orange slices and almonds.

Serves 4-6

Chocolate Macaroon Trifle

Metric/Imperial
6–8 macaroons
2 tablespoons rum
3 tablespoons orange juice
25 g/1 oz cornflour
450 ml/¾ pint milk
50 g/2 oz sugar
175 g/6 oz plain chocolate, broken into small pieces
150 ml/¼ pint double cream
To decorate:
whipped cream
blanched almonds

American
6–8 macaroons
2 tablespoons rum
3 tablespoons orange juice
¼ cup cornstarch
2 cups milk
¼ cup sugar
1 cup semi-sweet chocolate chips
⅔ cup heavy cream
To decorate:
whipped cream
blanched almonds

Put the macaroons into a serving bowl and sprinkle with the rum and orange juice.

Dissolve the cornflour (cornstarch) in the milk and pour into a saucepan. Add the sugar and heat, stirring, until the mixture thickens. Add the chocolate and stir until it has melted. Remove from the heat and cool, stirring occasionally. Stir in the cream.

Pour the chocolate mixture over the macaroons and chill until fairly firm. Decorate with whipped cream and almonds.

Serves 4–6

Strawberry Ratafias

Metric/Imperial
75 g/3 oz ratafias
2 tablespoons orange juice
2 tablespoons sweet sherry
225 g/8 oz strawberries
caster sugar
150 ml/¼ pint double cream

American
3 oz ratafias
2 tablespoons orange juice
2 tablespoons sweet sherry
½ lb strawberries
sugar
⅔ cup heavy cream

Set aside four of the ratafias. Divide the remainder between four tall glasses. Sprinkle over the orange juice and sherry and leave to soak for 1 hour.

Set aside 4 strawberries; slice the remainder. Pile the sliced strawberries on the soaked ratafias. Sprinkle over a little sugar.

Whip the cream until thick and spoon over the strawberries. Decorate with the reserved ratafias and strawberries.
Serves 4

Variation:

Divide all the ratafias between six glasses. Peel and segment 3 oranges and layer in the glasses with the strawberries, 50 g/2 oz (⅓ cup) brown sugar and 150 ml/¼ pint (⅔ cup) sour cream, ending with sour cream. Chill for 1 hour, then decorate with toasted desiccated (shredded) coconut.
Serves 6

Tipsy Fingers

Metric/Imperial
6 slices of light sponge cake, cut into
    fingers
jam
150 ml/¼ pint sweet white wine
150 ml/¼ pint double cream
toasted flaked almonds

American
6 slices of pound cake, cut into
    fingers
jam
⅔ cup sweet white wine
⅔ cup heavy cream
toasted slivered almonds

Arrange the cake fingers on a plate and spread them with a little jam.
Sprinkle over the wine and leave to soak for 5 minutes.

Whip the cream until thick and spread over the cake fingers. Sprinkle with
the almonds and serve.

Serves 4–6

Peach Trifle

Metric/Imperial
1 × 425 g/15 oz can peach halves
1 jam-filled Swiss roll, sliced
5–6 tablespoons sweet
    sherry
900 ml/1½ pints custard sauce (see
    page 213)
300 ml/½ pint whipping cream
grated chocolate to decorate

American
1 × 15 oz can peach halves
1 jelly roll, sliced
5–6 tablespoons sweet (cream)
    sherry
4 cups custard sauce (see page
    213)
1¼ cups whipping cream
grated chocolate to decorate

Drain the peach halves, reserving 150 ml/¼ pint (⅔ cup) of the syrup. Put the
peach halves in a glass serving bowl. Stand the Swiss (jelly) roll slices
around the edge of the bowl and over the peaches. Mix together the sherry
and reserved peach syrup and sprinkle over the cake slices. Pour over the
custard sauce and chill.

Just before serving, whip the cream until thick. Spread over the custard
layer and decorate with grated chocolate.

Serves 6

Macaroon and Banana Pudding

Metric/Imperial
600 ml/1 pint cold custard sauce (see
   page 213)
3 large macaroons, crumbled
2 large bananas, sliced
redcurrant jelly
150 ml/¼ pint double cream

American
2½ cups cold custard sauce (see
   page 213)
3 large macaroons, crumbled
2 large bananas, sliced
redcurrant jelly
⅔ cup heavy cream

Gently mix the custard sauce with the macaroons and bananas in a serving
bowl. Top with a layer of redcurrant jelly.

Whip the cream until thick and spread over the jelly. Chill lightly before
serving.

Serves 4

Apricot Cream Fondue

Metric/Imperial
1 × 425 g/15 oz can apricot halves
1 tablespoon cornflour
300 ml/½ pint double cream
65 g/2½ oz icing sugar
To serve:
small macaroons
sponge fingers
sponge cake cubes

American
1 × 15 oz can apricot halves
1 tablespoon cornstarch
1¼ cups heavy cream
½ cup confectioners' sugar
To serve:
small macaroons
ladyfingers
pound cake cubes

Drain the apricots, reserving the syrup. Put the apricots in the blender and
purée. Add enough of the reserved syrup to the purée to make it up to 300 ml/
½ pint (1¼ cups).

Dissolve the cornflour (cornstarch) in 2 tablespoons of the remaining
apricot syrup in a saucepan. Add the cream, sugar and apricot purée. Bring to
the boil, stirring, and simmer until thickened.

Serve in a fondue pot over a spirit burner, with the biscuits (cookies) and
cake.

Serves 4–5

Cream Trifle

Metric/Imperial
300 ml/½ pint double cream
2 tablespoons golden syrup, warmed
4 tablespoons rum
6 sponge fingers, sliced
sliced strawberries to decorate
juice of 1 lemon

American
1¼ cups heavy cream
2 tablespoons maple syrup, warmed
¼ cup rum
6 ladyfingers, sliced
sliced strawberries to decorate
juice of 1 lemon

Mix together the cream, syrup and rum. Place the sponge (lady) fingers in the bottom of four individual serving bowls and pour over the cream mixture. Decorate with strawberry slices. Chill for 1 hour.

Sprinkle with the lemon juice just before serving.

Serves 4

Chocolate Orange Fondue

Metric/Imperial
1 small can evaporated milk
225 g/8 oz plain chocolate, broken
   into pieces
2 tablespoons orange juice
To serve:
pieces of fresh fruit
sponge cake cubes
marshmallows

American
1 small can evaporated milk
1⅓ cups semi-sweet chocolate
   chips
2 tablespoons orange juice
To serve:
pieces of fresh fruit
pound cake cubes
marshmallows

Set aside 3 tablespoons of the milk and whip the rest until thick. Chill.

Melt the chocolate gently with the orange juice and reserved evaporated milk. When the mixture is smooth, fold in the whipped milk. Serve immediately, in a fondue pot over a very low spirit burner, with the fruit and cake for dipping.

Serves 4

Chocolate Fondue

Metric/Imperial
40 g/1½ oz cornflour
2 tablespoons sugar
600 ml/1 pint milk
100 g/4 oz plain chocolate, chopped
To serve:
banana slices
orange segments
grapes
apple wedges
sponge cake cubes
marshmallows

American
6 tablespoons cornstarch
2 tablespoons sugar
2½ cups milk
1⅓ cups semi-sweet chocolate chips
To serve:
banana slices
orange segments
grapes
apple wedges
pound cake cubes
marshmallows

Dissolve the cornflour (cornstarch) and sugar in a little of the milk. Heat the remaining milk in a saucepan and stir in the cornflour (cornstarch) mixture. Bring to the boil, stirring, and simmer for 1 minute. Reduce the heat and stir in the chocolate until melted.

Pour the chocolate mixture into a fondue pot and serve over a spirit burner with the fruit and cake cubes for dipping.
Serves 4–6

Variation:
Melt 225 g/8 oz plain chocolate (1⅓ cups semi-sweet chocolate chips) gently with 6 tablespoons double (heavy) cream and stir in 2 tablespoons rum or brandy.
Serves 4

Chocolate Nut Fondue

Metric/Imperial
225 g/8 oz plain chocolate, grated
150 ml/¼ pint double cream
4 tablespoons honey
75 g/3 oz blanched almonds,
    chopped
To serve:
sponge fingers
pieces of fresh fruit

American
1⅓ cups semi-sweet chocolate chips
⅔ cup heavy cream
¼ cup honey
¾ cup chopped blanched
    almonds
To serve:
ladyfingers
pieces of fresh fruit

Melt the chocolate gently with the cream and honey. Stir in the nuts. Pour into a fondue pot over a spirit burner and serve with the sponge (lady) fingers and fruit for dipping.
Serves 3–4

PUDDINGS

Hot Fresh Fruit Desserts

DESSERTS

Fruit Crumble

Metric/Imperial
500–600 g/1–1¼ lb prepared fruit
sugar to taste
Topping:
100 g/4 oz plain flour
50 g/2 oz butter
50 g/2 oz sugar

American
4–5 cups prepared fruit
sugar to taste
Topping:
1 cup all-purpose flour
4 tablespoons butter
¼ cup sugar

Put the fruit into a baking dish. If using soft berry fruit, add no water. For harder fruit, add 3 to 4 tablespoons of water. Sweeten to taste. Cook in a preheated moderate oven (180°C/350°F, Gas Mark 4) for 10 minutes. (To keep berry fruits firm, do not cook before adding the topping.)

For the topping, sift the flour into a bowl. Cut the butter into walnut-sized pieces and rub into the flour until the mixture resembles breadcrumbs, then stir in the sugar. Sprinkle the topping over the fruit and return to the oven. Bake for a further 25 to 30 minutes or until crisp and golden brown. Serve hot.

Serves 4

Variation:

Sift ½ to 1 teaspoon ground ginger, cinnamon or other spice with the flour, or add the grated rind of 1 to 2 oranges or lemons.

Brandied Apple Pots

Metric/Imperial
3 tablespoons brandy
1 tablespoon grated orange rind
150 ml/¼ pint orange juice
1.5 kg/3 lb cooking apples, peeled,
  cored and thinly sliced
2 tablespoons sugar
ground cinnamon
whipped cream to serve

American
3 tablespoons brandy
1 tablespoon grated orange rind
⅔ cup orange juice
3 lb tart apples, peeled, cored and
  thinly sliced
2 tablespoons sugar
ground cinnamon
whipped cream to serve

Mix together the brandy and orange rind and juice. Fold in the apple slices, then pack into six ramekin dishes. Sprinkle over the sugar. Place the dishes on a baking sheet and cover each with a small piece of greased greaseproof (wax) paper. Put a weight on top of each.

Bake in a preheated cool oven (150°C/300°F, Gas Mark 2) for 1½ hours.

Sprinkle with a little cinnamon and serve hot, with whipped cream.

Serves 6

Rhubarb and Ginger Crumble

Metric/Imperial
1 kg/2 lb rhubarb, chopped
1 cooking apple, peeled, cored and
  chopped
2 teaspoons ground ginger
50 g/2 oz brown sugar
25 g/1 oz crystallized ginger,
  chopped
Topping:
100 g/4 oz wholemeal flour
50 g/2 oz brown sugar
75 g/3 oz butter
1 tablespoon honey

American
2 lb rhubarb, chopped
1 tart apple, peeled, cored and
  chopped
2 teaspoons ground ginger
⅓ cup brown sugar
2 tablespoons chopped candied
  ginger
Topping:
1 cup wholewheat flour
⅓ cup brown sugar
6 tablespoons butter
1 tablespoon honey

Mix together the rhubarb and apple in a baking dish and sprinkle with the ground ginger, sugar and crystallized (candied) ginger.

For the topping, rub walnut-sized pieces of the butter into the flour until the mixture resembles breadcrumbs. Stir in the sugar and honey. Spread the topping over the fruit.

Bake in a preheated moderate oven (180°C/350°F, Gas Mark 4) for 45 minutes or until the top is crisp and golden.

Serves 4

Sultana (Raisin) and Apple Crumble

Metric/Imperial
1 kg/2 lb cooking apples, peeled,
  cored and sliced
175 g/6 oz sultanas
1 tablespoon grated orange rind
50 g/2 oz sugar
1 teaspoon ground mixed spice
Topping:
150 g/5 oz plain flour, sifted
75 g/3 oz sugar
75 g/3 oz butter
1 teaspoon ground mixed spice

American
2 lb tart apples, peeled, cored and
  sliced
1 cup seedless white raisins
1 tablespoon grated orange rind
¼ cup sugar
1 teaspoon apple pie spice
Topping:
1¼ cups all-purpose flour, sifted
6 tablespoons sugar
6 tablespoons butter
1 teaspoon apple pie spice

Mix together the apples and sultanas (raisins) in a baking dish and sprinkle with the orange rind, sugar and spice.

For the topping, rub walnut-sized pieces of the butter into the flour until the mixture resembles breadcrumbs. Stir in the sugar and spice, then spread the topping over the fruit mixture.

Bake in a preheated moderate oven (180°C/350°F, Gas Mark 4) for 40 minutes or until the topping is crisp and golden.
Serves 4

Plum Crunch

Metric/Imperial
1 kg/2 lb plums, halved and stoned
100 g/4 oz demerara sugar
50 g/2 oz Rice Krispies or
  cornflakes, lightly crushed

American
2 lb plums, halved and pitted
⅔ cup raw brown sugar
1½ cups Rice Krispies or cornflakes,
  lightly crushed

Put the plums in a shallow baking dish. Mix the sugar with the cereal and sprinkle over the fruit. Bake in a preheated moderately hot oven (190°C/375°F, Gas Mark 5) for 45 minutes.
Serves 4–6

Gooseberry and Almond Crumble

Metric/Imperial
500 g/1 lb gooseberries
2 tablespoons sugar
grated rind and juice of 1 orange
Topping:
50 g/2 oz butter
100 g/4 oz wholemeal flour or rolled
  oats
50 g/2 oz soft brown sugar
50 g/2 oz blanched almonds,
  chopped

American
1 lb gooseberries
2 tablespoons sugar
grated rind and juice of 1 orange
Topping:
4 tablespoons butter
1 cup wholewheat flour or 1⅓ cups
  rolled oats
⅓ cup light brown sugar
½ cup chopped blanched
  almonds

Put the gooseberries in a baking dish and sprinkle over the sugar and orange rind and juice.

For the topping, rub walnut-sized pieces of the butter into the flour or rolled oats, then stir in the sugar and almonds. Scatter over the gooseberries to cover them completely.

Bake in a preheated moderately hot oven (200°C/400°F, Gas Mark 6) for 30 minutes or until the crumble topping is crisp and browned.
Serves 4

Fruit Amber

Metric/Imperial
300 ml/½ pint sweetened thick fruit
  purée (such as apple or apricot)
25 g/1 oz butter
2 eggs, separated
65 g/2½ oz caster sugar

American
1¼ cups sweetened thick fruit purée
  (such as apple or apricot)
2 tablespoons butter
2 eggs, separated
5 tablespoons sugar

Heat the purée gently and stir in the butter until melted. Remove from the heat and beat in the egg yolks. Pour into a greased baking dish.

Beat the egg whites until stiff. Add 1 tablespoon of the sugar and continue beating for 1 minute, then fold in all but 1 tablespoon of the remaining sugar. Pile the meringue on top of the fruit mixture and sprinkle with the reserved sugar.

Bake in a preheated moderate oven (160°C/325°F, Gas Mark 3) for 30 minutes or until the top is golden and crisp. Serve hot or cold.
Serves 4

Fritter Batter

Metric/Imperial
100 g/4 oz plain flour
pinch of salt
1–2 eggs, beaten
150 ml/¼ pint mixed milk and water
1–2 teaspoons oil or melted butter

American
1 cup all-purpose flour
pinch of salt
1–2 eggs, beaten
⅔ cup mixed milk and water
1–2 teaspoons oil or melted butter

Sift the flour and salt into a bowl. Mix in the eggs, then stir in the liquid to make a smooth batter. Add the oil or melted butter just before using.
Serves about 4

Variation:
For a lighter batter, separate the egg(s) and add the yolk to the flour. Mix in the liquid and oil or melted butter. Beat the egg white until stiff and fold into the batter. Use immediately.

Apple Fritters

Metric/Imperial
4 large cooking apples, peeled,
    cored and cut into 1 cm/½ inch
    rings
plain flour
fritter batter (see above)
oil for deep frying
sugar

American
4 large tart apples, peeled,
    cored and cut into ½ inch
    rings
all-purpose flour
fritter batter (see above)
oil for deep frying
sugar

Coat the apple rings with flour, then dip them into the fritter batter. Hold them over the bowl of batter to allow the excess to drop back into the bowl. Deep fry for 4 to 5 minutes or until golden brown. Drain on paper towels and serve hot, sprinkled with sugar.
Note: the fritters may be shallow fried for 2 to 3 minutes on each side.
Serves 4

Variation:
Banana Fritters: Use 4 bananas, quartered, and use the lighter fritter batter. Dredge with sugar and serve hot.

Fruit and Nut Fritters

Metric/Imperial

3 apples, peeled, cored and finely
   chopped
25 g/1 oz dried apricots, finely
   chopped
25 g/1 oz sultanas
50 g/2 oz blanched almonds, finely
   chopped
3 tablespoons rum
oil for deep frying
Batter:
200 g/7 oz plain flour
25 g/1 oz sugar
200 ml/⅓ pint white wine
1 tablespoon oil
grated rind of 1 lemon
3 eggs, separated

American

3 apples, peeled, cored and finely
   chopped
3 tablespoons finely chopped dried
   apricots
3 tablespoons seedless white raisins
½ cup finely chopped blanched
   almonds
3 tablespoons rum
oil for deep frying
Batter:
1¾ cups all-purpose flour
2 tablespoons sugar
⅞ cup white wine
1 tablespoon oil
grated rind of 1 lemon
3 eggs, separated

Put the fruit and nuts in a bowl and sprinkle with the rum. Leave to marinate for 1 hour, stirring occasionally.

For the batter, sift the flour into a bowl and stir in the sugar. Gradually beat in the wine, oil and lemon rind, followed by the egg yolks. Leave for 30 minutes.

Beat the egg whites until stiff and fold into the batter with the fruit mixture. Deep fry tablespoonsful of the batter until golden brown. Drain on paper towels and serve hot.
Serves 4–6

Grapefruit Meringues

Metric/Imperial	American
2 large grapefruit	2 large grapefruit
sugar to taste	sugar to taste
2 tablespoons kirsch	2 tablespoons kirsch
2 egg whites	2 egg whites
100 g/4 oz caster sugar	½ cup sugar
2 glacé cherries, halved	2 candied cherries, halved

Cut the grapefruit in half and loosen the segments. Remove the segments and reserve. Scoop out all the membrane, then return the segments to the grapefruit shells. Sprinkle with sugar to taste and the kirsch.

Beat the egg whites until stiff. Add 2 tablespoons of the sugar and continue beating for 1 minute. Fold in the remaining sugar.

Pile the meringue on the grapefruit halves and brown under a hot grill (broiler) for about 5 minutes. Top each with a half cherry.

Serves 4

Apple and Cheese Crumble

Metric/Imperial	American
750 g/1½ lb cooking apples, peeled, cored and sliced	1½ lb tart apples, peeled, cored and sliced
175 g/6 oz Cheddar cheese, grated	1½ cups grated Cheddar cheese
½ teaspoon ground cinnamon	½ teaspoon ground cinnamon
50 g/2 oz soft brown sugar	⅓ cup light brown sugar
50 g/2 oz raisins	⅓ cup raisins
175 g/6 oz plain flour	1½ cups all-purpose flour
75 g/3 oz butter	6 tablespoons butter
50 g/2 oz caster sugar	¼ cup sugar

Put the apples in a greased baking dish and sprinkle with 100 g/4 oz (1 cup) of the cheese, the cinnamon, brown sugar and raisins.

Sift the flour into a bowl and rub in walnut-sized pieces of the butter until the mixture resembles breadcrumbs. Add the sugar and the remaining cheese and mix well.

Sprinkle the crumb topping over the apples and bake in a preheated moderately hot oven (200°C/400°F, Gas Mark 6) for 30 to 40 minutes or until the top is golden brown.

Serves 4–6

Flaming Apples

Metric/Imperial
8 apples, peeled
lemon juice
175 g/6 oz soft brown sugar
1 teaspoon ground cinnamon
1.2 litres/2 pints water
6 tablespoons rum, warmed

American
8 apples, peeled
lemon juice
1 cup light brown sugar
1 teaspoon ground cinnamon
1 quart water
6 tablespoons rum, warmed

Dip the apples in lemon juice to prevent discoloration.

Put the sugar, cinnamon and water in a saucepan and bring to the boil, stirring to dissolve the sugar. Add the apples, cover and simmer for 10 to 15 minutes or until just tender.

Transfer the apples to a heatproof serving dish and keep hot. Boil the cooking syrup until it begins to thicken. Pour the syrup over the apples followed by the rum. Set alight and serve flaming.
Serves 4

Variation:
Peel, core and slice 4 large apples. Melt 50 g/2 oz (4 tablespoons) butter in a frying pan (skillet) or chafing dish, add the apple slices and brown on all sides. Sprinkle over brown sugar to taste, followed by 3 tablespoons rum. Warm the rum then set alight. When the flames have died down, serve the apples. Stir 2 tablespoons apple jelly into the syrup in the pan and pour over the apples. Serve with whipped cream.
Serves 4

Plums with Port

Metric/Imperial
1 kg/2 lb plums, halved and stoned
100 g/4 oz brown sugar
150 ml/¼ pint port wine

American
2 lb plums, halved and pitted
⅔ cup brown sugar
⅔ cup port wine

Put the plums in a baking dish, sprinkle over the sugar and pour over the port. Cover and cook in a preheated cool oven (150°C/300°F, Gas Mark 2) for 45 minutes to 1 hour or until the plums are very tender.

Serve hot or lightly chilled, with whipped cream.
Serves 4–6

Scorched Oranges

Metric/Imperial	American
4 large oranges, peeled and thinly sliced	4 large oranges, peeled and thinly sliced
2 tablespoons orange liqueur	2 tablespoons orange liqueur
300 ml/½ pint double cream	1¼ cups heavy cream
300 ml/½ pint sour cream	1¼ cups sour cream
50 g/2 oz demerara sugar	⅓ cup raw brown sugar

Place the orange slices in a flameproof serving dish and sprinkle them with the liqueur.

Whip the double (heavy) cream lightly and mix with the sour cream. Spread over the oranges. Chill.

Sprinkle the sugar over the cream. Grill (broil) until the sugar has melted.
Serves 4–6

Baked Apples

Metric/Imperial	American
4 cooking apples, cored	4 tart apples, cored
3 tablespoons golden syrup	3 tablespoons light corn syrup
50 g/2 oz sultanas	⅓ cup seedless white raisins
grated rind of ½ lemon	grated rind of ½ lemon

Score the skin around the centre of each apple. Mix together the syrup, sultanas (raisins) and lemon rind and pack into the apples. Place them in a baking dish and bake in a preheated moderate oven (180°C/350°F, Gas Mark 4) for 25 to 30 minutes or until tender.
Serves 4

Variations:

Fill the apples with 50 g/2 oz (¼ cup) chopped dates, top each with a pat of butter and pour over 4 tablespoons golden (light corn) syrup. Bake as above.

Fill the apples with a mixture of 225 g/8 oz blackberries, the finely grated rind and juice of 1 large orange, 4 tablespoons brown sugar and 1 tablespoon chopped mint. Bake as above.

Fill the apples with a mixture of 3 tablespoons orange marmalade, the finely grated rind of 1 orange and 2 tablespoons orange juice. Bake as above. Just before serving, top each apple with a few orange segments and heat through in the oven.

Glazed Apples

Metric/Imperial
300 ml/½ pint water
juice of 1 lemon
strip of lemon rind
100 g/4 oz sugar
4 medium cooking apples, peeled
1 tablespoon orange liqueur
25 g/1 oz butter

American
1¼ cups water
juice of 1 lemon
strip of lemon rind
½ cup sugar
4 medium tart apples, peeled
1 tablespoon orange liqueur
2 tablespoons butter

Put the water, lemon juice and rind and sugar in a saucepan and heat, stirring to dissolve the sugar. Add the apples and poach gently until tender.

Add the liqueur and butter and stir gently until the butter has melted. Baste the apples with the syrup until they are glazed. Serve hot.
Serves 4

Baked Apple Meringues

Metric/Imperial
4 large cooking apples, cored
50 g/2 oz butter
100 g/4 oz raisins
100 g/4 oz sugar
150 ml/¼ pint sweet white wine
2 egg whites
few drops of anise liqueur or Pernod
2 tablespoons honey

American
4 large tart apples, cored
4 tablespoons butter
⅔ cup raisins
½ cup sugar
⅔ cup sweet white wine
2 egg whites
few drops of anise liqueur or Pernod
2 tablespoons honey

Place the apples in a greased baking dish and fill the centres with the butter and raisins. Sprinkle over some of the sugar. Pour around the wine and bake in a preheated moderate oven (180°C/350°F, Gas Mark 4) for about 40 minutes.

Meanwhile, beat the egg whites with all but 2 tablespoons of the remaining sugar and the liqueur until stiff.

Spoon a little honey over each apple and top with the meringue. Sprinkle with the rest of the sugar and bake for a further 10 minutes or until the apples are tender and the meringue is lightly browned.
Serves 4

Pears in Cream

Metric/Imperial
25 g/1 oz butter
4 ripe pears, peeled, cored and
  sliced
4 tablespoons vanilla sugar
6 tablespoons double cream

American
2 tablespoons butter
4 ripe pears, peeled, cored and
  sliced
¼ cup vanilla sugar
6 tablespoons heavy cream

Melt the butter in a flameproof dish. Add the pears, arranging them in one layer, and sprinkle with the sugar. Cook very gently for 10 to 15 minutes or until the pears are tender.

Stir in the cream and cook for 2 minutes, shaking the dish occasionally. Transfer the dish to a preheated moderate oven (180°C/350°F, Gas Mark 4) and cook for 5 minutes. Serve hot.

Serves 4

Strawberries Flambés

Metric/Imperial
thinly pared rind of 1 lemon
grated rind and juice of 2 oranges
100 g/4 oz sugar
500 g/1 lb strawberries, hulled
4–5 tablespoons brandy
vanilla ice cream to serve

American
thinly pared rind of 1 lemon
grated rind and juice of 2 oranges
½ cup sugar
1 lb strawberries, hulled
4–5 tablespoons brandy
vanilla ice cream to serve

Put the lemon rind, orange rind and juice and sugar in a saucepan and heat slowly, stirring to dissolve the sugar. Cook gently for 5 minutes, pressing the lemon rind to extract the flavour.

Discard the lemon rind, then add the strawberries to the pan. Spoon the syrup over the strawberries.

Pour the strawberries and syrup into a warmed serving dish. Warm the brandy, pour over the strawberries and set alight. Serve flaming, spooned over vanilla ice cream.

Serves 6

Caribbean Bananas

Metric/Imperial
8 bananas, halved lengthways
juice of 1 lemon
2 tablespoons water
50 g/2 oz dark brown sugar
3 tablespoons rum
whipped cream to serve

American
8 bananas, halved lengthwise
juice of 1 lemon
2 tablespoons water
⅓ cup dark brown sugar
3 tablespoons rum
whipped cream to serve

Put the bananas in a well buttered baking dish. Mix the lemon juice with the water and sprinkle over the bananas with the sugar. Bake in a preheated moderately hot oven (190°C/375°F, Gas Mark 5) for 20 minutes.

Sprinkle over the rum and bake for a further 2 minutes.

Serve hot, with cream.

Serves 4

Pineapple Liqueur Fritters

Metric/Imperial
8 canned or fresh pineapple rings
2 tablespoons kirsch
fritter batter made with 1 egg (see
    page 72)
oil for deep frying
3 tablespoons sugar
1 teaspoon ground cinnamon

American
8 canned or fresh pineapple rings
2 tablespoons kirsch
fritter batter made with 1 egg (see
    page 72)
oil for deep frying
3 tablespoons sugar
1 teaspoon ground cinnamon

Sprinkle the pineapple rings with the kirsch, then leave to marinate for 30 minutes.

Pat the pineapple rings dry with paper towels and dip them into the batter to coat well. Deep fry in oil heated to 190°C/375°F until golden. Drain on paper towels.

Mix together the sugar and cinnamon. Roll the fritters in this mixture and serve hot.

Serves 4

Cherry Grapefruit Alaska

Metric/Imperial	**American**
2 grapefruit, halved	2 grapefruit, halved
4–6 tablespoons canned black cherries	4–6 tablespoons canned bing cherries
sugar to taste	sugar to taste
vanilla ice cream	vanilla ice cream
2 egg whites	2 egg whites
100 g/4 oz caster sugar	½ cup sugar

Loosen the grapefruit segments, then remove them. Discard all the membrane from the grapefruit halves, then return the grapefruit segments to them with the cherries. Sweeten to taste. Put a scoop of ice cream on each grapefruit half.

Beat the egg whites until stiff. Add 2 tablespoons of the sugar and continue beating for 1 minute, then fold in the remaining sugar. Pile the meringue on top of the grapefruit halves and arrange them in a baking dish. Bake in a preheated hot oven (225°C/450°F, Gas Mark 8) for 4 to 5 minutes or until the meringue is lightly tinged brown. Serve immediately.

Serves 4

Baked Bananas

Metric/Imperial	**American**
50 g/2 oz butter	4 tablespoons butter
2 tablespoons brown sugar	2 tablespoons brown sugar
finely grated rind and juice of 1 orange	finely grated rind and juice of 1 orange
juice of ½ lemon	juice of ½ lemon
pinch of ground mixed spice	pinch of apple pie spice
4 large bananas, halved lengthways	4 large bananas, halved lengthwise
2 tablespoons desiccated coconut	2 tablespoons shredded coconut

Put the butter, sugar, orange rind and juice, lemon juice and spice in a saucepan and heat gently, stirring to dissolve the sugar.

Put the bananas in a baking dish and pour over the spiced mixture. Sprinkle with the coconut. Bake in a preheated moderate oven (180°C/350°F, Gas Mark 4) for 30 minutes.

Serves 4

Baked Oranges

Metric/Imperial
4 large oranges, peeled and halved
50 g/2 oz brown sugar
3 tablespoons rum
15 g/½ oz butter

American
4 large oranges, peeled and halved
⅓ cup brown sugar
3 tablespoons rum
1 tablespoon butter

Put the orange halves, cut sides up, in a well buttered baking dish. Sprinkle over the sugar and rum and dot with the butter. Bake in a preheated moderate oven (180°C/350°F, Gas Mark 4) for 20 to 25 minutes.
Serves 4

Baked Spiced Peaches

Metric/Imperial
4 large peaches, halved and stoned
juice of 2 oranges
2 tablespoons redcurrant jelly
1 cinnamon stick
2 cloves
½ teaspoon whole allspice berries
2–3 tablespoons brandy (optional)
Filling:
1 egg, beaten
50 g/2 oz ground almonds
1 tablespoon finely chopped
    preserved ginger
1 tablespoon soft brown sugar

American
4 large peaches, halved and pitted
juice of 2 oranges
2 tablespoons redcurrant jelly
1 cinnamon stick
2 cloves
½ teaspoon whole allspice berries
2–3 tablespoons brandy (optional)
Filling:
1 egg, beaten
½ cup ground almonds
1 tablespoon finely chopped candied
    ginger
1 tablespoon light brown sugar

Scoop some of the flesh from the centre of each peach half to make room for the filling. Mix together the scooped-out peach flesh with all the filling ingredients. Use to fill the peach halves, then arrange them in a baking dish.

Put the orange juice, redcurrant jelly and spices in a saucepan and heat gently to melt the jelly. Bring to the boil, then pour over the peaches.

Bake in a preheated moderate oven (180°C/350°F, Gas Mark 4) for about 20 minutes or until the peaches are tender.

Warm the brandy, if using, pour it over the peaches and set alight. Serve flaming.
Serves 4

Pacific Delight

Metric/Imperial
1 ripe medium pineapple
4–6 portions vanilla ice cream
4 egg whites
100 g/4 oz caster sugar

American
1 ripe medium pineapple
4–6 portions vanilla ice cream
4 egg whites
½ cup sugar

Cut the top from the pineapple and reserve. Slice the pineapple into 4 to 6 rings. Remove the skin and cut out the core. Put the first slice of pineapple on an ovenproof serving plate and fill the centre hole with ice cream. Top with the second pineapple slice and more ice cream. When the pineapple has been reassembled, keep it in the freezer while you make the meringue.

Beat the egg whites until stiff. Gradually beat in 50 g/2 oz (¼ cup) of the sugar, then fold in the remainder. Put the meringue in a piping (pastry) bag fitted with a 6 mm/¼ inch rose nozzle. Pipe the meringue all over the pineapple, pulling it out in little peaks so that it looks like the fruit skin. Be sure all the fruit and ice cream is covered.

Bake in a preheated very hot oven (240°C/475°F, Gas Mark 9) for 3 minutes or until the meringue is just tinged with golden brown. Put the top leafy part back on the pineapple and serve.
Serves 4–6

Grapefruit Grand Marnier

Metric/Imperial
2 large grapefruit
4 tablespoons clear honey
2 tablespoons Grand Marnier

American
2 large grapefruit
¼ cup clear honey
2 tablespoons Grand Marnier

Halve the grapefruit and loosen the segments. Turn the grapefruit halves upside-down on paper towels to drain off excess juice, then arrange, cut side up, in the grill (broiler) pan. Top each half with 1 tablespoon honey and ½ tablespoon Grand Marnier. Leave to soak for 30 minutes.

Grill (broil) gently for about 3 minutes or until the fruit is hot and golden on top.
Serves 4

Stuffed Peaches in Wine

Metric/Imperial
4 large peaches, peeled, halved and
 stoned
40 g/1½ oz macaroons, crushed
25 g/1 oz ground almonds
½ teaspoon finely grated orange rind
1 egg yolk
25 g/1 oz butter
120 ml/4 fl oz sweet white wine

American
4 large peaches, peeled, halved and
 pitted
¾ cup crushed macaroons
¼ cup ground almonds
½ teaspoon finely grated orange rind
1 egg yolk
2 tablespoons butter
½ cup sweet white wine

Arrange the peach halves, cut sides up, in a buttered baking dish.
 Mix together the macaroons, almonds and orange rind and bind with the
egg yolk. Use to fill the hollows in the peach halves. Dot with pieces of butter.
Pour the wine around the peaches.
 Bake in a preheated moderate oven (180°C/350°F, Gas Mark 4) for 30
minutes. Serve warm.
Serves 4

Fried Bananas with Rum

Metric/Imperial
25 g/1 oz butter
4 large bananas, halved lengthways
juice of ½ lemon
4 tablespoons rum or brandy,
 warmed
caster sugar

American
2 tablespoons butter
4 large bananas, halved lengthwise
juice of ½ lemon
¼ cup rum or brandy,
 warmed
sugar

Melt the butter in a frying pan. Add the bananas and cook gently for about 2
minutes on each side. Add the lemon juice, then pour over the rum or brandy
and set alight. Sprinkle with sugar and serve immediately, with cream.
Serves 4

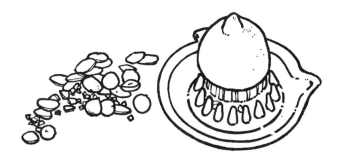

Hot Melon and Ginger

Metric/Imperial
1 melon, halved and seeded
juice of 1 lemon
150 ml/¼ pint water
50 g/2 oz sugar
3 tablespoons diced preserved or
   crystallized ginger

American
1 melon, halved and seeded
juice of 1 lemon
⅔ cup water
¼ cup sugar
3 tablespoons diced candied
   ginger

Scoop out the melon flesh with a melon-baller or cut it into cubes.
   Put the remaining ingredients in a saucepan and heat gently, stirring to dissolve the sugar. Add the melon and heat for a few minutes. Serve hot.
Serves 4

Variation:
Cut the melon into slices, remove the seeds and place in a baking dish. Sprinkle with orange juice and a little ground ginger and top with pieces of preserved or crystallized (candied) ginger. Warm in a preheated moderate oven (180°C/350°F, Gas Mark 4) for about 15 minutes.

Burgundy Bananas

Metric/Imperial
300 ml/½ pint red wine
100 g/4 oz brown sugar
1 teaspoon grated orange rind
½ teaspoon grated nutmeg
½ teaspoon ground cinnamon
4 bananas
3 tablespoons flaked almonds
4 tablespoons rum, warmed

American
1¼ cups red wine
⅔ cup brown sugar
1 teaspoon grated orange rind
½ teaspoon grated nutmeg
½ teaspoon ground cinnamon
4 bananas
3 tablespoons slivered almonds
¼ cup rum, warmed

Put the wine, sugar, orange rind and spices into a frying pan (skillet) or chafing dish. Heat, stirring to dissolve the sugar. Add the bananas and cook until they are just tender.
   Sprinkle over the almonds followed by the rum. Set alight and serve flaming, with cream or ice cream.
Serves 4

Cherries in Red Wine

Metric/Imperial
100 g/4 oz sugar
1 strip orange rind
pinch of ground cinnamon
1 tablespoon redcurrant jelly
150 ml/¼ pint red wine
500 g/1 lb large black cherries,
    stoned
25 g/1 oz butter
4 small thin slices of bread, crusts
    removed

American
½ cup sugar
1 strip orange rind
pinch of ground cinnamon
1 tablespoon redcurrant jelly
⅔ cup red wine
1 lb large bing cherries
    pitted
2 tablespoons butter
4 small thin slices of bread, crusts
    removed.

Put the sugar, orange rind, cinnamon, jelly and wine in a saucepan and bring to the boil, stirring to dissolve the sugar. Boil for 1 minute. Stir in the cherries and simmer gently for 10 to 15 minutes.

Meanwhile, melt the butter in a frying pan. Add the bread slices and fry until golden on both sides. Drain on paper towels and arrange on four individual serving plates. Place the cherries on the bread slices, using a slotted spoon. Keep hot.

Boil the cherry syrup until it thickens. Pour over the cherries.
Serves 4

Hot Fruit Compôte

Metric/Imperial
175 g/6 oz dried apricots
450 ml/¾ pint dry cider
3 tablespoons honey
150 ml/¼ pint water
1 cinnamon stick
2 cloves
50 g/2 oz raisins
1 large grapefruit, peeled and
  segmented
2 bananas, sliced

American
1 cup dried apricots
2 cups hard cider
3 tablespoons honey
⅔ cup water
1 cinnamon stick
2 cloves
⅓ cup raisins
1 large grapefruit, peeled and
  segmented
2 bananas, sliced

Soak the apricots in the cider for 2 to 3 hours.

Tip the apricots and cider into a saucepan and add the honey, water, cinnamon and cloves. Bring to the boil, then cover and simmer for 15 to 20 minutes or until the apricots are tender. Add the raisins and simmer for a further 5 minutes.

Discard the cinnamon stick and cloves. Add the grapefruit segments and bananas to the pan and heat through gently. Serve warm.
Serves 4

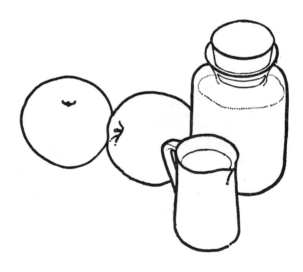

PUDDINGS

Cold Fresh Fruit Desserts

DESSERTS

Apple and Orange Bristol

Metric/Imperial
175 g/6 oz sugar
300 ml/½ pint water
4 apples, peeled, cored and
   quartered
2 oranges
whipped cream to serve

American
¾ cup sugar
1¼ cups water
4 apples, peeled, cored and
   quartered
2 oranges
whipped cream to serve

Put 50 g/2 oz (¼ cup) of the sugar in a saucepan and melt it gently. Heat until it turns a light golden brown, then pour onto a greased baking sheet, spreading it as thinly as possible. Cool until set, then crush with a rolling pin.

Put the remaining sugar in the saucepan with the water and stir to dissolve the sugar. Add the apples and poach until they are tender. Remove from the heat and cool the apples in the syrup until they are transparent.

Meanwhile, pare the rind from one of the oranges and cut it into thin shreds. Put it into a pan of water, bring to the boil and simmer for 10 minutes. Drain and refresh in cold water.

Peel the oranges, removing all the white pith, and slice them. Drain the apples and arrange the apples and oranges in a serving bowl. Pour over a little of the apple syrup. Sprinkle with the orange rind and the crushed caramel. Serve with whipped cream.
Serves 4–6

Fruity Apple Rings

Metric/Imperial
6 tablespoons mixed dried fruit
  (raisins, currants, etc)
2 tablespoons medium sherry or
  orange juice
4 apples, cored and cut into rings
orange juice

American
6 tablespoons mixed dried fruit
  (raisins, currants, etc)
2 tablespoons medium sherry or
  orange juice
4 apples, cored and cut into rings
orange juice

Put the fruit in a bowl and sprinkle with the sherry or orange juice. Leave to soak for 30 minutes.

Arrange the apple rings on four serving plates and sprinkle them with orange juice to prevent discoloration. Pile a little of the fruit in the centre of each apple ring. Serve with cream.

Serves 4

Creamy Apple Crunch

Metric/Imperial
100 g/4 oz sugar
150 ml/¼ pint water
4 medium cooking apples, peeled,
  cored and sliced
300 ml/½ pint soured cream
2½ tablespoons brown sugar
4–6 gingernut biscuits, crushed
2 tablespoons chopped almonds

American
½ cup sugar
⅔ cup water
4 medium tart apples, peeled, cored
  and sliced
1¼ cups sour cream
2½ tablespoons brown sugar
4–6 ginger snaps, crushed
2 tablespoons chopped almonds

Dissolve the sugar in the water. Add the apples and poach until just tender. Drain the apples and mix with the sour cream and 2 tablespoons of the brown sugar. Pour into a flameproof serving dish.

Mix together the crushed biscuits (cookies), almonds and remaining brown sugar and sprinkle over the apple mixture. Brown for 2 to 3 minutes under a hot grill (broiler). Serve cold.

Serves 4–6

Pink Poached Apples and Pears

Metric/Imperial
500 g/1 lb mixed red fruit
  (redcurrants, raspberries,
  loganberries, plums, etc)
sugar to taste
2 apples, peeled
2 pears, peeled

American
1 lb mixed red fruit (redcurrants,
  raspberries, loganberries, plums,
  etc)
sugar to taste
2 apples, peeled
2 pears, peeled

Poach the red fruit gently with just enough water to cover the bottom of the pan. When very soft, cool slightly, then tip into the blender. Blend to a smooth purée and sweeten to taste.

Put the apples and pears in a saucepan and pour over the red fruit sauce. Poach gently until they are just tender. Serve hot or cold.

Serves 4

Caramelized Oranges

Metric/Imperial
6 large oranges
300 ml/½ pint water
75 g/3 oz sugar

American
6 large oranges
1¼ cups water
6 tablespoons sugar

Peel the oranges. Remove all the white pith from the rind, then cut the rind into matchsticks. Put the rind and water into a saucepan and leave to soak for 30 minutes.

Bring the water to the boil and simmer for 20 minutes or until the rind is softened and the water is reduced to about 250 ml/8 fl oz (1 cup). Pour the water and rind into a bowl.

Put 3 tablespoons of the water back into the pan and add the sugar. Stir until dissolved, then boil until a golden caramel. Add the rest of the water with the rind and simmer for a few minutes.

Meanwhile, slice the oranges. Reshape them and secure with wooden cocktail sticks. Pour the caramel syrup over the oranges and chill well.

Serves 4

Apple Flake

Metric/Imperial	American
500 g/1 lb cooking apples, peeled, cored and chopped	1 lb tart apples, peeled, cored and chopped
100 g/4 oz caster sugar	½ cup sugar
300 ml/½ pint double cream	1¼ cups heavy cream
3 tablespoons golden syrup	3 tablespoons light corn syrup
50 g/2 oz cornflakes	2 cups cornflakes

Put the apples and sugar in a saucepan with just enough water to cover the bottom of the pan and cook gently until the apples have pulped. Beat until smooth, then divide between four serving dishes. Cool.

Whip the cream until thick and spread over the apples.

Warm the syrup in a saucepan. Add the cornflakes and toss gently to coat them with the syrup. Sprinkle the flakes over the cream. Chill well.
Serves 4–6

Pears in Cassis

Metric/Imperial	American
300 ml/½ pint medium or sweet white wine	1¼ cups medium or sweet white wine
100 g/4 oz blackcurrants	¼ lb blackcurrants
4 tablespoons honey	¼ cup honey
1 cinnamon stick	1 cinnamon stick
2 strips lemon rind	2 strips lemon rind
4–6 pears, peeled	4–6 pears, peeled
1 teaspoon arrowroot	1 teaspoon arrowroot

Put the wine, blackcurrants, honey, cinnamon stick and lemon rind in a saucepan and bring to the boil. Boil for 1 minute.

Put the pears into the pan, submerging them as much as possible in the liquid, cover the pan and cook gently for about 20 minutes or until the pears are tender.

Transfer the pears carefully to a serving bowl.

Discard the cinnamon stick and lemon rind from the liquid. Dissolve the arrowroot in a little water and add to the liquid. Bring to the boil, stirring, and simmer until thickened. Pour this sauce over the pears. Serve hot or cold.
Serves 4–6

Orange Salad

Metric/Imperial
6 juicy oranges
100 g/4 oz sugar
2 tablespoons brandy or orange
  liqueur

American
6 juicy oranges
½ cup sugar
2 tablespoons brandy or orange
  liqueur

Thinly pare the rind from one of the oranges and cut the rind into thin strips.
  Peel all the oranges, removing all the white pith, and divide them into
segments. Discard any seeds. Put the orange segments in a bowl.
  Put the orange rind strips and sugar in a saucepan and heat gently until the
sugar has melted and turned golden brown. Pour over the orange segments:
the sugar will set to a hard crust but will melt with the juice from the oranges.
Add the brandy or liqueur.
Serves 4

Variations:
Oranges in Kirsch: Pare the rind from one of 8 oranges, as above, and cut it
into strips. Peel all the oranges, slice them thinly, then reshape them and
secure with cocktail sticks. Put the oranges, orange rind strips and 120 ml/
4 fl oz (½ cup) kirsch in a bowl, cover and chill overnight. For the caramel,
melt 100 g/4 oz (½ cup) sugar until caramel coloured. Pour the caramel onto a
sheet of greased foil, spread out thinly and leave to set. Chop the caramel
with a sharp knife and sprinkle it over the oranges before serving.
Serves 8

Oranges and Grapes Grand Marnier: Peel and slice 6 oranges and arrange
decoratively in a serving dish. Halve and pip (seed) 225 g/8 oz grapes and
add to the oranges. Dissolve 225 g/8 oz (1 cup) sugar in 120 ml/4 fl oz (½ cup)
water and boil for 1 minute. Stir in the juice of 1 lemon and 6 tablespoons
Grand Marnier. Pour this syrup over the fruit and sprinkle with 50 g/2 oz (½
cup) flaked (slivered) almonds. Chill before serving.
Serves 6

Pears Belle Hélène

Metric/Imperial
225 g/8 oz sugar
300 ml/½ pint water
3 tablespoons honey
4 pears, peeled, halved and cored
vanilla ice cream
300 ml/½ pint chocolate sauce 1 (see
    page 215)

American
1 cup sugar
1¼ cups water
3 tablespoons honey
4 pears, peeled, halved and cored
vanilla ice cream
1¼ cups chocolate sauce 1 (see
    page 215)

Put the sugar and water in a saucepan and stir to dissolve the sugar. Stir in the honey. Add the pear halves and poach gently for 15 to 20 minutes or until tender. Drain and cool.

Put a scoop of ice cream in each of four individual serving dishes and arrange the pear halves on top. Pour over the chocolate sauce.
Serves 4

Hawaiian Nut Pudding

Metric/Imperial
6 canned pineapple rings
6 oranges, peeled
50 g/2 oz butter
50 g/2 oz caster sugar
150 ml/¼ pint pineapple syrup (from
    the can)
juice of 1 orange or 2 tablespoons
    orange liqueur
chopped nuts

American
6 canned pineapple rings
6 oranges, peeled
4 tablespoons butter
¼ cup sugar
⅔ cup pineapple syrup (from the
    can)
juice of 1 orange or 2 tablespoons
    orange liqueur
chopped nuts

Arrange the pineapple rings, in one layer, in a baking dish and place an orange on each ring.

Melt the butter in a saucepan and stir in the sugar until dissolved. Add the pineapple syrup and orange juice or liqueur and mix well. Pour over the oranges in the baking dish.

Cover the dish and bake in a preheated moderately hot oven (190°C/375°F, Gas Mark 5) for about 45 minutes.

Transfer the oranges and pineapple to a heated serving dish and pour over the liquid from the baking dish. Cover the oranges with chopped nuts and serve warm or cold with cream.
Serves 6

Casseroled Pears with Prunes

Metric/Imperial
225 g/8 oz prunes
300 ml/½ pint wine or cider
500 g/1 lb small pears, peeled, cored
  and quartered
grated rind and juice of 1 orange
100 g/4 oz sugar

American
½ lb prunes
1¼ cups wine or hard cider
1 lb small pears, peeled, cored and
  quartered
grated rind and juice of 1 orange
½ cup sugar

Put the prunes in a baking dish, pour over the wine or cider and leave to soak overnight.

The next day, add the pears, orange rind and juice and sugar to the dish and mix together gently. Cover and cook in a preheated moderate oven (160°C/325°F, Gas Mark 3) for 1 hour or until the fruit is tender. Serve hot or cold.
Serves 4–6

Steamed Pears

Metric/Imperial
4 large pears, peeled
4 tablespoons sugar
4 tablespoons honey
2 tablespoons cherry brandy

American
4 large pears, peeled
¼ cup sugar
¼ cup honey
2 tablespoons cherry brandy

Stand the pears in a saucepan and just cover with water. Bring to the boil, then simmer gently for 30 minutes.

Pour off half the water. Sprinkle the pears with the sugar and simmer for a further 10 minutes. Transfer the pears to a serving bowl and cool.

Pour off a further half of the water in the pan. Stir in the honey and brandy. Pour this sauce into a jug. Chill the pears and sauce for 2 hours before serving.
Serves 4

Caramel Bananas

Metric/Imperial
50 g/2 oz butter
150 g/5 oz dark brown sugar
4 large bananas, sliced
4 tablespoons single cream
vanilla ice cream to serve

American
4 tablespoons butter
¾ cup dark brown sugar
4 large bananas, sliced
¼ cup light cream
vanilla ice cream to serve

Melt the butter in a saucepan and stir in the sugar until dissolved. Add the bananas and cook gently for 5 minutes. Stir in the cream.
 Pour the banana mixture over scoops of vanilla ice cream.
Serves 4

Bananas with Kirsch and Cream

Metric/Imperial
4 large ripe bananas, sliced
caster sugar
2 tablespoons kirsch
4 tablespoons double cream

American
4 large ripe bananas, sliced
sugar
2 tablespoons kirsch
¼ cup heavy cream

Divide the bananas between four dishes and sprinkle with sugar to taste and the kirsch. Add the cream and fold together gently to be sure the banana slices are coated.
Serves 4

Baked Ginger Pears

Metric/Imperial
4 firm pears, peeled, halved and
 cored
450 ml/¾ pint ginger beer

American
4 firm pears, peeled, halved and
 cored
2 cups ginger ale

Arrange the pear halves in a baking dish and pour over the ginger beer (ale). Cover the dish and bake in a preheated moderate oven (180°C/350°F, Gas Mark 4) for about 1 hour.
Serves 4

Toffee Strawberries

Metric/Imperial
500 g/1 lb sugar
300 ml/½ pint water
225 g/8 oz strawberries

American
2 cups sugar
1¼ cups water
½ lb strawberries

Dissolve the sugar in the water, then bring to the boil. Boil until the syrup becomes pale gold. Remove from the heat.
    Dip the strawberries in the syrup, then leave to dry on greased plates. Serve within an hour of making.

Variation:
Toffee grapes may be made in the same way.

Raspberry Apple Sundae

Metric/Imperial
2–3 apples, cored and diced
2 teaspoons lemon juice
600 ml/1 pint raspberry yogurt
2 tablespoons raisins
2 tablespoons chopped nuts

American
2–3 apples, cored and diced
2 teaspoons lemon juice
2½ cups raspberry-flavored yogurt
2 tablespoons raisins
2 tablespoons chopped nuts

Put the apples and lemon juice into the blender and blend to a purée. Mix the purée into the yogurt, then fold in the raisins and nuts.
Serves 4

Strawberries Romanoff

Metric/Imperial
500 g/1 lb strawberries, hulled
6–8 tablespoons brandy or orange
    liqueur
150 ml/¼ pint double cream

American
1 lb strawberries, hulled
6–8 tablespoons brandy or orange
    liqueur
⅔ cup heavy cream

Put the strawberries in individual serving dishes and sprinkle over the brandy or orange liqueur.
    Whip the cream until thick and spoon over the strawberries.
Serves 4

Variation:
Use port wine instead of brandy or orange liqueur and whip the cream with 2 tablespoons sugar and a few drops of vanilla essence (extract).

Cidered Pears

Metric/Imperial
300 ml/½ pint dry cider
2 strips lemon rind
1 cinnamon stick
few drops of red food colouring
4 pears, peeled

American
1¼ cups dry hard cider
2 strips lemon rind
1 cinnamon stick
few drops of red food coloring
4 pears, peeled

Put the cider, lemon rind, cinnamon and food colouring in a saucepan and bring to the boil. Cover and boil for 1 minute.

Stand the pears in a baking dish and pour over the cider mixture. Cover the dish and bake in a preheated moderate oven (180°C/350°F, Gas Mark 4) for 30 to 40 minutes, basting from time to time. Serve hot or cold.

Serves 4

Fresh Cherry Compôte

Metric/Imperial
750 g/1½ lb dark red cherries, stoned
6 tablespoons red wine
3 tablespoons redcurrant jelly
1 tablespoon sugar
finely grated rind and juice of
    1 orange
pinch of ground cinnamon

American
1½ lb dark red cherries, pitted
6 tablespoons red wine
3 tablespoons redcurrant jelly
1 tablespoon sugar
finely grated rind and juice of
    1 orange
pinch of ground cinnamon

Put all the ingredients in a casserole, cover and cook in a preheated moderate oven (160°C/325°F, Gas Mark 3) for 35 minutes. Cool, then chill before serving.

Serves 6

Variation:

Redcurrant Compôte: Put 750 g/1½ lb redcurrants in a saucepan with 275 g/10 oz (1¼ cups) sugar and 1 tablespoon water. Stir gently to dissolve the sugar, then remove from the heat and stir in 2 tablespoons gin or brandy. Cool, then chill for 2 to 3 hours. Serve with whipped cream.

Baked Damsons

Metric/Imperial	American
500 g/1 lb damsons or other plums	1 lb damsons or other plums
½ teaspoon ground cinnamon	½ teaspoon ground cinnamon
grated rind and juice of 1 orange	grated rind and juice of 1 orange
2 tablespoons clear honey	2 tablespoons clear honey
1 tablespoon dry vermouth	1 tablespoon dry vermouth
2 tablespoons water	2 tablespoons water

Put the damsons in a baking dish. Put the remaining ingredients in a saucepan and bring to the boil. Pour over the damsons, cover the dish and bake in a preheated moderate oven (180°C/350°F, Gas Mark 4) for 30 minutes. Serve hot or cold.
Serves 4

Peaches alla Cardinale

Metric/Imperial	American
100 g/4 oz sugar	½ cup sugar
150 ml/¼ pint water	⅔ cup water
1 vanilla pod	1 vanilla bean
4 peaches, peeled, halved and stoned	4 peaches, peeled, halved and pitted
225 g/8 oz raspberries	½ lb raspberries
toasted flaked almonds to decorate	toasted slivered almonds to decorate

Dissolve the sugar in the water. Add the vanilla pod (bean), then bring to the boil and boil for 5 minutes, or until the syrup is thick. Remove from the heat. Place the peace halves in the pan, cut sides down, and coat with the syrup. Chill.

Purée the raspberries in a blender or sieve (strainer). Chill lightly.

Drain the peaches and place in four serving dishes. Coat with the raspberry purée and sprinkle with toasted almonds.
Serves 4

Variation:
Peach Melba: Add a scoop of vanilla ice cream to each dish before coating the peaches with the raspberry purée.

Peaches in Wine

Metric/Imperial	American
4 large ripe peaches, peeled, stoned and sliced	4 large ripe peaches, peeled, pitted and sliced
caster sugar	sugar
chilled rosé or white dessert wine	chilled rosé or white dessert wine

Put the peach slices into four goblets and sprinkle with plenty of sugar. Pour enough wine into the goblets to reach the top of the fruit and serve.
Serves 4

Peaches in Brandy

Metric/Imperial	American
100 g/4 oz sugar	½ cup sugar
300 ml/½ pint water	1¼ cups water
4 ripe peaches, peeled, halved and stoned	4 ripe peaches, peeled, halved and pitted
5 tablespoons brandy	5 tablespoons brandy

Dissolve the sugar in the water. Add the peach halves and simmer very gently until tender. Transfer the peaches to a serving bowl, using a slotted spoon.

Boil the sugar syrup until it is reduced by two-thirds. Stir in the brandy and pour over the peaches.
Serves 4

Gingered Pears

Metric/Imperial	American
150 ml/¼ pint water	⅔ cup water
100 g/4 oz sugar	½ cup sugar
1 teaspoon ground ginger	1 teaspoon ground ginger
few strips lemon rind	few strips lemon rind
4 Conference pears, peeled	4 Bartlett pears, peeled
50 g/2 oz flaked almonds	½ cup slivered almonds

Put the water, sugar, ginger and lemon rind in a saucepan and bring to the boil, stirring to dissolve the sugar. Boil for 1 minute.

Add the pears to the syrup and poach gently until tender. Cool, then tip the pears and syrup into a serving dish. Chill well.

Serve sprinkled with the almonds.
Serves 4

Peach Madrilènes

Metric/Imperial
150 ml/¼ pint double cream
sugar to taste
12 grapes, halved and pipped
1 orange, peeled and chopped
4 peaches, peeled, halved and
  stoned

American
⅔ cup heavy cream
sugar to taste
12 grapes, halved and seeded
1 orange, peeled and chopped
4 peaches, peeled, halved and
  pitted

Whip the cream until thick. Sweeten to taste, then fold in the grapes and orange. Pile on top of the peach halves.
Serves 4

Variations:
Use thick custard sauce (see page 213), sour cream or natural (unflavored) yogurt instead of cream.

Whip the cream with 1 tablespoon icing (confectioners') sugar and fold in 100 g/4 oz (1 cup) sliced strawberries. Pile on top of the peach halves and decorate each with a whole strawberry.

Honeyed Peaches

Metric/Imperial
6 peaches, peeled, halved and
  stoned
thinly pared rind and juice of 1 lemon
thinly pared rind of 1 orange
100 g/4 oz honey
150 ml/¼ pint water
whipped cream to serve

American
6 peaches, peeled, halved and
  pitted
thinly pared rind and juice of 1 lemon
thinly pared rind of 1 orange
⅓ cup honey
⅔ cup water
whipped cream to serve

Put the peach halves in a serving bowl and sprinkle with the lemon juice to prevent discoloration.
  Put the lemon and orange rinds, honey and water in a saucepan and bring to the boil. Boil for 5 minutes. Strain this syrup over the peaches. Cool, then chill well before serving, with whipped cream.
Serves 4–6

Danish Berry Dessert

Metric/Imperial
275 g/10 oz redcurrants
275 g/10 oz raspberries
600 ml/1 pint plus 4 tablespoons
   water
75 g/3 oz sugar
50 g/2 oz cornflour
250 ml/8 fl oz double cream

American
10 oz redcurrants
10 oz raspberries
2¾ cups water
6 tablespoons sugar
½ cup cornstarch
1 cup heavy cream

Put the fruit, 600 ml/1 pint (2½ cups) of the water and the sugar in a saucepan and heat, stirring to dissolve the sugar. Cook gently until the mixture forms a purée.

Dissolve the cornflour (cornstarch) in the remaining water and add to the pan. Bring to the boil, stirring, and simmer until very thick. Cool, then chill well until set.

Whip the cream until thick and spoon on top of the berry mixture.
Serves 4–6

Mangoes with Cream

Metric/Imperial
250 ml/8 fl oz water
100 g/4 oz sugar
1 small cinnamon stick
3 mangoes, peeled and thickly
   sliced lengthways
½ teaspoon vanilla essence
150 ml/¼ pint double cream
4 tablespoons rum or dry sherry

American
1 cup water
½ cup sugar
1 small cinnamon stick
3 mangoes, peeled and thickly
   sliced lengthwise
½ teaspoon vanilla extract
⅔ cup heavy cream
¼ cup rum or dry sherry

Put the water, 50 g/2 oz (¼ cup) of the sugar and the cinnamon stick into a saucepan and stir to dissolve the sugar. Bring to the boil, then simmer for 20 to 30 minutes or until the syrup thickens.

Add the mango slices and simmer for 7 to 10 minutes or until tender but not mushy. Remove from the heat. Discard the cinnamon stick. Stir in the vanilla. Cool, then chill for at least 1 hour.

Whip the cream with the remaining sugar and the rum or sherry. Spoon the fruit and syrup into serving dishes and top with the cream.
Serves 4

Stuffed Figs

Metric/Imperial	American
4 ripe figs	4 ripe figs
225 g/8 oz ricotta or sieved cottage cheese	1 cup ricotta or strained cottage cheese
1 large egg, separated	1 egg, separated
50 g/2 oz sugar	¼ cup sugar
1–2 tablespoons kirsch or brandy	1–2 tablespoons kirsch or brandy
4 unblanched almonds	4 unblanched almonds

Cut down the figs into quarters, not cutting right through but just enough to open out the fruit.

Mix together the cheese, egg yolk, sugar and kirsch or brandy, beating until light. Beat the egg white until stiff and fold in.

Pile the cheese mixture into the figs and top each with an almond. Chill before serving.

Serves 4

Melon Ambrosia

Metric/Imperial	American
1 small cantaloup melon, peeled, seeded and cut into balls or cubed	1 small cantaloup melon, peeled, seeded and cut into balls or cubed
1 small honeydew melon, peeled, seeded and cut into balls or cubed	1 small honeydew melon, peeled, seeded and cut into balls or cubed
2 oranges, peeled and segmented	2 oranges, peeled and segmented
2 bananas, sliced	2 bananas, sliced
225 g/8 oz strawberries, hulled	½ lb strawberries, hulled
small bunch of seedless green grapes	small bunch of seedless green grapes
small bunch of black or purple grapes, halved and pipped	small bunch of black or purple grapes, halved and seeded
2 peaches, peeled, stoned and chopped	2 peaches, peeled, pitted and chopped
50 g/2 oz sugar	¼ cup sugar
juice of 1 lemon	juice of 1 lemon
25 g/1 oz desiccated coconut	¼ cup shredded coconut

Put all the fruit into a serving bowl and add the sugar and lemon juice. Fold together gently, then chill well. Sprinkle with the coconut just before serving.

Serves 10–12

Italian Fruit Salad

Metric/Imperial

4 large peaches, peeled, stoned and
   sliced
12 apricots, peeled (optional),
   stoned and sliced
juice of 1 lemon
1 small ripe melon, peeled, seeded
   and cubed
8 fresh figs, chopped
sugar to taste
2 tablespoons brandy

American

4 large peaches, peeled, pitted and
   sliced
12 apricots, peeled (optional), pitted
   and sliced
juice of 1 lemon
1 small ripe melon, peeled, seeded
   and cubed
8 fresh figs, chopped
sugar to taste
2 tablespoons brandy

Put the peaches and apricots in a glass bowl and sprinkle with the lemon juice to prevent discoloration. Gently fold in the melon and figs, then add sugar to taste and the brandy. Cover and chill for about 4 hours.
Serves 6–8

Fruits in Sherry Syrup

Metric/Imperial

2 tablespoons sugar
4 tablespoons water
2 tablespoons dry sherry
2 teaspoons lemon or lime juice
½ teaspoon ground cinnamon
1 orange, peeled and segmented
1 medium pineapple, peeled, cored
   and cubed
1–2 mangoes or pawpaws, peeled
   and cubed
1 × 225 g/8 oz can lychees, drained

American

2 tablespoons sugar
¼ cup water
2 tablespoons dry sherry
2 teaspoons lemon or lime juice
½ teaspoon ground cinnamon
1 orange, peeled and segmented
1 medium pineapple, peeled, cored
   and cubed
1–2 mangoes or pawpaws, peeled
   and cubed
1 × ½ lb can litchis, drained

Dissolve the sugar in the water, then cool. Stir in the sherry, lemon or lime juice and cinnamon.
    Put all the fruit in a bowl and pour over the syrup. Fold together gently, then chill for 1 hour before serving.
Serves 6–8

Cointreau Fruit Salad

Metric/Imperial
1 large pineapple
2 apples, cored and sliced
2 pears, peeled, cored and sliced
2 oranges, peeled and chopped
1 × 100 g/4 oz jar maraschino
  cherries, drained
sugar to taste
1–2 tablespoons Cointreau

American
1 large pineapple
2 apples, cored and sliced
2 pears, peeled, cored and sliced
2 oranges, peeled and chopped
1 × ¼ lb jar maraschino cherries,
  drained
sugar to taste
1–2 tablespoons Cointreau

Cut the top from the pineapple. Scoop out the flesh, leaving a wall about 6 mm/¼ inch thick. Discard the core and cut the flesh into small pieces.

Mix the pineapple flesh with the apples, pears, oranges and cherries. Add sugar to taste and the Cointreau and stir until the sugar has dissolved. Pile the fruit into the pineapple shell for serving.
Serves 6–8

Sunshine Fruit Salad

Metric/Imperial
juice of 2 large oranges
juice of 1 lemon
2 tablespoons orange liqueur or
  brandy
225 g/8 oz strawberries, hulled and
  halved
2 large peaches, peeled, stoned and
  sliced
2 large bananas, sliced
2 passion fruit or pomegranates,
  halved

American
juice of 2 large oranges
juice of 1 lemon
2 tablespoons orange liqueur or
  brandy
½ lb strawberries, hulled and
  halved
2 large peaches, peeled, pitted and
  sliced
2 large bananas, sliced
2 passion fruit or pomegranates,
  halved

Mix together the orange and lemon juices and liqueur or brandy in a glass serving bowl. Add the strawberries, peaches and bananas and mix gently together. Remove the seeds and scoop the flesh out of the passion fruit or pomegranate shells and add to the bowl. Fold in gently. Chill before serving.
Serves 4

Melon with Raspberries and Mint

Metric/Imperial
1 honeydew melon
225 g/8 oz raspberries
2 tablespoons caster sugar
1 tablespoon chopped mint

American
1 honeydew melon
½ lb raspberries
2 tablespoons sugar
1 tablespoon chopped mint

Cut a slice off the top of the melon and scoop out the seeds. Scoop out the flesh with a melon baller, or cut it into cubes. Mix with the raspberries, sugar and mint. Spoon into the melon shell and serve soon after making.
Serves 4

Melon Fruit Cup

Metric/Imperial
2 oranges, peeled and segmented
1 small melon, peeled, seeded and
    diced
small bunch of seedless grapes
juice of 1 lemon
2 tablespoons sugar
mint leaves to decorate (optional)

American
2 oranges, peeled and segmented
1 small melon, peeled, seeded and
    diced
small bunch of seedless grapes
juice of 1 lemon
2 tablespoons sugar
mint leaves to decorate (optional)

Put the fruit in a serving bowl and add the lemon juice and sugar. Mix together gently, then chill well. Decorate with mint leaves, if liked, just before serving.
Serves 4–6

Grapefruit Raspberry Fluff

Metric/Imperial
2 grapefruit, peeled and segmented
225 g/8 oz raspberries
300 ml/½ pint double cream
sugar to taste

American
2 grapefruit, peeled and segmented
½ lb raspberries
1¼ cups heavy cream
sugar to taste

Mix together the grapefruit and raspberries. Whip the cream until thick. Fold in the fruit with sugar to taste.
Serves 4

Dessert Oranges

Metric/Imperial
4 large oranges
300 ml/½ pint double cream
75 g/3 oz walnuts, chopped
50 g/2 oz glacé cherries, chopped
50 g/2 oz plain chocolate, grated
few drops of orange liqueur
 (optional)

American
4 large oranges
1¼ cups heavy cream
¾ cup, chopped walnuts
⅓ cup chopped candied cherries
¼ cup grated semi-sweet chocolate
few drops of orange liqueur
 (optional)

Cut a slice from the top of each orange. Scoop out most of the orange flesh, leaving the skins intact. Chop the orange flesh and reserve 2 tablespoons of the juice. Put the chopped flesh back into the oranges.

Whip the cream with the reserved orange juice until thick. Fold in the nuts, cherries, chocolate and liqueur, if using. Spoon the cream mixture into the orange shells. Chill before serving.

Serves 4

Pineapple with Kirsch

Metric/Imperial
1 small ripe pineapple, peeled, cored
 and chopped
caster sugar
2 tablespoons kirsch

American
1 small ripe pineapple, peeled, cored
 and chopped
sugar
2 tablespoons kirsch

Put the pineapple in a serving bowl and sprinkle with sugar to taste and the kirsch. Fold together gently and serve, with cream.

Serves 4

Variation:

Glazed Pineapple: Peel the pineapple, cut it into slices about 1 cm/½ inch thick and remove the core. Sprinkle with 4 tablespoons kirsch and leave to marinate for 1 hour. Melt 75 g/3 oz (6 tablespoons) unsalted (sweet) butter in a frying pan, add the pineapple slices and kirsch and cook gently for about 10 minutes. Sprinkle with 100 g/4 oz (⅔ cup) brown sugar and 2 tablespoons warmed rum. Set alight and serve flaming, with whipped cream.

Chilled Melon Boat

Metric/Imperial
1 large melon or watermelon
mixture of fresh and canned fruit
   (pineapple, strawberries, pears,
   lychees, etc), peeled and chopped
   as necessary

American
1 large melon or watermelon
mixture of fresh and canned fruit
   (pineapple, strawberries, pears,
   litchis, etc), peeled and chopped
   as necessary

Cut a 5 cm/2 inch slice from the top of the melon. Remove the seeds and
scoop out the flesh with a melon-baller. Alternatively, the flesh may be
chopped into cubes. Mix the melon with the other fruit.

Scrape out the melon shell and scallop the edge, if you like. Put the fruit in
the melon shell, cover and chill for 2 to 3 hours.

Top with a few pieces of ice just before serving.
Serves 4–8

Summer Pudding

Metric/Imperial
750 g/1½ lb mixed soft fruit
   (raspberries, strawberries, red or
   black currants, etc)
75 g/3 oz caster sugar
3 tablespoons water
1 small white sliced loaf

American
1½ lb mixed soft fruit (raspberries,
   strawberries, red or black
   currants, etc)
6 tablespoons sugar
3 tablespoons water
1 small sliced loaf of white bread

Put the fruit, sugar and water in a saucepan and poach gently until the fruit is
just soft. Cool.

Remove the crusts from the bread and cut each slice in half diagonally. Use
most of the bread to line the bottom and sides of a greased 900 ml/1½ pint
(1 quart capacity) pudding basin or mould. Be sure the basin or mould is
completely covered. Tip in the fruit, reserving a few tablespoons of the syrup,
and cover with the rest of the bread slices. Place a saucer on top and press
down with a heavy weight or can. Chill overnight.

Unmould the pudding onto a serving plate. Drizzle the reserved syrup over
any white patches on the bread. Serve with whipped cream.
Serves 4–6

Variation:
Poach 350 g/12 oz strawberries, hulled, 350 g/12 oz black cherries, stoned
(pitted) and 1 cooking (tart) apple, peeled, cored and sliced with 175 g/6 oz
sugar. Use a raisin loaf instead of plain white bread.

Rhubarb Suèdoise

Metric/Imperial
500 g/1 lb rhubarb, chopped
225 g/8 oz sugar
25 g/1 oz cornflour
2 tablespoons water
sugar for sprinkling

American
1 lb rhubarb, chopped
1 cup sugar
¼ cup cornstarch
2 tablespoons water
sugar for sprinkling

Put the rhubarb in a bowl, sprinkle over the sugar and leave for about 1 hour, to draw out the juice. Tip the rhubarb mixture into a saucepan, add enough water just to cover and bring to the boil. Cover and simmer for 20 to 30 minutes or until the rhubarb is very soft and has almost disintegrated.

Dissolve the cornflour (cornstarch) in the water and add to the pan. Cook, stirring, until the mixture thickens and clears. Taste for sweetness, then pour into a dampened mould. Chill until set.

Turn out to serve and sprinkle with sugar.

Serves 4

Autumn Compôte

Metric/Imperial
50 g/2 oz sugar
150 ml/¼ pint water
pared rind and juice of 1 lemon
juice of 1 orange
1 large cooking apple, peeled, cored
   and sliced
100 g/4 oz blackberries
100 g/4 oz damsons, stoned
100 g/4 oz black plums, stoned
100 g/4 oz golden plums, stoned

American
¼ cup sugar
⅔ cup water
pared rind and juice of 1 lemon
juice of 1 orange
1 large tart apple, peeled, cored and
   sliced
1 cup blackberries
4–5 damsons, pitted
4–5 black plums, pitted
4–5 golden plums, pitted

Dissolve the sugar in the water. Add the lemon rind and juice and orange juice and bring to the boil. Add the fruit and cook gently until it is tender. Discard the lemon rind and serve hot or cold.

Serves 6

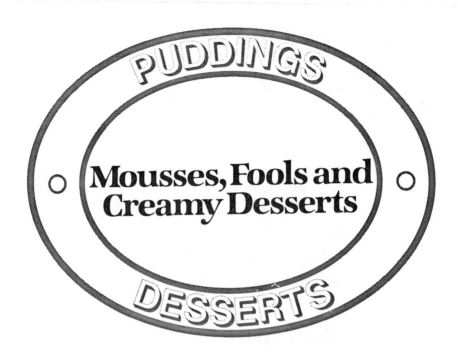

Raspberry Cream Crunch

Metric/Imperial
25 g/1 oz butter
6 digestive biscuits, crushed
50 g/2 oz sugar
50 g/2 oz wholewheat
   semolina
450 ml/¾ pint milk
150 ml/¼ pint raspberry yogurt
50 g/2 oz cream cheese
raspberries to decorate

American
2 tablespoons butter
6 graham crackers, crushed
¼ cup sugar
⅓ cup wholewheat semolina or
   cream of wheat
2 cups milk
⅔ cup raspberry-flavored yogurt
¼ cup cream cheese
raspberries to decorate

Melt the butter in a saucepan and stir in the biscuit (cracker) crumbs. Cool.

Put the sugar, semolina and milk in another saucepan and bring to the boil, stirring to dissolve the sugar. Simmer for 2 to 3 minutes. Cool slightly, then beat in the yogurt and cream cheese.

Pour the yogurt mixture into individual dishes and sprinkle over the crumb mixture. Chill until set.

Serve decorated with raspberries.

Serves 4

Cranberry Sherry Mousse

Metric/Imperial
1 × 382 g/13½ oz jar cranberry jelly
4 tablespoons dry sherry
150 ml/¼ pint double cream
25 g/1 oz walnuts, chopped

American
1 × 14 oz can cranberry jelly
¼ cup dry sherry
⅔ cup heavy cream
¼ cup chopped walnuts

Beat together the jelly and sherry until well mixed. Whip the cream until thick and fold into the jelly mixture. Pile into individual glasses. Decorate with the walnuts and chill before serving.
Serves 4

Rhubarb, Orange and Ginger Dessert

Metric/Imperial
500 g/1 lb rhubarb, chopped
finely grated rind and juice of 1
    orange
4 tablespoons soft brown sugar
150 ml/¼ pint milk
1 egg, beaten
1 tablespoon cornflour
1 tablespoon sugar
¼ teaspoon vanilla essence
150 ml/¼ pint natural yogurt
1 tablespoon finely chopped
    preserved ginger
orange slices to decorate

American
1 lb rhubarb, chopped
finely grated rind and juice of 1
    orange
¼ cup light brown sugar
⅔ cup milk
1 egg, beaten
1 tablespoon cornstarch
1 tablespoon sugar
¼ teaspoon vanilla extract
⅔ cup unflavored yogurt
1 tablespoon finely chopped candied
    ginger
orange slices to decorate

Put the rhubarb, orange rind and juice and brown sugar in a saucepan and cook gently until the rhubarb is tender. Mash to a pulp with a wooden spoon or purée in a blender. Cool.

Heat the milk in another saucepan. Mix together the egg, cornflour (cornstarch), sugar and vanilla. Gradually stir in the hot milk, then return to the saucepan. Bring to the boil, stirring, and cook gently until the custard thickens. Cool.

Beat the yogurt into the custard, then stir in the rhubarb purée and ginger. Pour into a serving bowl and chill. Serve decorated with orange slices.
Serves 4

Grape Brûlée

Metric/Imperial
750 g/1½ lb seedless white grapes
300 ml/½ pint whipping cream
3 tablespoons soft brown sugar

American
1½ lb seedless green grapes
1¼ cups whipping cream
3 tablespoons light brown sugar

Place the grapes in a flameproof serving dish. Whip the cream until thick and spread over the grapes. Chill.

Just before serving, sprinkle over the sugar. Melt the sugar under a preheated grill (broiler), then continue cooking until the sugar caramelizes.
Serves 6

Variation:
Other canned or fresh fruit may be used – either one kind or a mixture of fruits.

Brandied Peach Brûlée

Metric/Imperial
8 large peaches, peeled, stoned and
   sliced
50 g/2 oz caster sugar
2 tablespoons brandy
150–300 ml/¼–½ pint double cream
50–75 g/2–3 oz brown sugar

American
8 large peaches, peeled, pitted and
   sliced
¼ cup sugar
2 tablespoons brandy
⅔–1¼ cups heavy cream
⅓–½ cup brown sugar

Put the peach slices into four to six small individual flameproof serving dishes. Sprinkle over the sugar and brandy.

Whip the cream until thick and spoon over the fruit to cover it completely. The layer of cream should be at least 1 cm/½ inch thick. Chill well.

Sprinkle the cream with a thin layer of brown sugar, to cover it completely, and grill (broil) until the sugar has melted and formed a hard crust on top.
Serves 4–6

Variation:
Sour Cream Peach Brûlée: Peel, stone (pit) and slice 6 large peaches and divide between four individual flameproof serving dishes. Mix 2 tablespoons brown sugar with ½ teaspoon ground cinnamon and sprinkle over the peaches. Cover with 300 ml/½ pint (1¼ cups) sour cream. Sprinkle each serving with 1 tablespoon sugar, then grill (broil) until the sugar melts and caramelizes.
Serves 4

Yogurt Mallow

Metric/Imperial
2 egg whites
50 g/2 oz caster sugar
150 ml/¼ pint fruit-flavoured yogurt
1 tablespoon toasted desiccated
  coconut

American
2 egg whites
¼ cup sugar
⅔ cup fruit-flavored yogurt
1 tablespoon toasted shredded
  coconut

Beat the egg whites until stiff, then gradually beat in the sugar. Fold in the yogurt. Spoon the mixture into four glasses and sprinkle with the coconut. Serve immediately.
Serves 4

Banana and Ginger Dessert

Metric/Imperial
1 × 33 g/1⅓ oz packet vanilla
  blancmange powder
sugar
milk
100 g/4 oz apricot jam
4 bananas
75 g/3 oz preserved stem ginger,
  finely chopped
150 ml/¼ pint double cream
1 teaspoon caster sugar
½ teaspoon vanilla essence

American
1 × 2 oz package vanilla dessert
  mix
sugar
milk
⅓ cup apricot jam
4 bananas
½ cup finely chopped candied
  ginger
⅔ cup heavy cream
1 teaspoon sugar
½ teaspoon vanilla extract

Make up the blancmange (vanilla dessert) with sugar and milk according to the directions on the packet. Pour into a shallow serving dish and leave to set.

Heat the jam and rub it through a sieve (strainer). Cut the bananas in half lengthways, then scoop out a little 'trough' down the centre of each. Fill the troughs with most of the ginger and brush the cut surfaces of the banana halves with the jam. Arrange on the blancmange (vanilla dessert).

Whip the cream with the teaspoon of sugar and the vanilla essence (extract) until thick. Pipe the cream over the bananas and decorate with the rest of the ginger.
Serves 4

Grape Whisper

Metric/Imperial	American
225 g/8 oz green and black grapes, halved and pipped	½ lb green and purple grapes, halved and seeded
1½ tablespoons white wine	1½ tablespoons white wine
3 egg whites	3 egg whites
75 g/3 oz caster sugar	6 tablespoons sugar

Put the grapes in a bowl and sprinkle over the wine. Leave to marinate for about 1 hour, turning occasionally.

Beat the egg whites until stiff, then gradually beat in the sugar. Fold in the grapes. Spoon the mixture into individual glasses and serve immediately.
Serves 4

Variation:

Omit the wine and sugar, and use only 2 egg whites. Beat them until stiff and fold into 300 ml/½ pint (1¼ cups) apricot yogurt. Layer the yogurt mixture and grapes in dessert glasses.

Syllabub

Metric/Imperial	American
thinly pared rind of 1 lemon	thinly pared rind of 1 lemon
4 tablespoons lemon juice	¼ cup lemon juice
6 tablespoons sweet white wine or sherry	6 tablespoons sweet white wine or sherry
2 tablespoons brandy	2 tablespoons brandy
50 g/2 oz sugar	¼ cup sugar
300 ml/½ pint double cream	1¼ cups heavy cream
grated nutmeg	grated nutmeg

Put the lemon rind and juice, wine or sherry and brandy in a mixing bowl and leave to infuse overnight.

Discard the lemon rind. Stir the sugar into the lemon mixture until dissolved, then gradually stir in the cream. Beat until the mixture will hold a soft peak.

Spoon into four glasses and sprinkle with a little grated nutmeg.
Serves 4

Charlotte Malakoff

Metric/Imperial
2 tablespoons orange liqueur
1 tablespoon water
12–15 sponge finger biscuits
100 g/4 oz unsalted butter
100 g/4 oz caster sugar
100 g/4 oz ground almonds
finely grated rind of ½ orange
150 ml/¼ pint double cream
225 g/8 oz raspberries

American
2 tablespoons orange liqueur
1 tablespoon water
12–15 ladyfingers
8 tablespoons (1 stick) sweet butter
½ cup sugar
1 cup ground almonds
finely grated rind of ½ orange
⅔ cup heavy cream
½ lb raspberries

Line the bottom of a 900 ml/1½ pint (1 quart capacity) charlotte mould with a round of greaseproof (wax) paper.

Mix 1 tablespoon of the liqueur with the water. Dip the sponge (lady) fingers into the liquid, then use to line the mould, sugared side against the mould and standing upright.

Cream the butter and sugar together until light and fluffy. Beat in the almonds, orange rind and remaining liqueur. Whip the cream until thick and fold into the almond mixture. Spoon into the mould and smooth the top. Trim the tops of the sponge (lady) fingers if necessary so they are level with the top of the filling. Chill until set.

Meanwhile, purée the raspberries in a blender or sieve (strainer). Lightly chill the purée.

Turn out the charlotte onto a serving plate and serve with the raspberry purée as a sauce.
Serves 6–8

Coffee Cream Mousse

Metric/Imperial
2 × 75 g/3 oz packets cream cheese
4 large eggs, separated
150 ml/¼ pint double cream
3 tablespoons coffee essence
75 g/3 oz caster sugar
chocolate curls to decorate
  (optional)

American
2 × 3 oz packages cream cheese
4 eggs, separated
⅔ cup heavy cream
3 tablespoons coffee flavoring
6 tablespoons sugar
chocolate curls to decorate
  (optional)

Beat the cream cheese and egg yolks together until well mixed. Beat in the cream and coffee essence (flavoring).

Beat the egg whites until stiff, then gradually beat in the sugar. Fold in the coffee mixture. Spoon into six glasses and chill until set.

Serve decorated with curls of chocolate.

Serves 6

Chestnut Whip

Metric/Imperial
1 × 500 g/1 lb can unsweetened
  chestnut purée
¼ teaspoon vanilla essence
grated rind and juice of 1 small
  orange
2 tablespoons rum
100 g/4 oz soft brown sugar
2 egg whites
twisted orange slices to decorate

American
1 × 1 lb can unsweetened chestnut
  purée
¼ teaspoon vanilla extract
grated rind and juice of 1 small
  orange
2 tablespoons rum
⅔ cup light brown sugar
2 egg whites
twisted orange slices to decorate

Beat together the chestnut purée, vanilla, orange rind and juice, rum and sugar. Beat the egg whites until stiff and fold into the chestnut mixture. Spoon into serving dishes and chill.

Serve decorated with twisted orange slices.

Serves 6

Variation:
Chestnut Cream Whip: Mix a 225 g/8 oz can unsweetened chestnut purée with 300 ml/½ pint double cream (1¼ cups heavy cream), whipped. Fold in 25 g/1 oz (3 tablespoons) chopped marrons glacés. Beat 2 egg whites until stiff and fold in. Chill for 1 hour, then serve decorated with more marrons glacés and strawberries.

Serves 4

Chocolate Mousse

Metric/Imperial
225 g/8 oz plain chocolate, broken
   into pieces
2 tablespoons water
4 eggs, separated
1 tablespoon brandy (optional)
grated chocolate to decorate

American
1⅓ cups semi-sweet chocolate
   chips
2 tablespoons water
4 eggs, separated
1 tablespoon brandy (optional)
grated chocolate to decorate

Melt the chocolate gently with the water. Remove from the heat, cool slightly and beat in the egg yolks. Stir in the brandy, if using.

Beat the egg whites until stiff and fold into the chocolate mixture. Spoon into four individual ramekins and chill until set.

Serve decorated with grated chocolate.
Serves 4

Apricot Cream Fool

Metric/Imperial
500 g/1 lb apricots, halved and
   stoned
2 tablespoons water
150 ml/¼ pint cold custard sauce
   (see page 213)
sugar to taste
450 ml/¾ pint double cream
toasted flaked almonds to decorate

American
1 lb apricots, halved and
   pitted
2 tablespoons water
⅔ cup cold custard sauce (see page
   213)
sugar to taste
2 cups heavy cream
toasted slivered almonds to decorate

Put the apricots in a saucepan with the water and cook gently until soft. Tip into the blender and blend to a smooth purée. Stir in the custard, then sweeten if necessary.

Whip the cream until thick and fold into the apricot mixture. Spoon into four glasses and chill lightly. Serve sprinkled with almonds.
Serves 4

Orange Chocolate Mousse

Metric/Imperial
50 g/2 oz sugar
4 eggs, separated
1 tablespoon plain flour
4 tablespoons milk
50 g/2 oz butter
½ teaspoon vanilla essence
grated rind of 1 orange
225 g/8 oz plain chocolate, broken
 into pieces

To decorate:
whipped cream
orange pieces

American
¼ cup sugar
4 eggs, separated
1 tablespoon all-purpose flour
¼ cup milk
4 tablespoons butter
½ teaspoon vanilla extract
grated rind of 1 orange
1⅓ cups semi-sweet chocolate
 chips

To decorate:
whipped cream
orange pieces

Put the sugar, egg yolks, flour and milk in a saucepan and heat gently, stirring, until the mixture thickens. Stir in the butter until it has melted. Add the vanilla, orange rind and chocolate and continue stirring until the mixture is completely smooth. Remove from the heat and cool.

Beat the egg whites until stiff and fold into the chocolate mixture. Divide between four serving dishes and chill.

Serve decorated with whipped cream and orange pieces.

Serves 4

Banana Nut Cream

Metric/Imperial	American
2 large bananas, mashed	2 large bananas, mashed
2 tablespoons lemon juice	2 tablespoons lemon juice
4 tablespoons honey	¼ cup honey
300 ml/½ pint natural yogurt	1 ¼ cups unflavored yogurt
25 g/1 oz nuts, chopped	¼ cup chopped nuts

Mix the bananas with the lemon juice and honey. Add the yogurt and fold together well. Spoon into individual glasses and sprinkle with the nuts.
Serves 4

Banana Fluff

Metric/Imperial	American
4 bananas	4 bananas
2 teaspoons lemon juice	2 teaspoons lemon juice
1 tablespoon brown sugar	1 tablespoon brown sugar
150 ml/¼ pint double cream	⅔ cup heavy cream
2 egg whites	2 egg whites

Mash three of the bananas with 1 teaspoon of the lemon juice and the sugar. Whip the cream until thick and fold into the banana mixture. Beat the egg whites until stiff and fold into the banana mixture.

Divide the mixture between four glasses. Slice the remaining banana, sprinkle with the rest of the lemon juice to prevent discoloration, and arrange on top of each serving. Chill well.
Serves 4

Variation:

Strawberry Fluff: Set aside 8 good strawberries from 500 g/1 lb, then hull and mash the rest with 2 tablespoons sugar. Continue as above, using the mashed strawberries instead of the bananas, and decorating with the reserved strawberries.

Gooseberry Fool

Metric/Imperial
500 g/1 lb cooked fresh or canned
   gooseberries
450 ml/¾ pint cold custard sauce
   (see page 213)
sugar to taste
green food colouring (optional)

American
1 lb cooked fresh or canned
   gooseberries
2 cups cold custard sauce (see page
   213)
sugar to taste
green food coloring (optional)

Purée the gooseberries in a sieve (strainer) or blender. Fold the purée into the custard sauce with sugar to taste. Add a little green food colouring if necessary. Chill well.
Serves 4

Banana Syllabub

Metric/Imperial
3 ripe bananas
2 tablespoons lemon juice
2 tablespoons white wine
25 g/1 oz sugar
300 ml/½ pint double cream

American
3 ripe bananas
2 tablespoons lemon juice
2 tablespoons white wine
2 tablespoons sugar
1¼ cups heavy cream

Mash the bananas with the lemon juice, wine and sugar. Whip the cream until thick and fold into the banana mixture. Chill well.
Serves 6

Variation:
Use natural (unflavored) yogurt instead of whipped cream.

Atholl Brose

Metric/Imperial
4 tablespoons medium oatmeal
4 tablespoons whisky
2 tablespoons honey
1 tablespoon lemon juice
150 ml/¼ pint double cream

American
¼ cup medium oatmeal
¼ cup whiskey
2 tablespoons honey
1 tablespoon lemon juice
⅔ cup heavy cream

Toast the oatmeal under the grill (broiler) until it is golden brown, then cool.
   Mix together the whisky, honey and lemon juice. Add the cream and whip until the mixture is thick. Fold in the toasted oatmeal. Chill before serving.
Serves 4

Basque Chocolate Mousse

Metric/Imperial
4 tablespoons strong black coffee
100 g/4 oz plain chocolate, broken
  into pieces
50 g/2 oz butter
few drops of vanilla essence
3 eggs, separated
To decorate:
whipped cream
toasted flaked almonds

American
¼ cup strong black coffee
⅔ cup semi-sweet chocolate
  chips
4 tablespoons butter
few drops of vanilla extract
3 eggs, separated
To decorate:
whipped cream
toasted slivered almonds

Warm the coffee in a saucepan. Add the chocolate and melt it gently.
Remove from the heat and stir in the butter and vanilla. Gradually beat in the
egg yolks.

Beat the egg whites until stiff and fold into the chocolate mixture. Divide
between four serving dishes and chill.

Decorate with whipped cream and toasted almonds before serving.

Serves 4

Strawberry Cheese Fool

Metric/Imperial
500 g/1 lb strawberries, hulled
1 × 75 g/3 oz packet cream cheese
150 ml/¼ pint natural yogurt
sugar to taste

American
1 lb strawberries, hulled
1 × 3 oz package cream cheese
⅔ cup unflavored yogurt
sugar to taste

Purée the strawberries in a sieve (strainer) or blender. Beat the cream
cheese and yogurt into the purée and sweeten to taste. Divide between four
serving glasses and chill thoroughly before serving.

Serves 4

Redcurrant Cream

Metric/Imperial
150 ml/¼ pint double cream
2 egg whites
150 ml/¼ pint natural yogurt
2 tablespoons caster sugar
500 g/1 lb redcurrants or blueberries
2 tablespoons chopped mint

American
⅔ cup heavy cream
2 egg whites
⅔ cup unflavored yogurt
2 tablespoons sugar
1 lb redcurrants or blueberries
2 tablespoons chopped mint

Whip the cream until thick. Beat the egg whites until stiff. Fold the egg whites and yogurt into the cream with the sugar. Fold in the redcurrants or blueberries and mint. Serve soon after making.
Serves 4

Drambuie Clouds

Metric/Imperial
4 egg yolks
75 g/3 oz caster sugar
3 tablespoons Drambuie
200 ml/⅓ pint double cream

American
4 egg yolks
6 tablespoons sugar
3 tablespoons Drambuie
1 cup heavy cream

Put the egg yolks and sugar in a heatproof bowl over a pan of hot water or in a double boiler and beat until the mixture has thickened and doubled in volume. Add the Drambuie and continue beating until the mixture becomes thick again. Remove from the heat and cool.

Whip the cream until thick and fold into the Drambuie mixture. Pour into four glasses and chill well.
Serves 4

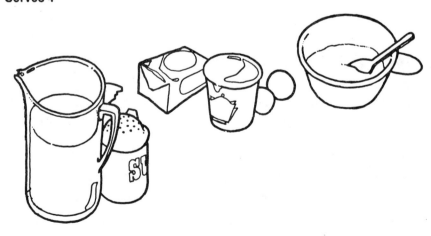

PUDDINGS

**Jellies,
Bavarian Creams
and
Moulded
Desserts**

DESSERTS

Champagne Jelly

Metric/Imperial
5 teaspoons gelatine
120 ml/4 fl oz water
50 g/2 oz caster sugar
*1 bottle Champagne or other
  sparkling white wine*
To decorate:
seedless green grapes
1 egg white, lightly beaten
caster sugar

American
2 envelopes unflavored gelatin
½ cup water
¼ cup sugar
*1 bottle Champagne or other
  sparkling white wine*
To decorate:
seedless green grapes
1 egg white, lightly beaten
sugar

Sprinkle the gelatine onto the water and heat gently until dissolved. Stir in the sugar until dissolved. Cool, then stir in the wine. The mixture will froth up; skim off the froth. Pour the skimmed mixture into glasses and chill until set.

For the decoration, dip the grapes in egg white then coat in a little sugar. Allow to dry.

Top each serving with sugared grapes.
Serves 4–6

Melon and Grape Jelly (Gelatin)

Metric/Imperial
1 large melon, halved and seeded
2 apples, peeled, cored and sliced
175 g/6 oz black grapes, halved and
  pipped
grated rind and juice of 2 limes
15 g/½ oz gelatine
2 tablespoons water
4 tablespoons honey

American
1 large melon, halved and seeded
2 apples, peeled, cored and sliced
6 oz purple grapes, halved and
  seeded
grated rind and juice of 2 limes
2 envelopes unflavored gelatin
2 tablespoons water
¼ cup honey

Scoop out the melon flesh in balls or cut it into cubes and mix with the apples and grapes. Scrape the melon shell halves clean of all flesh and reserve them. Chop the extra melon flesh.

Add the lime rind and juice to the fruit mixture. Dissolve the gelatine in the water over heat and add to the fruit mixture with the honey.

Put the chopped melon flesh in the bottom of the melon shell halves and pour over the fruit mixture. Chill until set.

Serve cut into wedges.

Serves 4–6

Grape Wine Jelly (Mould)

Metric/Imperial
15 g/½ oz gelatine
300 ml/½ pint water
175 g/6 oz sugar
thinly pared rind and juice of 1
  orange
thinly pared rind and juice of 1 lemon
300 ml/½ pint red or white wine
225 g/8 oz black or green grapes,
  peeled, halved and pipped

American
2 envelopes unflavored gelatin
1¼ cups water
¾ cup sugar
thinly pared rind and juice of 1
  orange
thinly pared rind and juice of 1 lemon
1¼ cups red or white wine
½ lb purple or green grapes, peeled,
  halved and seeded

Sprinkle the gelatine over 4 tablespoons of the water and heat gently until the gelatine has dissolved. Put the remaining water in a saucepan with the sugar and orange and lemon rind. Stir to dissolve the sugar, then bring to the boil and boil for 3 minutes. Remove from the heat and stir in the gelatine. Cool.

Stir the wine and orange and lemon juices into the gelatine mixture.

Arrange the grapes in the bottom of a dampened 900 ml/1½ pint (1 quart capacity) mould and strain in the gelatine mixture. Chill until set. Turn out to serve.

Serves 6–8

Jewelled Lime Mould

Metric/Imperial
1 packet lime jelly
orange or lemon juice
3 tablespoons chopped glacé
  cherries
2 tablespoons raisins
2 tablespoons chopped
  marshmallows
2 tablespoons chopped walnuts

American
1 package lime-flavored gelatin
orange or lemon juice
3 tablespoons chopped candied
  cherries
2 tablespoons raisins
2 tablespoons chopped
  marshmallows
2 tablespoons chopped walnuts

Make up the jelly (gelatin) according to the instructions on the packet, using orange or lemon juice in place of half the water. Leave until on the point of setting.

Fold in the remaining ingredients to distribute them evenly. Pour into a dampened mould and chill until set.

Serves 4

Strawberry Cheese Jelly

Metric/Imperial
1 packet strawberry
  jelly
300 ml/½ pint hot water
2 eggs, separated
50 g/2 oz caster sugar
100 g/4 oz strawberries, hulled and
  crushed
1 × 75 g/3 oz packet cream cheese

American
1 package strawberry-flavored
  gelatin
1¼ cups hot water
2 eggs, separated
¼ cup sugar
1 cup crushed and hulled
  strawberries
1 × 3 oz package cream cheese

Dissolve the jelly (gelatin) in the water. Set aside to thicken.

Beat the egg yolks and sugar together until pale and thick. Fold in the strawberries.

Beat together the cream cheese and a little of the jelly (gelatin). Add to the strawberry mixture with the rest of the jelly (gelatin) and combine thoroughly. Beat the egg whites until stiff and fold in. Pour into individual glasses and chill until set.

Serves 4

Variation:
Strawberry Jelly Whip: Make as above, omitting the strawberries and cream cheese and reducing the sugar to 25 g/1 oz (2 tablespoons).

Caramel Jelly (Gelatin)

Metric/Imperial	American
450 ml/¾ pint water	2 cups water
15 g/½ oz gelatine	2 envelopes unflavored gelatin
squeeze of lemon juice	squeeze of lemon juice
Caramel:	**Caramel:**
100 g/4 oz sugar	½ cup sugar
4 tablespoons water	¼ cup water

First make the caramel. Dissolve the sugar in the water, then boil until golden brown. Remove from the heat and stir in 3 tablespoons of the other quantity of water. Keep warm.

Heat 2 tablespoons of the remaining water and dissolve the gelatine in it, then add to the caramel mixture with the rest of the water and the lemon juice. Mix well. Pour into a mould and chill until set.

Serves 4–6

Fresh Lemon Jelly (Gelatin)

Metric/Imperial	American
grated rind and juice of 2 lemons	grated rind and juice of 2 lemons
600 ml/1 pint water	2½ cups water
1 tablespoon gelatine	1½ envelopes unflavored gelatin
50 g/2 oz sugar	¼ cup sugar
few drops of yellow food colouring	few drops of yellow food coloring
(optional)	(optional)

Put the lemon rind and water in a saucepan and bring to the boil. Simmer for 5 minutes, then strain and return to the pan. Bring back to the boil.

Dissolve the gelatine in the heated lemon juice. Stir in enough of the lemon rind liquid to make up to 600 ml/1 pint (2½ cups). Stir in the sugar and a little food colouring, if liked. Pour into a dampened mould and chill until set.

Turn out to serve.

Serves 4

Variations:

Use the grated rind and juice of 3 oranges instead of lemons, or a mixture of citrus fruits.

Quick Orange Jelly (Gelatin): Dissolve 1 tablespoon (1½ envelopes unflavored) gelatine in 120 ml/4 fl oz (½ cup) hot water. Stir in 300 ml/½ pint (1¼ cups) chilled orange juice and 6 crushed ice cubes. Stir until the ice melts, then pour into a dampened mould. Chill until set.

Banana Rum Jelly (Gelatin)

Metric/Imperial
1 packet lemon jelly
250 ml/8 fl oz double cream
2 large bananas, mashed
2 tablespoons rum
whipped cream to decorate

American
1 package lemon-flavored gelatin
1 cup heavy cream
2 large bananas, mashed
2 tablespoons rum
whipped cream to decorate

Make up the jelly (gelatin) according to the instructions on the packet. Chill until on the point of setting.

Whip the cream until thick. Add the cream to the jelly (gelatin) with the bananas and rum and mix well. Pour into a serving dish and chill until set.

Serve decorated with whipped cream.

Serves 6–8

Prune and Orange Ring

Metric/Imperial
225 g/8 oz prunes
finely grated rind of 1 orange
juice of 2 large oranges
15 g/½ oz gelatine
juice of 1 lemon
2 egg whites
orange slices to decorate

American
½ lb prunes
finely grated rind of 1 orange
juice of 2 large oranges
2 envelopes unflavored gelatin
juice of 1 lemon
2 egg whites
orange slices to decorate

Put the prunes and orange rind in a bowl. Make the orange juice up to 300 ml/ ½ pint (1¼ cups) with water and pour over the prunes. Leave to soak overnight.

The next day, tip the prune mixture into a saucepan and bring to the boil. Cover and simmer for 20 minutes or until the prunes are tender. Drain the prunes, reserving the juice. Make up the juice to 300 ml/½ pint (1¼ cups) with more water.

Remove the stones (pits) from the prunes, then put them in the blender with the juice. Blend to a purée.

Pour the lemon juice into a cup. Sprinkle the gelatine into the juice and stand the cup in a saucepan of hot water. Stir the mixture until the gelatine has completely dissolved then stir it into the prune mixture. Beat the egg whites until stiff and fold into the prune mixture. Pour into a ring mould and chill until set.

Turn out the prune and orange ring onto a serving plate and fill the centre with orange slices.

Serves 4–6

Raspberry Princess

Metric/Imperial
1 packet raspberry
  jelly
300 ml/½ pint boiling water
150 ml/¼ pint raspberries, crushed
3 egg whites
2 tablespoons caster sugar
raspberries to decorate

American
1 package raspberry-flavored
  gelatin
1¼ cups boiling water
⅔ cup crushed raspberries
3 egg whites
2 tablespoons sugar
raspberries to decorate

Dissolve the jelly (gelatin) in the boiling water and stir in the crushed raspberries. Cool until very slightly stiffened.

Beat the egg whites until stiff, then gradually beat in the sugar. Fold into the raspberry jelly (gelatin) mixture and spoon into dessert dishes. Chill until set.

Serve decorated with raspberries.

Serves 4–6

Orange Cherry Creams

Metric/Imperial
4 very large oranges
1 packet orange jelly
150 ml/¼ pint double cream
32 cherries, stoned

American
4 very large oranges
1 package orange-flavored gelatin
⅔ cup heavy cream
32 cherries, pitted

Cut a slice from the top of each orange and carefully scoop out the flesh. Reserve any juice in a measuring jug. Discard the seeds and membrane from the orange flesh and set it aside, with the orange shells.

Add enough water to the orange juice to make it up to 450 ml/¾ pint (2 cups) and heat. Dissolve the orange jelly (gelatin) in the juice mixture. Cool until on the point of setting.

Whip the cream until thick and beat in the orange jelly (gelatin).

Divide the reserved orange flesh between the orange shells and add 5 cherries to each. Top with the orange cream and leave to set.

Decorate with the remaining cherries.

Serves 4

Stuffed Apple Jelly (Gelatin)

Metric/Imperial
50 g/2 oz sugar
600 ml/1 pint water
6 small sweet apples, peeled and
  cored
15 g/½ oz candied angelica,
  chopped
25 g/1 oz glacé cherries,
  chopped
25 g/1 oz nuts, chopped
honey
1 packet orange jelly
whipped cream to decorate

American
¼ cup sugar
2½ cups water
6 small sweet apples, peeled and
  cored
1½ tablespoons chopped candied
  angelica
2 tablespoons chopped candied
  cherries
¼ cup chopped nuts
honey
1 package orange-flavored gelatin
whipped cream to decorate

Dissolve the sugar in the water in a saucepan and bring to the boil. Add the apples, cover the pan and simmer gently for 10 minutes. Remove from the heat and leave for a further 10 to 15 minutes or until the apples are soft but still firm and whole. Drain the apples, reserving the syrup.

Mix together the angelica, cherries and nuts with a little honey to bind and use to stuff the apples. Arrange in a serving dish.

Make up the syrup in which the apples were cooked to 450 ml/¾ pint (2 cups), heat, and dissolve the jelly (gelatin) in this. Leave until on the point of setting, then spoon the jelly (gelatin) over the apples to coat them completely. Pour any remaining jelly (gelatin) into the dish. Chill until set.

Decorate with whipped cream.
Serves 6

Chocolate Mocha Bavarian Cream

Metric/Imperial
4 eggs, separated
100 g/4 oz caster sugar
½ teaspoon cornflour
450 ml/¾ pint milk
75 g/3 oz plain or bitter eating
  chocolate, broken into pieces
15 g/½ oz gelatine
2 tablespoons strong black coffee
2 tablespoons orange liqueur
  (optional)
150 ml/¼ pint double cream

American
4 eggs, separated
½ cup sugar
½ teaspoon cornstarch
2 cups milk
½ cup semi-sweet chocolate
  chips
2 envelopes unflavored gelatin
2 tablespoons strong black coffee
2 tablespoons orange liqueur
  (optional)
⅔ cup heavy cream

Beat the egg yolks with 50 g/2 oz (¼ cup) of the sugar and the cornflour (cornstarch) until light and fluffy. Scald the milk, add the chocolate and stir until it has melted. Pour the chocolate milk slowly into the egg yolk mixture, stirring constantly, then return to the pan and heat gently, stirring, until thickened. Do not boil. Remove from the heat.

Dissolve the gelatine in the warmed coffee, then stir into the chocolate mixture with the liqueur, if using. Cool, stirring occasionally.

Beat the egg whites until stiff and beat in the remaining sugar. Fold into the chocolate mixture. Whip the cream until thick and fold in. Pour into a serving bowl and chill until set.
Serves 6

Rum Bavarian Cream

Metric/Imperial
600 ml/1 pint milk
1 egg
1 egg yolk
50 g/2 oz sugar
2 tablespoons light rum
15 g/½ oz gelatine
3 tablespoons water
150 ml/¼ pint double cream

American
2½ cups milk
1 egg
1 egg yolk
¼ cup sugar
2 tablespoons light rum
2 envelopes unflavored gelatin
3 tablespoons water
⅔ cup heavy cream

Put the milk, egg and egg yolk in a heatproof bowl over a pan of hot water or into a double boiler. Cook, stirring, until the custard is thick enough to coat the back of the spoon. Remove from the heat and stir in the sugar and rum.

Dissolve the gelatine in the water over heat and stir into the rum custard. Strain into a mixing bowl and cool.

Whip the cream until thick and fold into the rum mixture. Spoon into a dampened 600 ml/1 pint (2½ cup capacity) mould and chill until set. Turn out to serve.

Serves 4

Caramel Bavarian Cream

Metric/Imperial
1½ tablespoons gelatine
120 ml/4 fl oz water
175 g/6 oz sugar
200 ml/⅓ pint milk
2 eggs, separated
½ teaspoon vanilla essence
300 ml/½ pint whipping cream

American
1½ envelopes unflavored gelatin
½ cup water
¾ cup sugar
1 cup milk
2 eggs, separated
½ teaspoon vanilla extract
1¼ cups whipping cream

Sprinkle the gelatine onto 4 tablespoons of the water and heat until dissolved. Put the remaining water in a saucepan with the sugar and stir to dissolve. Bring to the boil and boil until the syrup turns a caramel colour.

Heat the milk in another saucepan. Stir in the caramel syrup and stir until well mixed. Remove from the heat and beat in the egg yolks. Stir in the gelatine and vanilla. Leave until on the point of setting.

Whip the cream until thick. Beat the egg whites until stiff. Fold the cream and egg whites into the caramel mixture. Spoon into a greased 1.5 litre/ 2½ pint (1½ quart capacity) mould and chill until set. Turn out to serve.

Serves 4

Orange Bavarian Cream

Metric/Imperial	American
150 ml/¼ pint milk	⅔ cup milk
1 egg	1 egg
1 egg yolk	1 egg yolk
15 g/½ oz gelatine	2 envelopes unflavored gelatin
3 tablespoons water	3 tablespoons water
150 ml/¼ pint orange juice	⅔ cup orange juice
juice of ½ lemon	juice of ½ lemon
50 g/2 oz caster sugar	¼ cup sugar
150 ml/¼ pint double cream	⅔ cup heavy cream

Put the milk, egg and egg yolk in a heatproof bowl over a pan of hot water or in a double boiler. Cook gently, stirring, until the custard is thick enough to coat the back of the spoon. Remove from the heat.

Dissolve the gelatine in the warmed water and stir into the custard with the orange and lemon juices and sugar. Whip the cream until thick and fold in. Pour into an oiled 600 ml/1 pint (2½ cup capacity) mould and chill until set.

Turn out to serve.

Serves 4

Variations:

Apricot Bavarian Cream: Use 150 ml/¼ pint (⅔ cup) apricot purée instead of the orange juice, and use only 7 g/¼ oz (1 envelope) gelatine.

Rum Bavarian Cream: Use 450 ml/¾ pint (2 cups) extra milk instead of the orange and lemon juices. Add 1 to 2 tablespoons rum.

Ribbon Bavarian Cream: Use 450 ml/¾ pint (2 cups) extra milk instead of the orange and lemon juices. Divide the mixture between three bowls. Add ½ teaspoon coffee essence (flavoring) to one bowl; add a few drops of vanilla essence (extract) to the second; add a few drops of almond essence (extract) with green food colouring to the third. Pour the first mixture into the mould and allow to set before adding the second mixture. When that has set, pour in the third mixture.

Charlotte Russe

Metric/Imperial
300 ml/½ pint liquid lemon jelly
about 12 sponge finger biscuits
1 quantity orange Bavarian cream
  mixture (see opposite)
whipped cream to decorate

American
1¼ cups liquid lemon-flavored gelatin
about 12 ladyfingers
1 quantity orange Bavarian cream
  mixture (see opposite)
whipped cream to decorate

Pour enough of the jelly (gelatin) into the bottom of a 600 ml/1 pint (2½ cup capacity) charlotte mould to make a 1 cm/½ inch layer. Arrange the sponge (lady) fingers standing upright around the side of the mould with their ends in the jelly (gelatin). Pour in the Bavarian cream mixture. Trim the sponge (lady) fingers if necessary to make them even with the top of the filling. Chill until set.

Turn out the charlotte onto a serving plate. Coarsely chop the remaining jelly (gelatin) which will have set and use to decorate the charlotte, with whipped cream.

Serves 4

Blackcurrant Dessert Mould

Metric/Imperial
1 packet blackcurrant
  jelly
100 g/4 oz blackcurrants
2 eggs, separated
50 g/2 oz caster sugar
1 × 75 g/3 oz packet cream cheese
whipped cream to decorate

American
1 package blackcurrant-flavored
  gelatin
¼ lb blackcurrants
2 eggs, separated
¼ cup sugar
1 × 3 oz package cream cheese
whipped cream to decorate

Dissolve the jelly (gelatin) according to the instructions on the packet, using half the water called for. Leave until on the point of setting.

Poach the blackcurrants in a little water until soft. Pour into the blender and blend to a purée.

Beat the egg yolks and sugar together until pale and fluffy. Fold in the fruit purée.

Cream the cream cheese with 1 tablespoon of the setting jelly (gelatin), then fold with the remaining jelly (gelatin) into the fruit mixture. Beat the egg whites until stiff and fold in. Pour into a dampened decorative mould and chill until set.

Turn out to serve, decorated with whipped cream.

Serves 4

Pineapple Cheese Whip

Metric/Imperial	American
2 tablespoons water	2 tablespoons water
1 tablespoon gelatine	1 envelope unflavored gelatin
1 × 425 g/15 oz can pineapple chunks	1 × 15 oz can pineapple chunks
2 eggs, separated	2 eggs, separated
100 g/4 oz sugar	½ cup sugar
grated rind of ½ lemon	grated rind of ½ lemon
350 g/12 oz cottage cheese, sieved	1½ cups cottage cheese, strained
1 tablespoon lemon juice	1 tablespoon lemon juice
150 ml/¼ pint double cream	⅔ cup heavy cream

Warm the water and soften the gelatine in it. Drain the pineapple chunks, reserving 150 ml/¼ pint (⅔ cup) of the syrup.

Beat the egg yolks and sugar together until pale and thick. Slowly beat in the reserved pineapple syrup. Pour the mixture into a saucepan, add the softened gelatine and stir over a low heat until dissolved. Stir in the lemon rind, remove from the heat and cool.

Mix in the cottage cheese and lemon juice and leave the mixture until it is beginning to set.

Beat the cheese mixture until it is smooth. Whip the cream and fold into the cheese mixture. Finely chop half the pineapple chunks. Beat the egg whites until stiff. Fold the pineapple into the cheese mixture followed by the egg whites. Pour into individual serving dishes and decorate with the remaining pineapple chunks. Chill until set.
Serves 4

Pineapple Cheese Cream

Metric/Imperial
1 × 400 g/14 oz can pineapple
  chunks
1 tablespoon gelatine
75 g/3 oz Edam cheese, grated
2 egg yolks
50 g/2 oz caster sugar
200 ml/⅓ pint double cream

American
1 × 14 oz can pineapple chunks

1 envelope unflavored gelatin
¾ cup grated Edam cheese
2 egg yolks
¼ cup sugar
1 cup heavy cream

Drain the pineapple chunks, reserving the syrup. Sprinkle the gelatine onto the syrup and heat gently until the gelatine has dissolved. Then pour into the blender. Add the pineapple chunks, cheese, egg yolks and sugar and blend until smooth. Pour into a bowl.

Whip the cream until thick and fold into the pineapple mixture. Pour into a 900 ml/1½ pint (1 quart capacity) mould and chill until set. Turn out to serve.
Serves 6

Mandarin Coffee Cream

Metric/Imperial
2 eggs
25 g/1 oz sugar
300 ml/½ pint warm milk
1 × 300 g/11 oz can mandarin
  oranges
1½ teaspoons sweetened coffee
  essence
15 g/½ oz gelatine
whipped cream to decorate

American
2 eggs
2 tablespoons sugar
1¼ cups warm milk
1 × 11 oz can mandarin oranges

1½ teaspoons sweetened coffee
  flavoring
2 envelopes unflavored gelatin
whipped cream to decorate

Beat the eggs with the sugar in a heatproof bowl or top of a double boiler. Stir in the milk, then put the bowl or pan over hot water and heat gently, stirring, until the custard thickens enough to coat the back of the spoon. Remove from the heat and cool.

Drain the mandarin oranges, reserving the syrup. Mix 150 ml/¼ pint (⅔ cup) of the syrup with the coffee essence (flavoring). Dissolve the gelatine in the syrup mixture over heat and cool.

Beat the syrup mixture into the custard and pour into a dampened mould. Chill until set.

Turn out to serve, decorated with the mandarin oranges and whipped cream.
Serves 4

Raspberry Cream Mould

Metric/Imperial
1 tablespoon gelatine
250 ml/8 fl oz water
100 g/4 oz sugar
500 g/1 lb raspberries
2 egg whites
150 ml/¼ pint whipping cream

American
1 envelope unflavored gelatin
1 cup water
½ cup sugar
1 lb raspberries
2 egg whites
⅔ cup whipping cream

Sprinkle the gelatine onto 120 ml/4 fl oz (½ cup) of the water and heat until dissolved. Put the remaining water and the sugar in a saucepan and stir to dissolve the sugar. Stir in the gelatine mixture.

Pour the gelatine mixture into the blender goblet and add the raspberries. Blend until a smooth purée. Pour into a bowl and leave until on the point of setting.

Beat the egg whites until stiff and fold into the raspberry mixture. Whip the cream until thick and fold in. Spoon into a greased 1.5 litre/2½ pint (1½ quart capacity) mould and chill, until set.
Serves 4

Chilled Mocha Pudding

Metric/Imperial
2 tablespoons water
1 tablespoon gelatine
2 tablespoons instant coffee powder
1 tablespoon cocoa powder
2 tablespoons sugar
300 ml/½ pint boiling water
200 ml/⅓ pint evaporated milk,
   chilled

American
2 tablespoons water
1 envelope unflavored gelatin
2 tablespoons instant coffee powder
1 tablespoon unsweetened cocoa
2 tablespoons sugar
1¼ cups boiling water
⅞ cup evaporated milk,
   chilled

Warm the water and soften the gelatine in it. Dissolve the coffee powder, cocoa powder and sugar in the boiling water. Add the gelatine and stir until it has dissolved. Allow to cool until the mixture is on the point of setting.

Beat the evaporated milk until it is thick and fluffy. Gradually beat in the coffee mixture, then pour into a dampened 1 litre/1¾ pint (1 quart capacity) mould. Chill until set.

Turn out to serve.
Serves 6–8

Country Junket

Metric/Imperial
1.2 litres/2 pints milk
4 junket tablets or 2 tablespoons
  rennet
2 tablespoons caster sugar
2 tablespoons rum
½ teaspoon grated nutmeg
½ teaspoon ground cinnamon
strawberry jam to decorate

American
5 cups milk
4 junket tablets or 2 tablespoons
  rennet
2 tablespoons sugar
2 tablespoons rum
½ teaspoon grated nutmeg
½ teaspoon ground cinnamon
strawberry jam to decorate

Make the junket with lukewarm milk and the junket tablets, according to the directions on the bottle. Stir in the sugar, rum and spices and pour into a warm bowl. Leave to set at room temperature for 30 minutes to 1 hour.

Serve topped with strawberry jam.

Serves 4

Apricot and Orange Cream

Metric/Imperial
500 g/1 lb apricots, halved and
  stoned
100 g/4 oz sugar
150 ml/¼ pint water
grated rind and juice of 2 large
  oranges
15 g/½ oz gelatine
300 ml/½ pint double cream
½ teaspoon demerara sugar

American
1 lb apricots, halved and
  pitted
½ cup sugar
⅔ cup water
grated rind and juice of 2 large
  oranges
2 envelopes unflavored gelatin
1¼ cups heavy cream
½ teaspoon raw brown sugar

Put the apricots, sugar and water in a saucepan and heat gently, stirring to dissolve the sugar. Poach until the apricots are tender. Cool slightly, then purée the apricots with the sugar syrup in a blender or sieve (strainer). Stir in the orange rind and half the orange juice.

Heat the remaining orange juice and dissolve the gelatine in it, then stir into the apricot mixture.

Whip all but 3 tablespoons of the cream until thick. Fold into the apricot mixture. Turn into a glass serving dish and chill until set.

Just before serving, pour over the reserved cream and sprinkle with the demerara (raw brown) sugar.

Serves 6

Normandy Mould

Metric/Imperial
300 ml/½ pint water
1 packet strawberry
  jelly
150 ml/¼ pint apple purée
150 ml/¼ pint whipping cream
whipped cream to decorate

American
1 cup water
1 package strawberry-flavored
  gelatin
⅔ cup apple sauce
⅔ cup whipping cream
whipped cream to decorate

Warm the water and dissolve the jelly (gelatin) in it. Cool slightly, then stir in the apple purée (sauce). Whip the cream until thick and fold into the apple mixture. Turn into a dampened mould and chill until set.

Remove from the mould to serve, decorated with whipped cream.
Serves 4–6

Variation:
Use lemon jelly (gelatin) and apricot purée and add 2 to 3 tablespoons finely chopped almonds.

Almond Junket

Metric/Imperial
1½ tablespoons gelatine
150 ml/¼ pint cold water
75 g/3 oz sugar
150 ml/¼ pint boiling water
450 ml/¾ pint evaporated milk
few drops of almond essence

American
2 envelopes unflavored gelatin
⅔ cup cold water
6 tablespoons sugar
⅔ cup boiling water
2 cups evaporated milk
few drops of almond extract

Sprinkle the gelatine onto the cold water and heat until dissolved. Add the sugar, then stir in the boiling water until the sugar has dissolved. Stir in the evaporated milk and almond essence (extract). Pour into four individual serving dishes. Cool, then chill until set.
Serves 4

Moulded Strawberry Cream

Metric/Imperial
500 g/1 lb strawberries, hulled
15 g/½ oz gelatine
2 tablespoons water
2 egg whites
75 g/3 oz caster sugar
300 ml/½ pint whipping cream
1 tablespoon lemon juice

American
1 lb strawberries, hulled
2 envelopes unflavored gelatin
2 tablespoons water
2 egg whites
6 tablespoons sugar
1¼ cups whipping cream
1 tablespoon lemon juice

Mash the strawberries to a smooth purée. Dissolve the gelatine in the water over heat. Beat the egg whites until soft peaks form. Gradually beat in the sugar and continue beating until stiff. Whip the cream until thick and fold into the egg white mixture. Fold in the strawberries, lemon juice and gelatine. Pour into a dampened mould and chill until set.
Serves 4

Gingered Pear and Yogurt Mousse

Metric/Imperial
1 kg/2 lb pears, peeled, cored and
   chopped
finely grated rind and juice of 1 lemon
¼ teaspoon ground ginger
3–4 pieces preserved ginger in syrup
2 eggs, separated
300 ml/½ pint natural yogurt
15 g/½ oz gelatine
2 tablespoons water

American
2 lb pears, peeled, cored and
   chopped
finely grated rind and juice of 1 lemon
¼ teaspoon ground ginger
3–4 pieces candied ginger in syrup
2 eggs, separated
1¼ cups unflavored yogurt
2 envelopes unflavored gelatin
2 tablespoons water

Put the pears, lemon rind and juice, ground ginger and 2 tablespoons of ginger syrup into a saucepan. Cover and cook gently for 10 to 15 minutes or until the pears are tender.

Pour the pear mixture into the blender, add the egg yolks and yogurt and blend to a smooth purée.

Dissolve the gelatine in the warmed water and stir into the pear mixture. Finely chop one or two pieces of the ginger and add to the pear mixture. Leave until on the point of setting.

Beat the egg whites until stiff and fold into the pear mixture. Spoon into individual dishes and chill until set.

Serve decorated with the remaining ginger, cut into thin slices.
Serves 6

Apple Lemon Mould

Metric/Imperial
grated rind and juice of 2 lemons
600 ml/1 pint hot thick apple purée
2 tablespoons gelatine
2 tablespoons golden
  syrup
lemon slices to decorate

American
grated rind and juice of 2 lemons
2½ cups hot thick apple sauce
2 envelopes unflavored gelatin
2 tablespoons light corn or maple
  syrup
lemon slices to decorate

Mix together the lemon rind and apple purée (sauce). Heat the lemon juice
and dissolve the gelatine in it and add to the apple mixture with the syrup.
Pour into a dampened mould and chill until set.
    Turn out to serve, decorated with lemon slices.
Serves 4

Dutch Chocolate Dessert

Metric/Imperial
225 g/8 oz unsalted
  butter
100 g/4 oz caster sugar
225 g/8 oz plain chocolate,
  melted
1 × 440 g/15½ oz can unsweetened
  chestnut purée
few drops of vanilla essence
150 ml/¼ pint milk
2 teaspoons gelatine
1 × 200 g/7 oz can mandarin
  oranges, drained

American
16 tablespoons (2 sticks) sweet
  butter
½ cup sugar
1⅓ cups semi-sweet chocolate chips,
  melted
1 × 15½ oz can unsweetened
  chestnut purée
few drops of vanilla extract
⅔ cup milk
1 envelope unflavored gelatin
1 × 7 oz can mandarin oranges,
  drained

Cream 100 g/4 oz (1 stick) of the butter with the sugar until pale and fluffy.
Beat in the melted chocolate, chestnut purée and vanilla. Pour into a greased
and lined 500 g/1 lb loaf pan and chill overnight.
    Put the remaining butter, the milk and gelatine in a heatproof bowl over a
pan of water or in a double boiler. Heat gently until the butter has melted and
the gelatine dissolved. Remove from the heat and beat for 1 minute. Chill for
2 to 3 hours.
    Turn out the chocolate loaf onto a serving plate. Whip the chilled milk
mixture well, then use to decorate the chocolate loaf, with the mandarin
orange segments.
Serves 8–10

Orange Rice Mould

Metric/Imperial	American
75 g/3 oz short grain rice	6 tablespoons pudding rice
600 ml/1 pint milk	2½ cups milk
25 g/1 oz sugar	2 tablespoons sugar
1 egg, separated	1 egg, separated
15 g/½ oz butter	1 tablespoon butter
1 packet orange jelly	1 package orange-flavored gelatin
150 ml/¼ pint boiling water	⅔ cup boiling water
glacé cherries to decorate	candied cherries to decorate

Put the rice, milk and sugar in a saucepan and bring to the boil, stirring to dissolve the sugar. Cover and simmer for 30 minutes.

Cool slightly, then beat in the egg yolk and butter

Dissolve the jelly (gelatin) in the boiling water. Cool slightly, then stir into the rice mixture. Beat the egg white until stiff and fold into the rice mixture. Pour into an oiled ring mould and chill until set.

Serve decorated with glacé (candied) cherries.

Serves 4–6

Variation:

Cherry Rice Mould: Cook 75 g/3 oz (6 tablespoons) rice with 1.2 litres/ 2 pints (5 cups) milk and 150 g/5 oz (⅔ cup) sugar as above, or until the rice is tender and most of the milk has been absorbed. Omit the butter and stir in 1 egg yolk with 1 teaspoon vanilla essence (extract). Dissolve 2 tablespoons (2 envelopes unflavored) gelatine in 4 tablespoons hot water and add to the rice mixture. Whip 300 ml/½ pint double cream (1¼ cups heavy cream) until thick and fold in, with 225 g/8 oz glacé cherries (1 cup candied cherries). halved. Pour into a mould and chill until set.

Serves 6-8

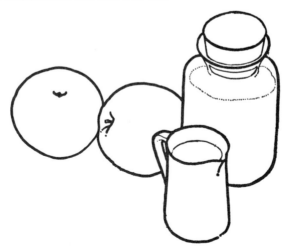

Fruit Chiffon

Metric/Imperial
2 tablespoons lemon juice
2 teaspoons gelatine
300 ml/½ pint sweetened thick fruit
   purée
150 ml/¼ pint double cream
2 egg whites
25 g/1 oz caster sugar

American
2 tablespoons lemon juice
1 envelope unflavored gelatin
1¼ cups sweetened thick fruit
   purée
⅔ cup heavy cream
2 egg whites
2 tablespoons sugar

Warm the lemon juice and dissolve the gelatine in it. Stir into the fruit purée, then leave until on the point of setting.

Whip the cream until thick and fold into the fruit mixture. Beat the egg whites until stiff and gradually beat in the sugar. Fold the egg whites into the fruit mixture.

Spoon into four or five glasses and chill until set.

Serves 4–5

Pots au Citron

Metric/Imperial
1 × 500 g/16 oz can sweetened
   condensed milk
1 × 225 g/8 oz packet cream cheese
grated rind and juice of 2 lemons
2 egg whites
15 g/½ oz gelatine
3 tablespoons water
chopped mixed nuts

American
1 × 1 lb can sweetened condensed
   milk
1 × ½ lb package cream cheese
grated rind and juice of 2 lemons
2 egg whites
2 envelopes unflavored gelatin
3 tablespoons water
chopped mixed nuts

Beat together the condensed milk and cream cheese. Mix in the lemon rind and juice. Beat the egg whites until stiff and fold into the lemon mixture.

Warm the water and dissolve the gelatine in it, then stir into the lemon mixture. Pour into four small pots and chill until set.

Just before serving, decorate with nuts.

Serves 4

Rhubarb Velvet

Metric/Imperial
1 kg/2 lb rhubarb, chopped
1 tablespoon grated orange rind
150 g/5 oz brown sugar
6 tablespoons water
350 ml/12 fl oz double cream
1 tablespoon gelatine
2 egg whites

American
2 lb rhubarb, chopped
1 tablespoon grated orange rind
⅞ cup brown sugar
6 tablespoons water
1½ cups heavy cream
2 envelopes unflavored gelatin
2 egg whites

Put the rhubarb in a saucepan with the orange rind, sugar and 4 tablespoons of the water. Simmer gently until the rhubarb has pulped. Cool.

Whip the cream until thick and fold into the rhubarb. Heat the remaining water and dissolve the gelatine in it and mix into the rhubarb mixture. Beat the egg whites until stiff and fold in. Spoon into a dampened mould and chill until set. Turn out to serve.

Serves 6

Summer Orange Whip

Metric/Imperial
300 ml/½ pint natural yogurt
1 × 175 g/6 oz can frozen
   concentrated orange juice, thawed
1 tablespoon gelatine
4 tablespoons water
grated rind and chopped flesh of 2
   oranges
2 egg whites
fresh mint sprigs to decorate

American
1¼ cups unflavored yogurt
1 × 6 oz can frozen concentrated
   orange juice, thawed
2 envelopes unflavored gelatin
¼ cup water
grated rind and chopped flesh of 2
   oranges
2 egg whites
fresh mint sprigs to decorate

Put the yogurt and orange juice in the blender and blend until well mixed. Warm the water and dissolve the gelatine in it.

Add the orange rind and flesh to the blender goblet with the gelatine and blend until thoroughly combined. Leave until beginning to set.

Beat the egg whites until stiff. Fold into the orange mixture and spoon into individual glasses. Chill until set.

Serve decorated with mint sprigs.

Serves 4–6

Banana and Lemon Cream

Metric/Imperial
1 packet lemon jelly
450 ml/¾ pint boiling water
2 teaspoons lemon juice
1 tablespoon sugar
300 ml/½ pint double cream
2 egg whites
3 small bananas, sliced
To decorate:
sponge fingers
whipped cream
glacé cherries

American
1 package lemon-flavored gelatin
2 cups boiling water
2 teaspoons lemon juice
1 tablespoon sugar
1¼ cups heavy cream
2 egg whites
3 small bananas, sliced
To decorate:
ladyfingers
whipped cream
candied cherries

Dissolve the jelly (gelatin) in the boiling water. Stir in the lemon juice and sugar, then leave until firm.

Beat the jelly (gelatin) until it is frothy. Whip the cream until thick and fold in. Beat the egg whites until stiff and fold in, with the bananas. Spoon into a dampened 1.2 litre/2 pint (1 quart capacity) mould and chill until set.

Turn out the cream onto a serving plate. Coat the unsugared side of the sponge (lady) fingers with whipped cream and press them against the side of the dessert. Decorate the top with more whipped cream and cherries.
Serves 4

Variation:

Honey Banana Cream: Mash 3 large bananas with 2 tablespoons lemon juice, 2 teaspoons grated lemon rind and 3 tablespoons honey. Beat in 300 ml/½ pint (1¼ cups) milk and 150 ml/¼ pint (⅔ cup) water. Dissolve 1 tablespoon (2 envelopes unflavored) gelatine in 2 tablespoons hot water and add to the banana mixture. Whip 300 ml/½ pint (1¼ cups) whipping cream until thick. When the banana mixture is on the point of setting, fold in the cream. Chill until set.
Serves 4

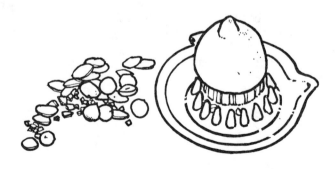

Jellied Apple Snow

Metric/Imperial
1 teaspoon gelatine
1 tablespoon water
300 ml/½ pint thick apple purée
2 tablespoons cider
150 ml/¼ pint double cream
3 egg whites

American
½ envelope unflavored gelatin
1 tablespoon water
1¼ cups thick apple sauce
2 tablespoons hard cider
⅔ cup heavy cream
3 egg whites

Dissolve the gelatine in the water over heat. Add to the apple purée (sauce) with the cider and mix well. Whip the cream until thick and fold half into the apple mixture.

Beat two of the egg whites until stiff and fold into the apple mixture. Spoon into individual serving dishes and chill until lightly set.

Beat the remaining egg white until stiff and fold into the rest of the cream. Pile on top of the apple snow and serve.

Serves 4

Pineapple in Sour Cream

Metric/Imperial
2 tablespoons gelatine
4 tablespoons hot water
250 ml/8 fl oz pineapple juice
175 g/6 oz fresh or canned
  pineapple, chopped
250 ml/8 fl oz sour cream
whipped cream to decorate

American
1½ envelopes unflavored gelatin
¼ cup hot water
1 cup pineapple juice
1 cup chopped fresh or canned
  pineapple
1 cup sour cream
whipped cream to decorate

Dissolve the gelatine in the hot water. Stir in the pineapple juice and chill until on the point of setting.

Fold the chopped pineapple and sour cream into the pineapple mixture. Divide between six glasses and chill until set.

Serve topped with whipped cream.

Serves 6

Plum Froth

Metric/Imperial	American
1 small can evaporated milk, chilled	1 small can evaporated milk, chilled
1 tablespoon gelatine	1½ envelopes unflavored gelatin
2 tablespoons water	2 tablespoons water
300 ml/½ pint sweetened plum purée	1¼ cups sweetened plum purée
2 egg whites	2 egg whites

Beat the evaporated milk until it has doubled in bulk. Dissolve the gelatine in the water over heat, then beat it into the evaporated milk. Fold in the plum purée.

Beat the egg whites until stiff and fold into the plum mixture. Spoon into a serving bowl and chill until set.

Serves 4

Orange Yogurt Sorbet

Metric/Imperial	American
300 ml/½ pint natural yogurt	1¼ cups unflavored yogurt
1 × 175 g/6 oz can frozen concentrated orange juice, thawed	1 × 6 oz can frozen concentrated orange juice, thawed
2 oranges	2 oranges
sugar to taste	sugar to taste
15 g/½ oz gelatine	2 envelopes unflavored gelatin
3 tablespoons water	3 tablespoons water
2 egg whites	2 egg whites
mint sprigs to decorate	mint sprigs to decorate

Mix together the yogurt and undiluted orange juice. Grate the rind from the oranges and add to the mixture with sugar to taste.

Dissolve the gelatine in the water over heat and add to the yogurt mixture. Leave until on the point of setting.

Beat the egg whites until stiff and fold into the yogurt mixture. Spoon into a freezer tray and freeze until set.

Peel the oranges and separate them into segments. Remove all the skin from the segments.

To serve, layer the sorbet and orange segments in dessert glasses and top each serving with a mint sprig.

Serves 4–6

Pashka

Metric/Imperial
350 g/12 oz curd cheese
1 × 75 g/3 oz packet cream cheese
100 g/4 oz sugar
150 ml/¼ pint double cream
50 g/2 oz glacé cherries, chopped
50 g/2 oz sultanas
50 g/2 oz chopped mixed peel
50 g/2 oz blanched almonds,
　chopped
1 tablespoon dry sherry
grated rind of 1 lemon
2 teaspoons gelatine
2 tablespoons water

American
1½ cups small-curd cottage cheese
1 × 3 oz package cream cheese
½ cup sugar
⅔ cup heavy cream
⅓ cup chopped candied cherries
⅓ cup seedless white raisins
⅓ cup chopped mixed candied peel
½ cup chopped blanched
　almonds
1 tablespoon dry sherry
grated rind of 1 lemon
1 envelope unflavored gelatin
2 tablespoons water

Beat together the cheeses and sugar. Whip the cream until thick and fold into the cheese mixture with the cherries, sultanas (raisins), peel, almonds, sherry and lemon rind. Mix well.

Dissolve the gelatine in the water over heat and add to the cheese mixture. Turn into a tall pashka mould lined with muslin (cheesecloth), cover with a small plate and put a weight on top. Chill overnight.

The next day, remove the pashka from the mould to serve.
Serves 6–8

Orange Creams

Metric/Imperial
1 tablespoon gelatine
3 tablespoons hot water
500 ml/16 fl oz orange juice, chilled
120 ml/4 fl oz double cream

American
1½ envelopes unflavored gelatin
3 tablespoons hot water
2 cups orange juice, chilled
½ cup heavy cream

Dissolve the gelatine in the hot water. Stir in the orange juice. Whip the cream until thick and mix into the orange mixture. Pour into four small dampened moulds and chill until set.
Serves 4

Mandarin Whip

Metric/Imperial
1 × 300 g/11 oz can mandarin
   oranges
1 packet orange jelly
3 eggs, separated
25 g/1 oz caster sugar

American
1 × 11 oz can mandarin
   oranges
1 package orange-flavored gelatin
2 eggs, separated
2 tablespoons sugar

Drain the oranges, reserving the syrup. Make up the syrup to 450 ml/¾ pint (2 cups) with water, heat the liquid then dissolve the jelly (gelatin) in it. Beat in the egg yolks, then leave until on the point of setting.

Beat the egg whites until stiff and gradually beat in the sugar. Fold the oranges into the jelly (gelatin) mixture followed by the egg whites. Spoon into a serving bowl and chill until set.
Serves 4–6

Variations:
Pineapple Whip: Use lemon jelly (gelatin) and canned diced pineapple rings or crushed pineapple.
Soft Fruit Whip: Use raspberry or strawberry jelly (gelatin) and uncooked berry fruit. Dissolve the jelly (gelatin) in 450 ml/¾ pint (2 cups) hot water.

Eugénie's Rice

Metric/Imperial
1.2 litres/2 pints milk
150 g/5 oz sugar
pinch of salt
75 g/3 oz short grain rice
1 teaspoon vanilla essence
300 ml/½ pint cold custard sauce
  (see page 213)
150 ml/¼ pint double cream
2 tablespoons gelatine
2 tablespoons water
50 g/2 oz flaked almonds
25 g/1 oz sultanas
2 tablespoons chopped glacé
  cherries

American
5 cups milk
⅔ cup sugar
pinch of salt
½ cup short grain rice
1 teaspoon vanilla extract
1¼ cups cold custard sauce (see
  page 213)
⅔ cup heavy cream
2 envelopes unflavored gelatin
2 tablespoons water
½ cup slivered almonds
2½ tablespoons seedless white
  raisins
2 tablespoons chopped candied
  cherries

Put the milk, sugar and salt in a saucepan and bring to the boil. Gradually stir in the rice and simmer for 45 minutes to 1 hour or until the rice is tender and most of the milk has been absorbed. Stir in the vanilla and cool.

Beat the custard into the rice mixture. Whip the cream until thick and fold in. Dissolve the gelatine in the water over heat and add to the rice mixture. Fold in the almonds, sultanas (raisins) and cherries.

Pour into a dampened ring mould and chill until set.
Serves 6

Orange Praline Mould

Metric/Imperial
2 sugar lumps
2 juicy oranges
900 ml/1½ pints milk
175 g/6 oz sugar
6 eggs, separated
2 teaspoons cornflour
25 g/1 oz gelatine
2 tablespoons water
25 g/1 oz unblanched almonds

American
2 sugar lumps
2 juicy oranges
4 cups milk
¾ cup sugar
6 eggs, separated
2 teaspoons cornstarch
3 envelopes unflavored gelatin
2 tablespoons water
¼ cup unblanched almonds

Rub the sugar lumps over the orange rind to extract the zest (oil). Quarter the oranges and squeeze out the juice; there should be 6 tablespoons.

Put the sugar lumps in a saucepan with the milk and 50 g/2 oz (¼ cup) of the sugar. Heat, stirring to dissolve the sugar, until the milk is at boiling point. Mix together the egg yolks and cornflour (cornstarch) and stir in a little of the hot milk. Return this mixture to the pan and cook gently until thickened. Remove from the heat.

Dissolve the gelatine in the orange juice over heat and add to the custard. Leave until on the point of setting.

Meanwhile, dissolve the remaining sugar in the water and stir in the almonds. Cook briskly until the mixture is a deep golden brown, stirring frequently. Turn onto an oiled baking sheet and leave until set, then crush finely with a rolling pin.

Beat the egg whites until stiff and fold into the orange mixture with half the crushed praline. Spoon into a dampened decorative mould and chill until set.

Turn out to serve, decorated with the rest of the praline.
Serves 6

Sorbet-Filled Oranges

Metric/Imperial	American
600 ml/1 pint water	2½ cups water
225 g/8 oz sugar	1 cup sugar
300 ml/½ pint orange juice	1¼ cups orange juice
1 egg white	1 egg white
6–8 oranges	6–8 oranges
2 tablespoons orange liqueur	2 tablespoons orange liqueur

Put the water and sugar in a saucepan and stir to dissolve the sugar. Bring to the boil and boil for 3 minutes. Cool, then stir in the orange juice. Pour into a freezer tray and freeze until mushy.

Beat the egg white until stiff. Beat the orange ice with a fork to break down the ice crystals. Fold the egg white into the orange ice. Return to the freezer and freeze until set.

Slice the tops off the oranges and hollow out the flesh. Cut a slice off the bottoms so the oranges have a flat base.

Allow the sorbet to soften slightly, then use it to fill the orange shells. Sprinkle over the liqueur and serve.
Serves 6–8

Coffee Sorbet

Metric/Imperial
1 tablespoon caster sugar
600 ml/1 pint water
1 tablespoon coffee essence
2 egg whites

American
1 tablespoon sugar
2½ cups water
1 tablespoon coffee flavoring
2 egg whites

Dissolve the sugar in the water. Stir in the coffee essence (flavoring). Pour into a freezer tray and freeze until mushy.

Beat the egg whites until stiff. Tip the coffee mixture into a bowl and beat with a fork to break down the ice crystals. Fold in the egg whites. Return to the freezer tray and freeze until set.

Serve 4–6

Elderflower Sorbet

Metric/Imperial
900 ml/1½ pints water
350 g/12 oz caster sugar
16 elderflower heads
juice of 2 lemons
1 large egg white

American
3¾ cups water
1½ cups sugar
16 elderflower heads
juice of 2 lemons
1 egg white

Put the water and sugar in a saucepan and bring to the boil, stirring to dissolve the sugar. Add the elderflowers, cover the pan and remove from the heat. Leave to infuse for 30 minutes.

Strain the liquid and stir in the lemon juice. Pour into a freezer tray and freeze until mushy.

Beat the elderflower mixture to break down the ice crystals. Beat the egg white until stiff and fold into the elderflower mixture. Return to the freezer and freeze until firm.

Serves 6

Variations:
Mint Sorbet: Dissolve 75 g/3 oz (6 tablespoons) sugar in 300 ml/½ pint (1¼ cups) water, add 6 large mint sprigs and infuse for 20 minutes. Strain and add the juice of 1 lemon. Continue as above.
Serves 4
Grapefruit and Mint Sorbet: Dissolve 50 g/2 oz (¼ cup) sugar in 150 ml/ ¼ pint (⅔ cup) water, add 3 mint sprigs and infuse for 20 minutes. Strain and add the juice of 2 large grapefruit. Continue as above.
Serves 4

Blackcurrant Sorbet

Metric/Imperial
1 × 425 g/15 oz can blackcurrants
175 g/6 oz sugar
grated rind and juice of 1 lemon
1 teaspoon gelatine
1 tablespoon water
2 egg whites

American
1 × 15 oz can blackcurrants
¾ cup sugar
grated rind and juice of 1 lemon
1 envelope unflavored gelatin
1 tablespoon water
2 egg whites

Drain the blackcurrants, reserving the syrup. Make the syrup up to 450 ml/¾ pint (2 cups) with water. Put the syrup in a saucepan with the sugar and heat, stirring to dissolve the sugar. Bring to the boil and boil for 2 minutes. Cool, then stir in the lemon rind and juice.

Purée the blackcurrants in a sieve (strainer). Stir the purée into the syrup mixture. Dissolve the gelatine in the water over heat and add to the blackcurrant mixture. Pour into a freezer tray and freeze until mushy.

Beat the blackcurrant ice with a fork to break down the ice crystals. Beat the egg whites until stiff and fold into the blackcurrant ice. Continue freezing until set.

Serves 6

Frosted Apple

Metric/Imperial
4 cooking apples, peeled, cored and
    chopped
sugar to taste
2 eggs, separated
chopped nuts to decorate

American
4 tart apples, peeled, cored and
    chopped
sugar to taste
2 eggs, separated
chopped nuts to decorate

Put the apples in a saucepan with just enough water to cover the bottom of the pan. Cook gently until the apples have pulped. Beat to a smooth purée, then sweeten to taste. Cool.

Beat the egg yolks into the apple purée. Beat the egg whites until stiff and fold in. Spoon into freezerproof serving dishes and freeze until just set. Serve topped with nuts.

Serves 6

Pineapple Sorbet

Metric/Imperial	American
1 × 1.5 kg/3 lb pineapple	1 × 3 lb pineapple
grated rind and juice of 1 large orange	grated rind and juice of 1 large orange
sugar to taste	sugar to taste
2 egg whites	2 egg whites

Cut the pineapple in half lengthways, leaving the green leaves intact. Scoop out the flesh and discard the core. Reserve the shells for serving.

Put the pineapple flesh in the blender goblet with the orange rind and juice and blend to a smooth purée. Sweeten to taste. Pour into a freezerproof bowl and freeze until mushy.

Beat the egg whites until stiff. Break down the ice crystals in the pineapple mixture, then fold in the egg whites. Spoon into the pineapple shells and freeze until set.

Allow the sorbet to soften slightly before serving.

Serves 6–8

Variation:

Remove the pineapple flesh as above, then chop it finely and mix with the juice of 1½ lemons. Make a thin syrup with 175 g/6 oz (¾ cup) sugar and 450 ml/¾ pint (2 cups) water. Stir in the pineapple mixture, then freeze until mushy. Break down the ice crystals by beating with a fork, then continue freezing until set. Serve in the pineapple shell as above.

Lemon Water Ice

Metric/Imperial	American
3 tablespoons golden syrup	3 tablespoons light corn syrup
75 g/3 oz sugar	6 tablespoons sugar
450 ml/¾ pint water	2 cups water
thinly pared rind and juice of 1 lemon	thinly pared rind and juice of 1 lemon
4 teaspoons gelatine	1½ envelopes unflavored gelatin

Put the syrup, sugar and 300 ml/½ pint (1¼ cups) of the water in a saucepan and bring to the boil, stirring to dissolve the sugar. Add the lemon rind, then boil for about 5 minutes.

Meanwhile, dissolve the gelatine in the remaining water and the lemon juice over heat. Strain the sugar syrup onto the gelatine mixture and cool. Pour into a freezer tray and freeze until thick and mushy.

Break down the ice crystals with a fork, then freeze until completely set.

Serves 4

Apple Water Ice

Metric/Imperial
500 g/1 lb cooking apples, chopped
thinly pared rind and juice of 1 lemon
300 ml/½ pint water
100 g/4 oz sugar
2 teaspoons gelatine
green food colouring
1 egg white

American
1 lb tart apples, chopped
thinly pared rind and juice of 1 lemon
1¼ cups water
½ cup sugar
1 envelope unflavored gelatin
green food coloring
1 egg white

Put the apples into a saucepan with the lemon rind, water and sugar. Stir to dissolve the sugar, then cook gently until the apples are soft. Sieve (strain) the mixture to make a smooth purée.

Dissolve the gelatine in the lemon juice, then add to the apple mixture. Tint it a pale green with a little food colouring. Pour into a freezer tray and freeze until mushy.

Beat the egg white until stiff. Break down the ice crystals in the apple mixture, then fold in the egg whites. Return to the freezer and freeze until set.
Serves 6

Variations:
Use other fruit in place of apples. Plums, rhubarb, gooseberries, etc should be cooked, but soft fruit such as raspberries and strawberries should be used raw and blended with sugar syrup. A combination of two fruits may also be used.

Italian Lemon Gelato

Metric/Imperial
400 g/14 oz sugar
4 tablespoons lemon juice
1.5 litres/ 2½ pints water
grated rind of 1 lemon
300 ml/½ pint double cream

American
1¾ cups sugar
¼ cup lemon juice
5 cups water
grated rind of 1 lemon
1¼ cups heavy cream

Put the sugar, lemon juice, water and lemon rind in a saucepan and bring to the boil, stirring to dissolve the sugar. Boil for 15 minutes, then strain and cool.

Whip the cream until thick and fold into the lemon mixture. Pour into a freezer tray and freeze, stirring from time to time. When the cream is added to the lemon mixture, the two will not combine; however, the stirring during the freezing process will mix them thoroughly.
Serves 6

Blackcurrant and Orange Sherbet

Metric/Imperial
225 g/8 oz blackcurrants
finely grated rind and juice of
    1 orange
6–8 mint leaves
4 tablespoons soft brown sugar
300 ml/½ pint natural yogurt
2 eggs, separated
mint sprigs to decorate

American
½ lb blackcurrants
finely grated rind and juice of
    1 orange
6–8 mint leaves
¼ cup light brown sugar
1¼ cups unflavored yogurt
2 eggs, separated
mint sprigs to decorate

Put most of the blackcurrants in the blender with the orange rind and juice, mint leaves, sugar, yogurt and egg yolks. Blend until smooth. Pour into a freezerproof bowl and freeze until mushy.

Beat the egg whites until stiff. Break down the ice crystals in the blackcurrant mixture, then fold in the egg whites. Freeze until set.

Allow the sherbet to soften slightly before serving, decorated with mint leaves and the remaining blackcurrants.

Serves 4–6

Apricot Sherbet

Metric/Imperial
1 × 500 g/1 lb can apricot halves,
    drained
2 eggs, separated
pinch of grated nutmeg
4 tablespoons single cream
25 g/1 oz caster sugar

American
1 × 1 lb can apricot halves,
    drained
2 eggs, separated
pinch of grated nutmeg
¼ cup light cream
2 tablespoons sugar

Purée the apricots in a blender or sieve (strainer). Stir in the egg yolks, nutmeg and cream. Beat the egg whites until stiff and beat in 1 tablespoon of the sugar. Fold in the remaining sugar, then fold the egg whites into the apricot mixture.

Pour into a freezer tray and freeze until set.

Serves 4–6

Vanilla Cream

Metric/Imperial	American
500 ml/16 fl oz double cream	2 cups heavy cream
1 vanilla pod, split, or 1 teaspoon vanilla essence	1 vanilla bean, split, or 1 teaspoon vanilla extract
50 g/2 oz caster sugar	¼ cup sugar
4 tablespoons water	¼ cup water
3 eggs, separated	3 eggs, separated

Put the cream and vanilla pod (bean) in a saucepan and heat gently until lukewarm. Remove from the heat, cover and leave to infuse for about 15 minutes. Strain the cream and allow to cool.

Dissolve the sugar in the water in another saucepan, then bring to the boil and boil until the temperature reaches 110°C/220°F. To test without a thermometer, cool a little of the syrup, then draw it out between your thumb and finger; it should form a thread.

Cool the syrup for 1 minute, then beat it into the egg yolks. Continue beating until the mixture is pale and thick.

Whip the cream until thick. Beat the egg whites until stiff. Fold the cream and then the egg whites, with the vanilla essence (extract) if using, into the egg yolk mixture. Pour into a freezer tray and freeze for 45 minutes.

Turn the mushy ice cream into a bowl and beat briskly to break down the ice crystals. Return to the freezer tray and freeze until set.

Makes 600 ml/1 pint (2½ cups)

Variations:

Chocolate Ice Cream: Melt 100 g/4 oz plain chocolate (⅔ cup semi-sweet chocolate chips) and fold into the egg yolk mixture with the cream. Add 2 tablespoons rum, if liked.

Coffee Ice Cream: Dissolve 4 teaspoons instant coffee powder in 1 tablespoon hot water and fold into the egg yolk mixture with the cream.

Soft Fruit Ice Cream: Add 150 ml/¼ pint (⅔ cup) raspberry, strawberry or blackcurrant purée to the ice cream before freezing.

Citrus Ice Cream: Add 2 tablespoons lemon or orange juice and 2 teaspoons grated rind to the egg yolk mixture with the cream.

Ginger Ice Cream: Fold 50 g/2 oz (⅓ cup) chopped crystallized (candied) ginger and 2 teaspoons ginger syrup into the egg yolk mixture with the cream.

Praline Ice Cream: Dissolve 50 g/2 oz (¼ cup) sugar in 2 tablespoons water, add 50 g/2 oz (½ cup) unblanched almonds and cook briskly until the mixture is a deep golden brown, stirring frequently. Turn onto an oiled baking sheet and leave until set, then pulverize in a blender or crush with a rolling pin. Stir into the mushy ice cream.

Black Forest Bombe

Metric/Imperial
Chocolate ice cream:
2 × 75 g/3 oz packets cream cheese
90 g/3½ oz caster sugar
100 g/4 oz plain chocolate,
    melted
250 ml/8 fl oz milk
150 ml/¼ pint double cream
Cherry ice cream:
1 × 75g/3 oz packet cream cheese
40 g/1½ oz caster sugar
5 tablespoons milk
5 tablespoons double cream
1 × 215 g/7½ oz can cherry pie filling
Plain ice cream:
1 × 75 g/3 oz packet cream cheese
40 g/1½ oz caster sugar
150 ml/¼ pint milk
2 tablespoons double cream

American
Chocolate ice cream:
2 × 3 oz packages cream cheese
7 tablespoons sugar
⅔ cup semi-sweet chocolate chips,
    melted
1 cup milk
⅔ cup heavy cream
Cherry ice cream:
1 × 3 oz package cream cheese
3 tablespoons sugar
5 tablespoons milk
5 tablespoons heavy cream
1 × 7½ oz can cherry pie filling
Plain ice cream:
1 × 3 oz package cream cheese
3 tablespoons sugar
⅔ cup milk
2 tablespoons heavy cream

First make the chocolate ice cream: mix the cream cheese and sugar together until smooth, then stir in the chocolate. Gradually beat in the milk and cream, then pour into a freezer tray. Freeze for 40 minutes.

For the cherry ice cream, mix the cream cheese and sugar together until smooth. Gradually beat in the milk, cream and pie filling, pour into a freezer tray and freeze for 40 minutes.

For the plain ice cream, beat the cream cheese and sugar together until smooth. Gradually beat in the milk and cream. Pour into a freezer tray and freeze for 40 minutes.

Chill a 15 cm/6 inch loose-bottomed cake tin (springform pan).

Cover the bottom and sides of the tin (pan) with the chocolate ice cream and freeze for 15 minutes.

Line the chocolate ice cream with the cherry ice cream and freeze for 15 minutes.

Fill the centre cavity with the plain ice cream and freeze for 1½ to 2 hours.

Quickly dip the tin (pan) into hot water to loosen the bombe and turn it out onto a serving plate.
Serves 6–8

Cassata

Metric/Imperial	American
2.4 litres/4 pints vanilla ice cream	2½ quarts vanilla ice cream
juice of 1 lemon	juice of 1 lemon
2 tablespoons sugar	2 tablespoons sugar
1 banana, sliced	1 banana, sliced
50 g/2 oz glacé cherries, chopped	⅓ cup chopped candied cherries
2 glacé apricots, chopped	2 candied apricots, chopped
1 slice glacé pineapple, chopped	1 slice candied pineapple, chopped
50 g/2 oz plain chocolate	⅓ cup semi-sweet chocolate chips
25 g/1 oz cocoa powder	¼ cup unsweetened cocoa
1 tablespoon water	1 tablespoon water
1 teaspoon rum	1 teaspoon rum
25 g/1 oz butter	2 tablespoons butter
50 g/2 oz flaked almonds	½ cup slivered almonds
few drops of almond essence	few drops of almond extract

Divide the ice cream into three bowls. Allow to soften slightly.

Mix together the lemon juice, 1 tablespoon sugar, the banana and glacé (candied) fruits. Mix into one bowl of ice cream. Spread on the bottom of a foil-lined freezerproof 23 × 12.5 cm/9 × 5 inch loaf tin. Freeze until firm.

Melt the chocolate and mix in the cocoa, water, rum and remaining sugar. Stir into the second bowl of ice cream. Spread over the fruit ice cream in the tin and freeze until firm.

Melt the butter in a saucepan, add the almonds and fry until golden brown. Drain on paper towels and cool. Add the almonds to the third bowl of ice cream and flavour to taste with almond essence (extract). Spread over the chocolate ice cream in the tin and freeze until firm.

Turn out to serve, cut into slices.

Serves 10–12

Chocolate Mint Ice

Metric/Imperial
600 ml/1 pint milk
100 g/4 oz sugar
½ teaspoon peppermint essence
2 egg whites
50 g/2 oz plain chocolate,
  chopped

American
2½ cups milk
½ cup sugar
½ teaspoon mint flavoring
2 egg whites
2 squares semi-sweet chocolate,
  chopped

Put the milk, sugar and peppermint essence (mint flavoring) in a saucepan and bring to the boil, stirring to dissolve the sugar. Cool, then pour into a freezer tray and freeze until mushy.

Beat the egg whites until stiff. Tip the mint ice into a bowl and beat with a fork to break down the ice crystals. Fold in the egg whites, then return to the freezer tray. Freeze until set.

To serve, layer scoops of the mint ice with the chocolate in glasses.
Serves 4

Fresh Peach Ice

Metric/Imperial
100 g/4 oz sugar
150 ml/¼ pint water
4 large peaches, peeled, halved and
  stoned
juice of 1 lemon

American
½ cup sugar
⅔ cup water
4 large peaches, peeled, halved and
  pitted
juice of 1 lemon

Bring the sugar and water to the boil, stirring to dissolve the sugar. Boil for 5 minutes, then remove from the heat and cool.

Purée the peaches in a blender or sieve (strainer). Stir in the lemon juice and sugar syrup and pour into a freezer tray. Freeze until mushy.

Beat the peach ice to break down the ice crystals, then return to the freezer. Continue freezing until firm.
Serves 4

Variations:
Melon Ice: Use the flesh of a ripe cantaloup melon instead of the peaches. After peeling and seeding, the flesh should weigh about 750 g/1½ lb.
Pineapple and Maraschino Ice: Use the flesh of 1 medium pineapple and increase the sugar to 225 g/8 oz (1 cup). Add the grated rind of the lemon as well as the juice. After beating the mushy ice to break down the ice crystals, stir in 2 tablespoons maraschino liqueur and 10 maraschino cherries, halved. Freeze until firm.

Raspberry Coupe

Metric/Imperial
100 g/4 oz sugar
7 tablespoons water
1 teaspoon gelatine
500 g/1 lb raspberries
100 g/4 oz strawberries
100 g/4 oz blackberries
Sorbet:
100 g/4 oz sugar
300 ml/½ pint water
juice of ½ lemon
225 g/8 oz raspberries or
   strawberries
2 egg whites

American
½ cup sugar
7 tablespoons water
1 envelope unflavored gelatin
1 lb raspberries
¼ lb strawberries
¼ lb blackberries
Sorbet:
½ cup sugar
1¼ cups water
juice of ½ lemon
½ lb raspberries or
   strawberries
2 egg whites

First make the sorbet: dissolve the sugar in the water, then bring to the boil and boil for 10 minutes. Stir in the lemon juice and cool. Sieve (strain) the fruit to a purée and stir into the cooled syrup. Pour into a freezerproof container and freeze until mushy. Beat the egg whites until stiff and fold into the fruit mixture. Freeze until firm.

Meanwhile, dissolve the sugar in 6 tablespoons of the water, then bring to the boil and boil for 10 minutes. Dissolve the gelatine in the remaining water over heat and stir into the syrup. Lightly crush 350 g/12 oz of the raspberries and pour over the gelatine mixture. Fold together thoroughly. Cool, then sieve (strain) to a smooth purée and chill.

To serve, divide scoops of the sorbet between individual serving dishes and top with the remaining raspberries and the strawberries. Sprinkle with a little extra sugar to taste, then pour over the raspberry gelatine mixture and top with the blackberries.

Serves 6

Coffee Pear Alaska

Metric/Imperial
block of coffee ice cream (to serve
   4), frozen solid
2 pears, peeled, quartered and cored
4 egg whites
100 g/4 oz caster sugar

American
block of coffee ice cream (to serve
   4), frozen solid
2 pears, peeled, quartered and cored
4 egg whites
½ cup sugar

Put the ice cream in the centre of an ovenproof serving dish and surround
with the pear quarters.

Beat the egg whites until stiff. Add 50 g/2 oz (¼ cup) of the sugar and
continue beating for 1 minute, then fold in the remaining sugar. Pile on the ice
cream and fruit, spreading the meringue to cover completely.

Bake in a preheated very hot oven (240°C/475°F, Gas Mark 9) for 3 to 5
minutes or until lightly browned. Serve immediately.
Serves 4

Variation:
Put the ice cream and pears on a sponge (plain) cake layer. If you like,
moisten the cake with a little sweetened black coffee or coffee liqueur.

Iced Pineapple Ring

Metric/Imperial
1 packet lemon jelly
150 ml/¼ pint boiling water
1 × 400 g/14 oz can crushed
   pineapple, drained
600 ml/1 pint vanilla ice cream,
   softened
225 g/8 oz strawberries or other
   soft fruit

American
1 package lemon-flavored gelatin
½ cup boiling water
1 × 14 oz can crushed pineapple,
   drained
1 pint vanilla ice cream,
   softened
½ lb strawberries or other
   soft fruit

Dissolve the jelly (gelatin) in the boiling water. Cool slightly, then stir in the
pineapple and ice cream. Pour into a freezerproof 20 cm/8 inch fluted ring
mould. Cover with foil and freeze until set.

Turn out the ring onto a serving plate and fill the centre with the fruit.
Serves 4–6

Raspberry and Honey Ice Cream

Metric/Imperial	American
500 g/1 lb raspberries	1 lb raspberries
150 ml/¼ pint double cream	⅔ cup heavy cream
150 ml/¼ pint natural yogurt	⅔ cup unflavored yogurt
2 tablespoons lemon juice	2 tablespoons lemon juice
150 ml/¼ pint clear honey	⅔ cup clear honey
pinch of salt	pinch of salt
3 egg whites	3 egg whites

Purée the raspberries in a sieve (strainer) or blender. There should be 300 ml/½ pint (1¼ cups) purée. Stir in the cream, yogurt, lemon juice, honey and salt and pour into a freezer tray. Freeze until mushy.

Beat the raspberry mixture with a fork to break down the ice crystals. Beat the egg whites until stiff and fold into the raspberry mixture. Return to the freezer tray and freeze until set.

Allow to soften slightly before serving.
Serves 8

Frozen Almond Meringue Desserts

Metric/Imperial	American
2 egg whites	2 egg whites
100 g/4 oz caster sugar	½ cup sugar
100 g/4 oz blanched almonds, toasted and chopped	1 cup toasted and chopped blanched almonds
300 ml/½ pint double cream	1¼ cups heavy cream
2 tablespoons brandy	2 tablespoons brandy

Beat the egg whites until stiff. Add 4 teaspoons of the sugar and continue beating for 1 minute, then fold in the rest of the sugar and all but 2 tablespoons of the almonds.

Whip the cream with the brandy until thick. Fold in the almond meringue mixture and spoon into six individual freezerproof moulds. Sprinkle over the reserved almonds and freeze until set.
Serves 6

Praline Ice Cream Fingers

Metric/Imperial
6 tablespoons golden syrup
3 tablespoons coarsely chopped
  peanuts or almonds
1 block vanilla ice cream (to serve 4)

American
6 tablespoons light corn syrup
3 tablespoons coarsely chopped
  peanuts or almonds
1 block vanilla ice cream (to serve 4)

Bring the syrup to the boil in a saucepan and boil until it turns a little darker. Stir in the nuts.

Put the block of ice cream on a serving dish and pour over the nut mixture. Cut into fingers to serve.

Serves 4

Iced Honey and Brandy Mousse

Metric/Imperial
3 eggs, separated
2 tablespoons honey
2 tablespoons lemon juice
2 tablespoons brandy
2 tablespoons water
150 ml/¼ pint double cream

American
3 eggs, separated
2 tablespoons honey
2 tablespoons lemon juice
2 tablespoons brandy
2 tablespoons water
⅔ cup heavy cream

Beat the egg yolks, honey, lemon juice, brandy and water together until the mixture is pale and very thick, and has doubled or tripled in volume.

Whip the cream until thick and fold into the honey mixture. Beat the egg whites until stiff and fold in. Spoon into a 600 ml/1 pint (2½ cup capacity) freezerproof serving dish and freeze until firm.

Serves 6

Frosted Almond Creams

Metric/Imperial
2 eggs, separated
50 g/2 oz soft brown sugar
50 g/2 oz blanched almonds,
  chopped and toasted
300 ml/½ pint natural yogurt
2 tablespoons Grand Marnier
25 g/1 oz flaked almonds, toasted

American
2 eggs, separated
⅓ cup light brown sugar
½ cup chopped toasted
  almonds
1¼ cups unflavored yogurt
2 tablespoons Grand Marnier
¼ cup toasted slivered almonds

Beat together the egg yolks and sugar until fluffy. Stir in the chopped almonds, yogurt and Grand Marnier. Beat the egg whites until stiff and fold into the almond mixture. Pour into six individual freezerproof serving dishes and freeze until set.

Thirty mintues before serving, transfer the creams to the refrigerator and leave to soften slightly. Sprinkle with the flaked (slivered) almonds.
Serves 6

Ice Cream Gâteau

Metric/Imperial
25 g/1 oz cornflour
300 ml/½ pint milk
75 g/3 oz caster sugar
3 egg yolks
¼ teaspoon vanilla essence
50 g/2 oz mixed glacé fruits, chopped
25 g/1 oz glacé cherries,
  chopped
1 block chocolate ice cream (to
  serve 4–6)

American
¼ cup cornstarch
1¼ cups milk
6 tablespoons sugar
3 egg yolks
¼ teaspoon vanilla extract
⅓ cup chopped mixed candied fruits
2½ tablespoons chopped candied
  cherries
1 block chocolate ice cream (to
  serve 4–6)

Mix together the cornflour (cornstarch), milk and sugar in a saucepan and bring to the boil, stirring until thickened. Cool slightly, then beat in the egg yolks. Pour into a heatproof bowl over a pan of hot water or a double boiler and cook, stirring, until thick and creamy. Stir in the vanilla, then cover with dampened greaseproof (wax) paper and cool.

Stir in most of the fruit and cherries. Put the ice cream in a serving bowl and pour over the fruit mixture. Decorate with the remaining fruit and cherries.
Serves 4–6

Iced Sicilian Dessert

Metric/Imperial
4 eggs, separated
100 g/4 oz icing sugar, sifted
300 ml/½ pint double cream
100 g/4 oz raisins
100 g/4 oz glacé cherries, chopped
50 g/2 oz glacé pineapple, chopped
25 g/1 oz candied angelica,
  chopped
50 g/2 oz preserved ginger, chopped

American
4 eggs, separated
1 cup confectioners' sugar, sifted
1¼ cups heavy cream
⅔ cup raisins
⅔ cup chopped candied cherries
⅓ cup chopped candied pineapple
2½ tablespoons chopped candied
  angelica
⅓ cup chopped candied ginger

Beat the egg yolks and sugar together until pale and fluffy. Whip the cream until thick. Beat the egg whites until stiff. Fold the cream and egg whites into the egg yolk mixture. Pour into a freezer tray and freeze for 1 hour.

Tip the cream mixture into a bowl and beat well to break down the ice crystals. Fold in the raisins, cherries, pineapple, angelica and ginger. Pour into a freezerproof mould and freeze for 4 hours or until set.

Turn out to serve.
Serves 6–8

Orange and Pear Caprice

Metric/Imperial
75 g/3 oz sugar
150 ml/¼ pint water
1 × 175 ml/6 fl oz can frozen
  concentrated orange juice, thawed
1 egg white
1 pear, peeled, cored and sliced
lemon juice
2 oranges, peeled and segmented

American
6 tablespoons sugar
⅔ cup water
1 × 6 fl oz can frozen concentrated
  orange juice, thawed
1 egg white
1 pear, peeled, cored and sliced
lemon juice
2 oranges, peeled and segmented

Dissolve the sugar in the water. Remove from the heat and stir in the undiluted orange juice. Pour into a freezer tray and freeze until mushy.

Break down the ice crystals in the orange ice. Beat the egg white until stiff and fold into the orange ice. Return to the freezer and freeze until firm.

Sprinkle the pear slices with a little lemon juice to prevent discoloration.

Scoop the ice into glasses and decorate with the orange segments and pear slices.
Serves 4

Iced Cream Cheese

Metric/Imperial
1 × 225 g/8 oz packet cream cheese
250 ml/8 fl oz double cream
finely grated rind of 1 lemon
caster or icing sugar

American
1 × ½ lb package cream cheese
1 cup heavy cream
finely grated rind of 1 lemon
granulated or confectioners' sugar

Sieve (strain) the cream cheese. Whip the cream until thick and mix with the cheese until smooth. Stir in the lemon rind and sugar to taste.

Press the mixture into a muslin or cheesecloth-lined mould, cover and freeze for 1 to 2 hours.

Turn out the cheese mould and serve with fresh berry fruits.
Serves 6

Chestnut Sundae

Metric/Imperial
6 tablespoons sweetened chestnut
    purée
2 tablespoons single cream or
    natural yogurt
4 large scoops of vanilla or
    strawberry ice cream
2 meringue shells, coarsely crushed

American
6 tablespoons sweetened chestnut
    purée
2 tablespoons light cream or
    unflavored yogurt
4 large scoops of vanilla or
    strawberry ice cream
2 meringue shells, coarsely crushed

Mix together the chestnut purée and cream or yogurt. Put the ice cream into four glasses and top with the chestnut mixture and crushed meringue.
Serves 4

Pineapple Macaroon Sundae

Metric/Imperial
4 large macaroons
4 scoops of vanilla ice cream
4 heaped tablespoons canned
  crushed pineapple, well drained
4 glacé or maraschino cherries

American
4 large macaroons
4 scoops of vanilla ice cream
4 heaped tablespoons canned
  crushed pineapple, well drained
4 candied or maraschino cherries

Put the macaroons in four sundae glasses and top each with a scoop of ice cream. Spoon over the pineapple and decorate with the cherries.
Serves 4

Variations:
Use a tart apple or apricot purée instead of the pineapple.

Brown Bread Ice Cream

Metric/Imperial
300 ml/½ pint double cream
150 ml/¼ pint single cream
75 g/3 oz icing sugar, sifted
100 g/4 oz fresh brown breadcrumbs
2 eggs, separated
1 tablespoon dark rum (optional)

American
1¼ cups heavy cream
⅔ cup light cream
¾ cup confectioners' sugar, sifted
2 cups fresh brown breadcrumbs
2 eggs, separated
1 tablespoon dark rum (optional)

Whip the creams together until thick, then fold in the sugar and breadcrumbs. Beat the egg yolks with the rum, if using, and stir into the cream mixture. Beat the egg whites until stiff and fold into the cream mixture. Pour into a freezer tray and freeze until set.
Serves 4–6

Simple Orange Ice Cream

Metric/Imperial
300 ml/½ pint double cream
300 ml/½ pint orange juice
caster sugar to taste

American
1¼ cups heavy cream
1¼ cups orange juice
sugar to taste

Whip the cream until thick. Gradually beat in the orange juice, then sweeten to taste. Pour into a freezerproof container and freeze until mushy.
    Beat the ice with a fork to break down the ice crystals, then return to the freezer and freeze until set.
Serves 4

Chocolate Sundae

Metric/Imperial
vanilla ice cream (to serve 4)
120 ml/4 fl oz double cream
chocolate sauce 1 or 2 (see page 215)
chopped toasted nuts or salted peanuts

American
vanilla ice cream (to serve 4)
½ cup heavy cream
chocolate sauce 1 or 2 (see page 215)
chopped toasted nuts or salted peanuts

Divide the ice cream between four sundae glasses. Whip the cream until thick and pile half of it on top of the ice cream. Drizzle over the chocolate sauce and top with the remaining whipped cream. Sprinkle with the nuts and serve.
Serves 4

Banana Ice Cream

Metric/Imperial
4 large bananas, mashed
350 g/12 oz sugar
pinch of salt
120 ml/4 fl oz pineapple juice
juice of 1 lemon
2 tablespoons rum
1 teaspoon ground ginger
300 ml/½ pint double cream

American
4 large bananas, mashed
1½ cups sugar
pinch of salt
½ cup pineapple juice
juice of 1 lemon
2 tablespoons rum
1 teaspoon ground ginger
1¼ cups heavy cream

Mix together the bananas, sugar, salt, pineapple and lemon juices, rum and ginger. Whip the cream until thick and fold into the banana mixture. Pour into a freezer tray and freeze until mushy.

Beat the banana mixture with a fork to break down the ice crystals, then return to the freezer and freeze until set.
Serves 6–8

Matzo Apple Dessert

Metric/Imperial
100 g/4 oz medium matzo meal
50 g/2½ oz sugar
½ teaspoon ground cinnamon
2 eggs, beaten
2 medium cooking apples, peeled,
  cored and grated
grated rind and juice of ½ lemon
65 g/2½ oz butter

American
1 cup medium matzo meal
5 tablespoons sugar
½ teaspoon ground cinnamon
2 eggs, beaten
2 medium tart apples, peeled, cored
  and grated
grated rind and juice of ½ lemon
5 tablespoons butter

Mix together the matzo meal, 50 g/2 oz (¼ cup) of the sugar and the cinnamon. Beat in the eggs, apples and lemon rind and juice. Melt 50 g/2 oz (4 tablespoons) of the butter and stir into the apple mixture with a little water if necessary to make a soft consistency. Pour into a greased 900 ml/1½ pint (1 quart capacity) baking dish, sprinkle with the rest of the sugar and dot with the remaining butter.

Bake in a preheated moderately hot oven (190°C/375°F, Gas Mark 5) for 1 hour.
Serves 4

Fruit Taj

Metric/Imperial
2 large oranges, peeled and
  segmented
2 large bananas, sliced
lemon juice
150 ml/¼ pint vanilla ice cream,
  softened
1 egg yolk
150 ml/¼ pint whipping cream
1 tablespoon rum
1 tablespoon thinly sliced dates

American
2 large oranges, peeled and
  segmented
2 large bananas, sliced
lemon juice
¾ cup vanilla ice cream,
  softened
1 egg yolk
⅔ cup whipping cream
1 tablespoon rum
1 tablespoon thinly sliced dates

Divide the orange segments and banana slices between individual serving dishes. Sprinkle the banana with a little lemon juice to prevent discoloration.

Stir together the ice cream and egg yolk. Whip the cream until thick and stir into the ice cream mixture with the rum. Spoon over the fruit and decorate with the dates.

Serves 4

Oranges Che Yang

Metric/Imperial
1 × 300 g/11 oz can mandarin
  oranges, drained
300 ml/½ pint sweetened apple purée
25 g/1 oz preserved stem ginger,
  chopped
1 teaspoon grated nutmeg
1 tablespoon clear honey
2 teaspoons lemon juice
2 tablespoons ginger syrup
crème chantilly to serve (see page
  218)

American
1 × 11 oz can mandarin oranges,
  drained
1¼ cups sweetened apple sauce
2½ tablespoons chopped candied
  ginger
1 teaspoon grated nutmeg
1 tablespoon clear honey
2 teaspoons lemon juice
2 tablespoons ginger syrup
crème chantilly to serve (see page
  218)

Mix together all the ingredients and spoon into dessert glasses. Serve with crème chantilly.

Serves 4

Meringue Chantilly

Metric/Imperial
3 egg whites
100 g/4½ oz caster sugar
150 ml/¼ pint double cream
few drops of vanilla essence

American
3 egg whites
½ cup plus 1 tablespoon sugar
⅔ cup heavy cream
few drops of vanilla extract

Beat 2 of the egg whites until stiff. Add 2 tablespoons of the sugar and continue beating for 1 minute, then fold in all but 1 tablespoon of the remaining sugar. Put the meringue into a piping bag fitted with a 1 cm/½ inch plain nozzle and pipe about eight mounds on a baking sheet lined with non-stick silicone paper. Dry out in a preheated very cool oven (120°C/250°F, Gas Mark ½) for 3 to 4 hours or until the meringues are crisp. Cool on a wire rack.

Whip the cream until thick. Stir in the remaining sugar and the vanilla. Beat the remaining egg white until stiff and fold into the cream. Use to sandwich the meringues together in pairs.
Serves 4

Granita al Caffè

Metric/Imperial
600 ml/1 pint strong black coffee
50 g/2 oz sugar
2 tablespoons Bénédictine (optional)

American
2½ cups strong black coffee
¼ cup sugar
2 tablespoons Bénédictine (optional)

Mix the coffee and sugar together until the sugar has dissolved. Stir in the liqueur, if using. Pour into a freezer tray and freeze until mushy – about 2 to 3 hours. Stir the granita every hour to break down the ice crystals.

Spoon the half-frozen mixture into glasses and serve immediately.
Serves 4

Variations:
Granita di Limone: Dissolve 175 g/6 oz (¾ cup) sugar in 450 ml/¾ pint (2 cups) water, cool and stir in the grated rind of 1 lemon and the juice of 4 large lemons. Freeze as above.
Granita di Arancia: Make as granita di limone, using the juice of 2 large lemons, the juice of 2 medium oranges and the grated rind of 1 orange, with the sugar syrup.
Granita di Agrumi: Make as granita di limone, using the juice of 2 large lemons, the juice of 1 large orange, the juice of 1 medium grapefruit and 1 teaspoon grated grapefruit rind, with the sugar syrup.

Date Crisps

Metric/Imperial
30 dates, stoned
30 walnut halves
30 wonton skins
1½ tablespoons brown sugar
oil for deep frying
3 tablespoons icing sugar

American
30 dates, pitted
30 walnut halves
30 wonton skins
1½ tablespoons brown sugar
oil for deep frying
3 tablespoons confectioners' sugar

Fill each date with a walnut half. Place each date on a wonton wrapping (skin) and sprinkle with a little brown sugar. Moisten the edges of the wonton, then roll and seal by twisting the ends.

Deep fry the rolls in oil heated to 160°C/325°F until they are golden brown. Drain on paper towels and sprinkle with the icing (confectioners') sugar. Cool before serving.
Makes 30

Note:
Wonton skins are paper-thin squares of dough which can be bought ready-made at Chinese supermarkets or delicatessens.

Clafoutis aux Cerises

Metric/Imperial
750 g/1½ lb black cherries, stoned
4 eggs, beaten
pinch of salt
100 g/4 oz sugar
50 g/2 oz plain flour
50 g/2 oz butter
250 ml/8 fl oz milk
sugar

American
1½ lb bing cherries, pitted
4 eggs, beaten
pinch of salt
½ cup sugar
½ cup all-purpose flour
4 tablespoons butter
1 cup milk
sugar

Spread out the cherries in a greased wide, shallow baking dish.

Beat the eggs with the salt and sugar, then sift in the flour and beat until smooth. Melt 25 g/1 oz (2 tablespoons) of the butter and stir into the egg mixture followed by the milk.

Pour the batter over the cherries and dot with the remaining butter. Bake in a preheated moderately hot oven (200°C/400°F, Gas Mark 6) for 35 to 40 minutes or until set.

Sprinkle with sugar and serve hot or warm.
Serves 6

Zabaglione

Metric/Imperial
4 egg yolks
100 g/4 oz caster sugar
150 ml/¼ pint Marsala

American
4 egg yolks
½ cup sugar
⅔ cup Marsala

Put all the ingredients in a large heatproof bowl placed over a pan of simmering water. Beat or whisk until the mixture is thick and foamy. Do not let the bowl get too hot or the egg yolks will scramble. Serve immediately.
Serves 4

Variation:
Iced Zabaglione: Beat the egg yolks until pale and fluffy before adding the sugar and Marsala. When the mixture is thick, pour it into individual freezerproof dishes, cool quickly and freeze until firm.

Zuppa Inglese

Metric/Imperial
8 large macaroons, roughly broken up
120 ml/4 fl oz Marsala
1 teaspoon finely grated orange rind
450 ml/¾ pint plus 3 tablespoons milk
4 eggs, beaten
3 tablespoons sugar
few drops of vanilla essence
450 ml/¾ pint double cream
2 tablespoons chopped pistachio nuts

American
8 large macaroons, roughly broken up
½ cup Marsala
1 teaspoon finely grated orange rind
2 cups plus 3 tablespoons milk
4 eggs, beaten
3 tablespoons sugar
few drops of vanilla extract
2 cups heavy cream
2 tablespoons chopped pistachio nuts

Put the macaroons into a glass serving bowl and sprinkle with the Marsala and orange rind.

Heat the 450 ml/¾ pint (2 cups) milk. Mix together the eggs and sugar in a bowl. Gradually stir in the milk, then return to the pan. Heat gently, stirring, until the custard thickens enough to coat the spoon. Do not boil. Stir in the vanilla. Allow the custard to cool, then pour it over the macaroons. Chill.

Whip the cream with the remaining milk until thick. Spread over the custard and sprinkle with the nuts.
Serves 6–8

Délice de L'Auberge

Metric/Imperial
200 ml/⅓ pint double cream
40 g/1½ oz icing sugar
600 ml/1 pint coffee ice cream,
  softened
50 g/2 oz flaked almonds, toasted
150 ml/¼ pint Grand Marnier
Spun sugar:
225 g/8 oz sugar (preferably lump)
150 ml/¼ pint water
pinch of cream of tartar

American
1 cup heavy cream
⅓ cup confectioners' sugar
1 pint coffee ice cream,
  softened
½ cup slivered almonds, toasted
⅔ cup Grand Marnier
Spun sugar:
1 cup sugar (preferably lump)
⅔ cup water
pinch of cream of tartar

Whip the cream and icing (confectioners') sugar together until fluffy. Spread a 3 cm/1¼ inch layer of ice cream in a 1.2 litre/2 pint (1 quart capacity) freezerproof container. Cover with a 1 cm/½ inch layer of the whipped cream. Sprinkle with some of the almonds and Grand Marnier. Continue making layers in this way, ending with almonds. Freeze for at least 6 hours.

For the spun sugar, dissolve the sugar in the water, then bring to the boil and boil until the syrup reaches 155°C/312°F and turns a light golden brown. Remove from the heat, stir in the cream of tartar and cool.

To serve, place portions of the ice cream mixture in tall glasses or sundae dishes. Melt the caramelized syrup gently, then using an oiled wooden spoon, pick up strands of the caramel and twirl them over the ice cream from a height to form threads. The caramel should harden enough as it falls to build into a web over the dessert.
Serves 4–5

Blintzes

Metric/Imperial	American
100 g/4 oz plain flour	1 cup all-purpose flour
¼ teaspoon salt	¼ teaspoon salt
1 egg	1 egg
300 ml/½ pint milk	1¼ cups milk
1 tablespoon oil	1 tablespoon oil
oil for frying	oil for frying
15 g/½ oz butter	1 tablespoon butter
Filling:	**Filling:**
225 g/8 oz curd cheese	1 cup small curd cottage cheese
1 egg	1 egg
2 tablespoons sugar (or more to taste)	2 tablespoons sugar (or more to taste)
1 tablespoon sultanas	1 tablespoon seedless white raisins

Sift the flour and salt into a bowl. Add the egg, milk and oil and beat until smooth.

Mix together the ingredients for the filling.

Lightly oil a shallow frying pan. Pour in just enough batter to cover the bottom of the pan thinly. Fry until lightly browned underneath.

Turn the blintz out onto a plate, add a spoonful of the filling and fold up to make a parcel. Repeat until all the batter and filling have been used.

Arrange the blintzes in a buttered baking dish and dot with the butter. Bake in a preheated moderately hot oven (190°C/375°F, Gas Mark 5) for 30 minutes.

Serves 3–4

Alternative Fillings:

Coconut and Raisin Filling: Mix together 100 g/4 oz (1 cup) desiccated (shredded) coconut, 100 g/4 oz (⅔ cup) raisins, 1 tablespoon orange juice, 1 teaspoon lemon juice, 1 tablespoon sugar and 1 small cooking apple, peeled, cored and grated.

Cherry Filling: Drain 1 × 225 g/8 oz can black cherries, reserving the syrup. Stone (pit) the cherries. Dissolve 1½ teaspoons cornflour (cornstarch) in 2 tablespoons of the syrup. Heat the remaining syrup, stir in the cornflour (cornstarch) and boil, stirring, until thickened. Stir in the cherries and 1 teaspoon lemon juice. Serve the cherry blintzes with sour cream.

Kissel

Metric/Imperial
2½ tablespoons cornflour
pinch of salt
2 tablespoons white wine
1 tablespoon lemon juice
450 ml/¾ pint fruit purée, sweetened
  to taste (redcurrants, cherries,
  strawberries or other fruit may be
  used)

American
2½ tablespoons cornstarch
pinch of salt
2 tablespoons white wine
1 tablespoon lemon juice
2 cups fruit purée, sweetened to
  taste (redcurrants, cherries,
  strawberries or other fruit may be
  used)

Mix together the cornflour (cornstarch), salt, wine and lemon juice. Bring the fruit purée to the boil and stir in the wine mixture. Simmer, stirring, until thickened. Cool, then chill before serving.
Serves 4

Pain Perdu

Metric/Imperial
150 ml/¼ pint milk
few drops of vanilla essence
2 thick slices of stale bread
knob of butter
1 egg, beaten
2 tablespoons caster sugar
pinch of ground cinnamon

American
⅔ cup milk
few drops of vanilla extract
2 thick slices of stale bread
pat of butter
1 egg, beaten
2 tablespoons sugar
pinch of ground cinnamon

Mix the milk with the vanilla in a shallow bowl. Add the bread slices and leave to soak for 5 minutes.

Melt the butter in a frying pan. Dip the bread in the beaten egg and coat on both sides, using two spoons to turn it. Put the bread in the pan and fry until crisp and golden brown on both sides.

Transfer the bread to a heated serving plate and sprinkle with the sugar and cinnamon.
Serves 1–2

Riz à l'Impératrice

Metric/Imperial
100 g/4 oz short grain
  rice
900 ml/1½ pints milk
½ teaspoon vanilla essence
100 g/4 oz sugar
25 g/1 oz butter
100 g/4 oz mixed glacé fruit, finely
  chopped
3 tablespoons kirsch
300 ml/½ pint double cream
4 egg yolks, beaten
15 g/½ oz gelatine
fresh fruit to decorate

American
½ cup plus 2 tablespoons pudding
  rice
4 cups milk
½ teaspoon vanilla extract
½ cup sugar
2 tablespoons butter
⅔ cup finely chopped mixed candied
  fruit
3 tablespoons kirsch
1¼ cups heavy cream
4 egg yolks, beaten
2 envelopes unflavored gelatin
fresh fruit to decorate

Put the rice into a saucepan, cover with water and bring to the boil. Simmer for 2 to 3 minutes, then drain the rice. Return it to the saucepan and add 600 ml/1 pint (2½ cups) of the milk and the vanilla. Bring to the boil, then cover and simmer gently until the rice is tender and the milk has been absorbed. Stir occasionally during the cooking. Stir in 50 g/2 oz (¼ cup) of the sugar and the butter, then leave to cool.

Soak the fruit in the kirsch.

Whip the cream until thick and fold into the rice mixture.

Put the egg yolks and remaining sugar in a bowl and mix well together. Heat the remaining milk in a saucepan, then stir it gradually into the egg yolk mixture. Stir in the gelatine until dissolved. Cool.

Strain the custard into the rice mixture, add the soaked fruit and fold together thoroughly. Spoon into a greased 1 litre/2½ pint (1 quart capacity) decorative mould and chill until set.

Turn out onto a serving plate and serve decorated with fresh fruit, such as pear slices. Alternatively, serve with a fruit sauce.

Serves 4–6

Chestnuts in Marsala

Metric/Imperial
500 g/1 lb chestnuts, peeled and
  skinned
2 tablespoons sugar
300 ml/½ pint Marsala
4 tablespoons red wine
50 g/2 oz sultanas

American
1 lb chestnuts, peeled and
  skinned
2 tablespoons sugar
1¼ cups Marsala
¼ cup red wine
⅓ cup seedless white raisins

Put the chestnuts in a saucepan and add the sugar, Marsala and red wine.
Bring to the boil, then simmer gently for about 30 minutes.

Stir in the sultanas (raisins) and continue simmering until the chestnuts are
tender and the wine sauce is syrupy. Serve hot or cold, with cream.
Serves 4–6

Oeufs en Neige

Metric/Imperial
1 vanilla pod
1 litre/1¾ pints milk
8 eggs, separated
350 g/12 oz caster sugar
spun sugar (see page 173)

American
1 vanilla bean
1 quart milk
8 eggs, separated
1½ cups sugar
spun sugar (see page 173)

Put the milk and vanilla pod (bean) in a wide shallow pan and heat gently
until almost boiling. Meanwhile, beat the egg whites until stiff and fold in
225 g/8 oz (1 cup) of the sugar.

Drop spoonsful of the meringue onto the milk and poach gently for 4 to 5
minutes. Lift out the meringues with a slotted spoon and drain on a clean
cloth.

Beat the egg yolks with the remaining sugar until pale. Gradually strain in
the milk, beating constantly. Return to the pan and cook gently, stirring, until
the custard is thick enough to coat the back of the spoon. Pour the custard
into a serving bowl and float the meringues on top.

Lift up fine threads of the spun sugar caramel syrup using a fork, and loop
them over an oiled rolling pin. Gather the loops carefully together and drape
them over the dessert. Serve cold.
Serves 6

Variation:
Put 2 bananas, sliced, in the bottom of the serving bowl, sprinkle them with
lemon juice and then pour over the custard. Omit the spun sugar and sprinkle
the top with grated plain (semi-sweet) or milk chocolate.
Serves 4

Crema de Mascherpone

Metric/Imperial
225 g/8 oz soft cream cheese
2 eggs, separated
50 g/2 oz caster sugar
2 tablespoons orange liqueur,
    brandy or rum
225 g/8 oz strawberries or
    raspberries

American
1 cup soft cream cheese
2 eggs, separated
¼ cup sugar
2 tablespoons orange liqueur,
    brandy or rum
½ lb strawberries or
    raspberries

Beat the cream cheese with the egg yolks and sugar, then beat in the liqueur, brandy or rum. Beat the egg whites until stiff and fold into the cream mixture.

Pile the cheese dessert into individual serving dishes and top with strawberries or raspberries.

Serves 4

Crème Chamonix

Metric/Imperial
4 egg whites
225 g/8 oz caster sugar
grated chocolate to decorate
Filling:
300 ml/½ pint double cream
¼ teaspoon vanilla essence
3 tablespoons sugar
2 tablespoons brandy
1 × 225 g/8 oz can unsweetened
    chestnut purée

American
4 egg whites
1 cup sugar
grated chocolate to decorate
Filling:
1¼ cups heavy cream
¼ teaspoon vanilla extract
3 tablespoons sugar
2 tablespoons brandy
1 × ½ lb can unsweetened chestnut
    purée

Beat the egg whites until stiff. Add 4 tablespoons of the sugar and continue beating for 1 minute. Fold in the remaining sugar.

Trace six 7.5 cm/3 inch circles on a baking sheet lined with non-stick silicone paper. Use about half the meringue to fill the six circles, then pipe the remaining meringue around the edge of the circles to form nests. Dry out in a preheated cool oven (140°C/275°F, Gas Mark 1) for about 1 hour or until set. Cool.

For the filling, whip the cream until thick. Set aside about one-third of the cream for the decoration; beat the remaining filling ingredients into the rest of the cream. Pipe the filling into the meringue nests.

Decorate with the reserved cream and grated chocolate.

Serves 6

Bisquit Tortoni

Metric/Imperial
1 large egg white
300 ml/½ pint double cream
4 tablespoons icing sugar, sifted
3 tablespoons brandy or liqueur
40 g/1½ oz flaked almonds, toasted

American
1 egg white
1¼ cups heavy cream
¼ cup confectioners' sugar, sifted
3 tablespoons brandy or liqueur
⅓ cup slivered almonds, toasted

Beat the egg white until stiff. Whip the cream with the sugar and brandy or liqueur until thick. Fold in the egg white.

Spoon the mixture into six to eight freezerproof sundae glasses and top with the toasted almonds. Cover loosely with foil and freeze for about 3 hours or until firm.

About 30 minutes before serving, transfer the ices to the refrigerator to soften a little.
Serves 6–8

Caramel Apples

Metric/Imperial
6 apples, peeled, cored and
  quartered
40 g/1½ oz plain flour
15 g/½ oz cornflour
2 egg whites
oil for deep frying
100 g/4 oz sugar
2 tablespoons water
1 tablespoon oil
1 tablespoon sesame seeds

American
6 apples, peeled, cored and
  quartered
6 tablespoons all-purpose flour
2 tablespoons cornstarch
2 egg whites
oil for deep frying
½ cup sugar
2 tablespoons water
1 tablespoon oil
1 tablespoon sesame seeds

Dust the apple quarters with a little of the flour. Sift the remaining flour and the cornflour (cornstarch) into a bowl. Add the egg whites and mix to a paste. Fold in the apple quarters to coat with the paste. Deep fry in hot oil until golden. Drain on paper towels and keep hot.

Put the sugar and water in a saucepan and stir to dissolve the sugar. Add the oil and continue heating slowly until the syrup is a light golden brown. Stir in the sesame seeds, then fold in the apples. Serve immediately in oiled individual dishes.

Put a bowl of cold water on the table so that each piece of apple can be dipped in it before eating, to harden the caramel.
Serves 4

Baked Alaska

Metric/Imperial
1 plain sponge or sandwich cake
2–3 tablespoons liqueur (optional)
6 egg whites
350 g/12 oz caster sugar
1 large block neapolitan or other ice
cream, frozen solid

American
1 plain or layer cake
2–3 tablespoons liqueur (optional)
6 egg whites
1½ cups sugar
1 large block neapolitan or other ice
cream, frozen solid

Place the cake on an ovenproof serving plate and sprinkle with the liqueur, if using.

Beat the egg whites until frothy. Gradually add the sugar, beating constantly, and continue beating until the meringue will hold a peak.

Place the ice cream on the cake and cover both the cake and ice cream completely with the meringue. Bake immediately in a preheated hot oven (225°C/450°F, Gas Mark 8) for 3 to 5 minutes or until the meringue is lightly browned. Serve immediately.
Serves 8–10

Variation:

Baked Marsala Alaska: Line the bottom and sides of a shallow ovenproof serving dish with 4 to 6 sponge (pound) cake slices cut about 1 cm/½ inch thick. Sprinkle with 5 tablespoons Marsala. Soften 600 ml/1 pint vanilla or strawberry ice cream, then mix in another 5 tablespoons Marsala. Spread the ice cream over the cake, smooth the top and sides and freeze until solid.

Beat 3 egg whites until stiff and beat in 75 g/3 oz (6 tablespoons) caster sugar. Spread the meringue over the cake and ice cream. Bake as above.

Sprinkle over 1 tablespoon sugar, then pour over 2 tablespoons warmed brandy. Set alight and serve flaming.
Serves 6

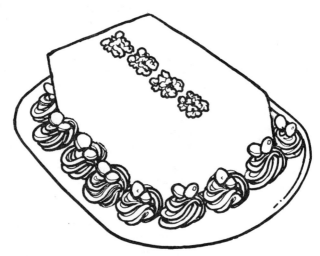

Eight-Treasure Rice Pudding

Metric/Imperial
225 g/8 oz pudding rice
40 g/1½ oz lard
2 tablespoons sugar
15 dried red dates, stoned
30 raisins
10 walnut halves
10 glacé cherries
10 pieces candied angelica, chopped
1 × 225 g/8 oz can sweetened
  chestnut purée, or red bean paste
Syrup:
3 tablespoons sugar
300 ml/½ pint plus 2 tablespoons
  water
1 tablespoon cornflour

American
1¼ cups sweet pudding rice
3 tablespoons lard
2 tablespoons sugar
15 dried red dates (jujubes), pitted
30 raisins
10 walnut halves
10 candied cherries
10 pieces candied angelica, chopped
1 × ½ lb can sweetened chestnut
  purée, or 1 cup red bean paste
Syrup:
3 tablespoons sugar
1¼ cups plus 2 tablespoons
  water
1 tablespoon cornstarch

Put the rice in a saucepan, cover with water and bring to the boil. Cover the pan tightly and cook for 10 to 15 minutes or until the water has been absorbed. Add 25 g/1 oz (2 tablespoons) of the lard and the sugar to the rice and mix well.

Use the remaining lard to grease a 900 ml/1½ pint (1 quart capacity) mould or pudding basin (steaming mold). Cover the bottom and sides with a thin layer of the rice mixture. Gently press a layer of the fruits and nuts, attractively arranged in rows, into the rice so they will show through when the pudding is turned out.

Cover the fruits and nuts with another layer of rice, much thicker this time. Fill the centre with the chestnut purée or bean paste and cover with the remaining rice. Press gently to flatten the top. Cover with greaseproof (wax) paper or foil and tie on with string. Steam for 1 hour.

A few minutes before the pudding is ready, make the syrup. Dissolve the sugar in the 300 ml/½ pint (1¼ cups) water, then bring to the boil. Dissolve the cornflour (cornstarch) in the remaining 2 tablespoons water and add to the pan. Simmer, stirring, until thickened.

Turn out the pudding onto a warmed serving plate and pour over the syrup.
Serves 6–8

Coeur à la Crème

Metric/Imperial
225 g/8 oz cottage cheese
300 ml/½ pint double cream
2 teaspoons sifted icing
  sugar
225 g/8 oz strawberries, hulled
1 teaspoon lemon juice
2 tablespoons caster sugar

American
1 cup cottage cheese
1¼ cups heavy cream
2 teaspoons sifted confectioners'
  sugar
½ lb strawberries, hulled
1 teaspoon lemon juice
2 tablespoons sugar

Rub the cottage cheese through a sieve (strainer) into a mixing bowl. Beat in the cream and icing (confectioners') sugar. Press into six coeur à la crème moulds or into a muslin-lined sieve (cheesecloth-lined strainer). Leave to drain overnight.

The next day, turn the coeur à la crème out onto a serving plate. Arrange the strawberries on the plate and sprinkle them with the lemon juice and sugar.
Serves 6

Lochshen Pudding

Metric/Imperial
100 g/4 oz lochshen (egg noodles)
40 g/1½ oz sugar
50 g/2 oz sultanas
1 tablespoon red wine
¼ teaspoon grated lemon rind
40 g/1½ oz butter, melted
1 egg, beaten

American
¼ lb lochshen (egg noodles)
3 tablespoons sugar
⅓ cup seedless white raisins
1 tablespoon red wine
¼ teaspoon grated lemon rind
3 tablespoons butter, melted
1 egg, beaten

Cook the lochshen in boiling salted water for 5 minutes. Drain and rinse with cold water. Mix the lochshen with the remaining ingredients and pour into a greased 900 ml/1½ pint (1 quart capacity) baking dish.

Bake in a preheated moderately hot oven (190°C/375°F, Gas Mark 5) for 45 minutes.
Serves 3

Chinese Rice Dumplings in Syrup

Metric/Imperial
50 g/2 oz sago
225 g/8 oz pudding rice powder
Filling:
175 g/6 oz canned sweetened chestnut purée
1 tablespoon sesame seeds
Syrup:
100 g/4 oz brown sugar
1.2 litres/2 pints water

American
⅓ cup sago
½ lb pudding rice powder
Filling:
½ cup sweetened chestnut purée
1 tablespoon sesame seeds
Syrup:
⅔ cup brown sugar
2½ pints water

Soak the sago in cold water for at least 6 hours. Drain in a sieve (strainer) for 30 minutes, then knead and pound until fine. Knead in the rice powder to make a smooth dough. Roll the dough into a sausage about 2.5 cm/1 inch in diameter and cut into 1 cm/½ inch slices.

Flatten each slice of dough and place ½ teaspoon of chestnut purée and a few sesame seeds in the centre. Carefully draw the edges of the dough over the filling and shape into a small ball by rolling in the palms of your hands.

For the syrup, dissolve the sugar in the water in a large saucepan. Bring to the boil, then drop in the dumplings. Bring back to the boil and when all the dumplings float to the surface, reduce the heat and simmer gently for 10 minutes. Serve hot.
Serves 4

Carrot Ingberlach

Metric/Imperial
500 g/1 lb carrots, grated
juice of 1 lemon
500 g/1 lb sugar
50 g/2 oz blanched almonds,
  chopped
½ teaspoon ground ginger
sugar for sprinkling

American
1 lb carrots, grated
juice of 1 lemon
2 cups sugar
½ cup chopped almonds
½ teaspoon ground ginger
sugar for sprinkling

Put the carrots on a sheet of foil, sprinkle with the lemon juice and fold up tightly. Bake in a preheated moderately hot oven (190°C/375°F, Gas Mark 5) for 1 hour.

Tip the carrots into a saucepan and add the sugar, almonds and ginger. Cook gently until the mixture is thick – about 15 to 20 minutes. Turn the mixture onto a sugared board and sprinkle with more sugar. Just before it is really hard, cut it into squares or diamonds.

Serves 4

Gaufres à la Flamande

Metric/Imperial
7 g/¼ oz fresh yeast
2 teaspoons sugar
3 tablespoons lukewarm water
225 g/8 oz plain flour
pinch of salt
4 eggs
25 g/1 oz butter, melted
1 tablespoon brandy
150 ml/¼ pint single cream
sugar for sprinkling

American
⅓ cake (¼ oz) compressed yeast
2 teaspoons sugar
3 tablespoons lukewarm water
2 cups all-purpose flour
pinch of salt
4 eggs
2 tablespoons butter, melted
1 tablespoon brandy
⅔ cup light cream
sugar for sprinkling

Mash the yeast with 1 teaspoon of the sugar, then cream in the water and a sprinkling of the flour. Leave until the surface is covered with bubbles.

Sift the remaining flour and the salt into a bowl. Add the eggs and remaining sugar and beat well. Beat in the yeast mixture, butter, brandy and cream until smooth. Cover and leave in a warm place for 1½ to 2 hours or until the batter is light.

Lightly oil a waffle iron and heat thoroughly. Spoon some of the batter onto the centre of the iron and cook until the waffle is golden brown.

Serve the waffles hot, sprinkled with sugar.

Serves 4

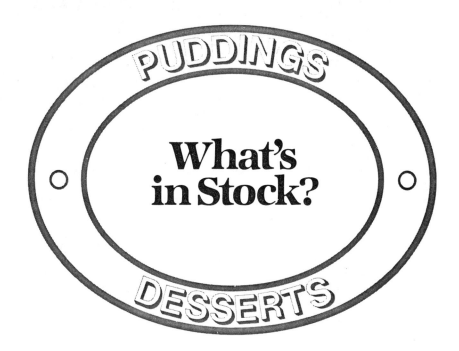

PUDDINGS

What's in Stock?

DESSERTS

Fruit Nut Whip

Metric/Imperial
2 × 75 g/3 oz packets cream cheese
50 g/2 oz caster sugar
2 eggs, separated
1 × 500 g/1 lb can fruit such as
   gooseberries, drained
150 ml/¼ pint double cream
50 g/2 oz hazelnuts, chopped

American
2 × 3 oz packages cream cheese
¼ cup sugar
2 eggs, separated
1 × 1 lb can fruit such as
   gooseberries, drained
⅔ cup heavy cream
½ cup chopped hazelnuts

Mix together the cream cheese and sugar, then beat in the egg yolks. Chop half the fruit, reserving the rest, and stir the chopped fruit into the cream cheese mixture.

Whip the cream until thick. Beat the egg whites until stiff. Fold most of the cream and all the egg whites into the fruit mixture.

Spread 25 g/1 oz (¼ cup) of the nuts in a serving bowl. Pour over half the cream cheese mixture and cover with the reserved fruit. Add the remaining cream cheese mixture. Decorate with the rest of the nuts and the reserved whipped cream. Chill well.
Serves 4–6

Danish Plum Crumble

Metric/Imperial
100 g/4 oz butter
100 g/4 oz fresh wholemeal
  breadcrumbs
175 g/6 oz macaroons, crushed
1 × 750 g/1½ lb can plums
2 teaspoons arrowroot or cornflour
whipped cream to decorate

American
8 tablespoons (1 stick) butter
2 cups fresh wholewheat
  breadcrumbs
1½ cups crushed macaroons
1 × 1½ lb can plums
2 teaspoons arrowroot or cornstarch
whipped cream to decorate

Melt the butter and stir in the breadcrumbs and macaroons. Press half this mixture over the bottom of a greased serving dish. Chill for 10 minutes.

Drain the plums, reserving 300 ml/½ pint (1¼ cups) of the syrup. Arrange the plums on top of the chilled crumb layer. Cover with the rest of the crumb mixture and chill for 10 minutes or until the topping is firm.

Dissolve the arrowroot or cornflour (cornstarch) in the reserved plum syrup in a saucepan. Bring to the boil, stirring, and simmer until thickened. Cool.

Decorate the plum crumble with whipped cream and serve with the syrup sauce.
Serves 6–8

Variation:
Other canned fruit, such as apricots, peaches or apple pie filling, may be used instead of plums.

Almond Lake with Mandarin Oranges

Metric/Imperial
600 ml/1 pint milk
100 g/4 oz sugar
1 teaspoon almond essence
50 g/2 oz ground rice
1 × 300 g/11 oz can mandarin
  oranges, drained
25 g/1 oz flaked almonds, toasted

American
2½ cups milk
½ cup sugar
1 teaspoon almond extract
⅓ cup ground rice
1 × 11 oz can mandarin oranges,
  drained
¼ cup slivered almonds, toasted

Put the milk, sugar, almond essence (extract) and rice in a saucepan and bring to the boil, stirring. Simmer for 5 minutes. Pour into a bowl, cover and cool.

Spoon the almond rice into individual serving dishes. Place the mandarin oranges on top and scatter over the almonds.
Serves 4

Mincemeat Oat Crumble

Metric/Imperial
100 g/4 oz mincemeat
150 ml/¼ pint plus 1 tablespoon
  water
grated rind of 1 orange
2 teaspoons cornflour
1 tablespoon rum or brandy
2 teaspoons sugar
Crumble topping:
100 g/4 oz butter
50 g/2 oz demerara sugar
100 g/4 oz quick cook oats
To decorate:
whipped cream
chopped walnuts

American
½ cup mincemeat
⅔ cup plus 1 tablespoon
  water
grated rind of 1 orange
2 teaspoons cornstarch
1 tablespoon rum or brandy
2 teaspoons sugar
Crumble topping:
8 tablespoons (1 stick) butter
⅓ cup raw brown sugar
⅔ cup quick cook oats
To decorate
whipped cream
chopped walnuts

Put the mincemeat, 150 ml/¼ pint (⅔ cup) of the water and the orange rind in a saucepan and cook gently for 5 minutes. Dissolve the cornflour (cornstarch) in the remaining water and add to the pan with the rum or brandy and sugar. Bring to the boil, stirring, and cook for 1 minute. Allow to cool.

For the topping, melt the butter in a saucepan and stir in the sugar and oats. Spread half the oat mixture on the bottom of a serving bowl and cover with the mincemeat mixture. Top with the rest of the oat mixture.

Serve decorated with whipped cream and walnuts.
Serves 4

Curried Fruit with Sour Cream

Metric/Imperial
1 × 1 kg/2 lb can fruit cocktail,
  drained
100 g/4 oz butter
175 g/6 oz brown sugar
2 teaspoons garam masala
1 teaspoon mild curry powder
250 ml/8 fl oz sour cream

American
1 × 2 lb can fruit cocktail,
  drained
8 tablespoons (1 stick) butter
1 cup brown sugar
2 teaspoons garam masala
1 teaspoon mild curry powder
1 cup sour cream

Put the fruit cocktail in a baking dish. Melt the butter in a saucepan and add the sugar. Stir until dissolved. Stir in the spices, then pour the mixture over the fruit. Bake in a preheated moderate oven (180°C/350°F, Gas Mark 4) for 25 minutes.

Stir in the sour cream and serve.
Serves 4–6

French Toasts

Metric/Imperial	American
1 egg	1 egg
1 tablespoon milk	1 tablespoon milk
few drops of vanilla essence	few drops of vanilla extract
4 slices of white bread, crusts removed and cut into fingers	4 slices of white bread, crusts removed and cut into fingers
1–2 tablespoons sugar	1–2 tablespoons sugar
butter for frying	butter for frying

Beat together the egg, milk and vanilla in a wide shallow bowl. Dip the bread fingers into the egg to coat both sides, then into the sugar.

Melt the butter in a frying pan, add the bread fingers and fry until golden brown and crisp on both sides.

Serve 4

Variation:

Lemon French Toasts: Butter the slices of bread and sandwich them together with 2 tablespoons lemon curd (cheese). Cut the two sandwiches into triangles. Beat together 2 eggs, 4 tablespoons milk and the grated rind of 1 lemon. Dip the sandwich triangles into the egg mixture and fry as above. Serve sprinkled with sugar.

Creamed Rice

Metric/Imperial	American
1.2 litres/2 pints milk	5 cups milk
150 g/5 oz sugar	⅔ cup sugar
½ teaspoon salt	½ teaspoon salt
75 g/3 oz rice	½ cup rice
½ teaspoon vanilla essence	½ teaspoon vanilla extract

Put the milk, sugar and salt in a saucepan and bring to the boil, stirring to dissolve the sugar. Gradually stir in the rice, then cover and cook very gently until the rice is tender and about two-thirds of the liquid has been absorbed. Stir in the vanilla and serve hot.

Serves 4–6

Chilled Semolina Pudding

Metric/Imperial
600 ml/1 pint milk
pinch of salt
50 g/2 oz semolina
25 g/1 oz sugar
25 g/1 oz butter
50 g/2 oz blanched almonds,
    chopped
50 g/2 oz dates, stoned and chopped
50 g/2 oz raisins
grated rind of ¼ orange
grated rind of ¼ lemon
To decorate:
glacé cherries
blanched almonds

American
2½ cups milk
pinch of salt
⅓ cup semolina or cream of wheat
2 tablespoons sugar
2 tablespoons butter
½ cup chopped almonds
⅓ cup chopped pitted dates
⅓ cup raisins
grated rind of ¼ orange
grated rind of ¼ lemon
To decorate:
candied cherries
blanched almonds

Bring the milk to the boil with the salt. Mix together the semolina and sugar and sprinkle over the milk. Cook gently, stirring, until the mixture thickens. Stir in the remaining ingredients and pour into individual serving dishes.

Cool, then chill before serving, decorated with cherries and almonds.
Serves 4

Gingered Fruit

Metric/Imperial
1 × 425 g/15 oz can pineapple
    chunks, drained
1 × 300 g/11 oz can lychees, drained
1 tablespoon chopped glacé
    cherries
2 tablespoons chopped crystallized
    ginger
25 g/1 oz flaked almonds, toasted

American
1 × 15 oz can pineapple chunks,
    drained
1 × 11 oz can litchis, drained
1 tablespoon chopped candied
    cherries
2 tablespoons chopped candied
    ginger
¼ cup slivered almonds, toasted

Mix together the pineapple, lychees, cherries and ginger in a serving bowl. Chill well.

Sprinkle over the almonds just before serving.
Serves 4

Tipsy Peaches

Metric/Imperial
1 × 425 g/15 oz can peach halves,
   drained
1 × 75 g/3 oz packet cream cheese
3 digestive biscuits, crushed
25 g/1 oz ground almonds
120 ml/4 fl oz white wine or cider

American
1 × 15 oz can peach halves,
   drained
1 × 3 oz package cream cheese
3 graham crackers, crushed
¼ cup ground almonds
½ cup white wine or cider

Arrange the peaches, hollow sides up, in a baking dish. Mix together the cream cheese, biscuits (crackers) and almonds and use to fill the hollows in the peaches. Pour around the wine or cider.

Bake in a preheated moderate oven (180°C/350°F, Gas Mark 4) for 10 to 15 minutes. Serve hot or cold.

Serves 4

Italian Chocolate Pudding

Metric/Imperial
100 g/4 oz unsalted butter
100 g/4 oz cocoa powder
100 g/4 oz ground almonds
100 g/4 oz sugar
3 tablespoons water
1 egg
100 g/4 oz digestive biscuits,
   crumbled but not crushed
sifted icing sugar

American
8 tablespoons (1 stick) sweet butter
1 cup unsweetened cocoa
1 cup ground almonds
½ cup sugar
3 tablespoons water
1 egg
1 cup crumbled, not crushed, plain
   sweet cookies
sifted confectioners' sugar

Cream together the butter and cocoa until soft. Beat in the almonds. Dissolve the sugar in the water over heat, then add to the creamed mixture with the egg. Mix well, then fold in the biscuits (cookies). Turn into a greased ring mould and chill until set.

Turn out to serve, sprinkled with icing (confectioners') sugar.

Serves 6

Dried Apricots Baked with Almonds

Metric/Imperial
225 g/8 oz dried apricots
450 ml/¾ pint water
50 g/2 oz sugar
1 vanilla pod or few drops of vanilla
    essence
50 g/2 oz blanched almonds, split

American
½ lb dried apricots
2 cups water
¼ cup sugar
1 vanilla bean or few drops of vanilla
    extract
¼ cup blanched split almonds

Put the apricots and water in a casserole and leave to soak for 1 hour.
    Add the sugar and vanilla to the casserole, cover and cook in a preheated cool oven (150°C/300°F, Gas Mark 2) for 1¾ hours.
    Stir in the almonds and cook for a further 15 minutes. Remove the vanilla pod (bean), if used, and serve hot or cold.
Serves 4

Spiced Fruit Compôte

Metric/Imperial
500 g/1 lb mixed dried fruit (apples,
    apricots, peaches, pears, figs,
    prunes, sultanas)
300 ml/½ pint orange juice
300 ml/½ pint water
1 cinnamon stick
2 cloves
50 g/2 oz flaked almonds

American
1 lb (about 3 cups) mixed dried fruit
    (apples, apricots, peaches, pears,
    figs, prunes, raisins)
1¼ cups orange juice
1¼ cups water
1 cinnamon stick
2 cloves
½ cup slivered almonds

Put the fruit in a bowl and pour over the orange juice and water. Add the spices and leave to soak overnight.
    The next day, tip the fruit mixture into a saucepan and bring to the boil. Cover and cook gently for about 20 minutes or until the fruit is tender. Add more water if necessary.
    Stir in the almonds and serve warm or cold.
Serves 4–6

Apricot Whip

Metric/Imperial
225 g/8 oz dried apricots, soaked
  overnight
1 large can evaporated milk, chilled
2 tablespoons orange juice
50 g/2 oz icing sugar, sifted

American
½ lb dried apricots, soaked
  overnight
1 large can evaporated milk, chilled
2 tablespoons orange juice
½ cup confectioners' sugar, sifted

Tip the apricots and their soaking water into a saucepan and simmer until tender. Drain the apricots and purée in a blender or sieve (strainer).

Beat the evaporated milk until it is beginning to thicken. Stir in the orange juice, sugar and apricot purée. Chill well.
Serves 4

Mandarin Surprise

Metric/Imperial
1 × 500 g/1 lb can mandarin oranges,
  drained
50 g/2 oz flaked almonds
250 ml/8 fl oz sour cream
2 tablespoons chopped crystallized
  ginger

American
1 × 1 lb can mandarin oranges,
  drained
½ cup slivered almonds
1 cup sour cream
2 tablespoons chopped candied
  ginger

Mix together the oranges, almonds and sour cream. Sprinkle over the ginger and chill for 15 minutes before serving.
Serves 4

Quick Stuffed Peaches

Metric/Imperial
1 × 400 g/14 oz can peach halves
4 tablespoons double cream
2 tablespoons chopped mixed
  peel

American
1 × 14 oz can peach halves
¼ cup heavy cream
2 tablespoons chopped mixed
  candied peel

Drain the peach halves, reserving the syrup. Put the peach halves, cut sides up, in two serving bowls.

Whip the cream until thick and fold in the peel. Put a tablespoon of the cream mixture into each peach half and pour over a little of the reserved peach syrup.
Serves 2

Cherries Jubilee

Metric/Imperial
1 × 500 g/1 lb can cherries
1 tablespoon sugar
1 small cinnamon stick
2 teaspoons arrowroot
1 tablespoon water
4–6 tablespoons brandy or cherry
   brandy
vanilla ice cream to serve

American
1 × 1 lb can cherries
1 tablespoon sugar
1 small cinnamon stick
2 teaspoons arrowroot
1 tablespoon water
4–6 tablespoons brandy or cherry
   brandy
vanilla ice cream to serve

Drain the cherries, reserving the syrup. Pour the syrup into a saucepan and add the sugar and cinnamon stick. Bring to the boil, stirring to dissolve the sugar, and simmer for 3 minutes. Strain and return to the saucepan.

Dissolve the arrowroot in the water and stir into the cherry syrup. Simmer, stirring, until the sauce thickens. Add the cherries and heat through.

Warm the brandy, stir into the cherry mixture and set alight. Spoon the sauce immediately over servings of vanilla ice cream.
Serves 4

Variations:

Jamaican Cherries: Drain the cherries, reserving the syrup. Sprinkle the cherries with 150 ml/¼ pint (⅔ cup) rum and leave to marinate for several hours. Boil the cherry syrup until reduced to about two-thirds the original quantity. Dissolve 1 teaspoon cornflour (cornstarch) in 1 tablespoon water and add to the cherry syrup. Bring to the boil, stirring, and simmer until thickened. Add the cherries with the rum and 1 teaspoon orange liqueur. Heat through, then set alight and serve flaming.
Serves 6

Apricots Jubilee: Drain a 425 g/15 oz can apricot halves, reserving the syrup. Put the syrup into a saucepan with 2 lemon slices and ¼ teaspoon ground cloves and boil until reduced by half. Strain the apricot syrup and return to the pan. Add the apricot halves and 4 to 5 tablespoons brandy and heat through. Set alight and serve flaming, over scoops of vanilla ice cream. Sprinkle each portion with a crushed macaroon.
Serves 6

Pêches Flambés

Metric/Imperial	American
50 g/2 oz unsalted butter	4 tablespoons sweet butter
8 canned peach halves	8 canned peach halves
6 tablespoons brandy	6 tablespoons brandy
150 ml/¼ pint syrup from the peaches	⅔ cup syrup from the peaches
300 ml/½ pint double cream	1¼ cups heavy cream

Melt the butter in a frying pan, add the peach halves and brown lightly on both sides. Sprinkle over 3 tablespoons of the brandy. Warm it, then set alight. Extinguish the flames before they die out, and transfer the peaches to warmed serving dishes.

Add the peach syrup to the pan with the remaining brandy and bring to the boil. Stir in the cream and cook gently until the sauce thickens. Pour the sauce over the peaches and serve.

Serves 4

Butterscotch Whip

Metric/Imperial	American
150 g/5 oz golden syrup	½ cup light corn syrup
25 g/1 oz butter	2 tablespoons butter
600 ml/1 pint milk	2½ cups milk
40 g/1½ oz cornflour	6 tablespoons cornstarch
1 egg, separated	1 egg, separated
½ teaspoon vanilla essence	½ teaspoon vanilla extract
whipped cream to decorate	whipped cream to decorate

Put the syrup and butter in a saucepan and cook gently until a rich golden brown. Gradually stir in 450 ml/¾ pint (2 cups) of the milk. Dissolve the cornflour (cornstarch) in the remaining milk and stir into the syrup mixture. Bring to the boil, stirring.

Remove from the heat and beat in the egg yolk. Cool, then stir in the vanilla.

Beat the egg white until stiff and fold into the butterscotch mixture. Divide between four serving glasses and chill thoroughly. Decorate with whipped cream before serving.

Serves 4

Dried Fruit and Nut Salad

Metric/Imperial
100 g/4 oz prunes
100 g/4 oz dried apricots
100 g/4 oz dried figs
50 g/2 oz raisins
900 ml/1½ pints water
25 g/1 oz walnut halves
25 g/1 oz blanched almonds
25 g/1 oz pine nuts (optional)

American
⅔ cup prunes
⅔ cup dried apricots
⅔ cup dried figs
⅓ cup raisins
4 cups water
¼ cup walnut halves
¼ cup blanched almonds
¼ cup pine nuts (optional)

Put the dried fruit into a casserole, pour over the water and leave to soak overnight.

The next day, cover the casserole and cook in a preheated cool oven (150°C/300°F, Gas Mark 2) for 1 hour. Stir in the nuts, then cool. Chill before serving.
Serves 6–8

Berry Sour Cream Dessert

Metric/Imperial
1 × 500 g/1 lb can strawberries,
   loganberries, fruit cocktail, etc.
600 ml/1 pint sour cream
100 g/4 oz sugar
1½ teaspoons cornflour
1 teaspoon lemon juice

American
1 × 1 lb can strawberries,
   loganberries, fruit cocktail, etc.
2½ cups sour cream
½ cup sugar
1½ teaspoons cornstarch
1 teaspoon lemon juice

Drain the fruit, reserving the syrup. Purée the fruit in a blender or sieve (strainer). Mix the purée with the sour cream and sugar and pour into a greased baking dish. Bake in a preheated moderate oven (180°C/350°F, Gas Mark 4) for 15 minutes. Cool.

Dissolve the cornflour (cornstarch) in 2 tablespoons of the fruit syrup. Put the rest of the syrup in a saucepan with the lemon juice and bring to the boil. Add the cornflour (cornstarch) and simmer, stirring, until thickened. Cool, then pour over the sour cream mixture in the dish. Chill lightly before serving.
Serves 6–8

Ginger Cream Roll

Metric/Imperial
150 ml/¼ pint double cream
150 ml/¼ pint single cream
3 tablespoons brandy or whisky
1 tablespoon caster sugar
350 g/12 oz ginger nut biscuits
sliced crystallized ginger to decorate

American
⅔ cup heavy cream
⅔ cup light cream
3 tablespoons brandy or whiskey
1 tablespoon sugar
¾ lb ginger snaps
sliced candied ginger to decorate

Whip creams together until thick. Add the brandy or whisky and sugar and
beat in well. Put about 1 heaped teaspoon of the cream mixture on each
biscuit (cookie) and press them together into two rolls on a serving plate.
Spread the remaining cream mixture all over the rolls. Chill for 3 hours.

Decorate with ginger before serving.

Serves 4–6

Peaches with Cherry Sauce

Metric/Imperial
1 × 425 g/15 oz can peach halves
1 × 425 g/15 oz can black cherries
1 teaspoon arrowroot or cornflour
juice of 1 lemon
2 tablespoons redcurrant or apple
  jelly

American
1 × 15 oz can peach halves
1 × 15 oz can bing cherries
1 teaspoon arrowroot or cornstarch
juice of 1 lemon
2 tablespoons redcurrant or apple
  jelly

Drain the peaches, reserving the syrup. Put the peaches in a serving bowl.

Drain the cherries, reserving the syrup. Mix together the peach and cherry
syrups in a saucepan. Dissolve the arrowroot or cornflour (cornstarch) in the
lemon juice and add to the pan with the redcurrant or apple jelly. Bring to the
boil, stirring, and simmer until clear and slightly thickened. Stir in the cherries
and heat through.

Pour the cherry sauce over the peaches.

Serves 4

PUDDINGS

Treats for Children

DESSERTS

Caramel Dumplings

Metric/Imperial
150 g/5 oz self-raising flour
pinch of salt
25 g/1 oz butter
50 g/2 oz sugar
4 tablespoons milk
1 teaspoon vanilla essence
Sauce:
25 g/1 oz butter
225 g/8 oz brown sugar
pinch of salt
450 ml/¾ pint water

American
1¼ cups self-rising flour
pinch of salt
2 tablespoons butter
¼ cup sugar
¼ cup milk
1 teaspoon vanilla extract
Sauce:
2 tablespoons butter
1⅓ cups brown sugar
pinch of salt
2 cups water

Sift the flour and salt into a bowl. Rub in the butter until the mixture resembles breadcrumbs, then stir in the sugar. Bind to a soft dough with the milk and vanilla.

For the sauce, put all the ingredients in a saucepan and bring to the boil, stirring to dissolve the sugar. Drop tablespoonsful of the dough into the sauce and simmer for 20 minutes or until they are cooked through. Serve hot.
Serves 4

Crispy Chocolate Pie

Metric/Imperial
25 g/1 oz butter
2 tablespoons golden syrup
75 g/3 oz plain chocolate, melted
100 g/4 oz cornflakes
ice cream

American
2 tablespoons butter
2 tablespoons light corn syrup
½ cup semi-sweet chocolate chips
4 cups cornflakes
ice cream

Melt the butter with the syrup in a saucepan. Stir in the chocolate, then fold in the cornflakes. Spoon into a 20 cm/8 inch pie pan and press gently but evenly over the bottom and up the sides. Chill until firm.

Just before serving, fill the pie shell with scoops of your favourite ice cream.
Serves 4–6

Variation:
Fill the pie shell with a packaged dessert mix. Add some fresh or canned fruit, if liked.

Apple Ice Lollies (Popsicles)

Metric/Imperial
apples, peeled, cored and chopped
water
sugar or honey to taste
green food colouring (optional)

American
apples, peeled, cored and chopped
water
sugar or honey to taste
green food coloring (optional)

Put the apples in a saucepan and add just enough water to cover the bottom of the pan. Simmer gently until very tender. Sieve (strain) or blend to make a very smooth purée and sweeten to taste with sugar or honey. Add a few drops of food colouring, if necessary. Cool, then pour into lolly (popsicle) moulds or ice cube trays and freeze until mushy.

Add sticks and continue freezing until set.

Variations:
Half fill the moulds with the apple purée and freeze until set. Pour in enough chilled orange juice to fill the moulds and freeze until mushy. Add the sticks and continue freezing until the orange juice is set.

Other fruit purées, such as sieved fresh raspberries or strawberries, black or red currants or cooked plums, may be used.

Orange Ice Lollies (Popsicles)

Metric/Imperial
oranges
sugar (if necessary)

American
oranges
sugar (if necessary)

Squeeze the juice from oranges, or rub the pulp through a sieve (strainer), or blend the pulp to give a smooth purée. Sweeten, if necessary. Pour into lolly (popsicle) moulds or ice cube trays and freeze until mushy.
   Add sticks and continue freezing until set.

Variations:
Other fruit juices, such as grapefruit or pineapple, or rosehip or blackcurrant syrup, may be used.

Banana Ice Cream Sundae

Metric/Imperial
2 large ripe bananas, mashed
4 large scoops vanilla ice cream,
   softened
grated milk chocolate

American
2 large ripe bananas, mashed
4 large scoops vanilla ice cream,
   softened
grated milk chocolate

Beat the bananas into the ice cream. If the mixture is too soft, chill it in the freezer for a few minutes. Divide the ice cream between four sundae glasses and sprinkle with grated chocolate.
Serves 4

Gondolas

Metric/Imperial
4 large firm bananas
little apricot jam
squeeze of lemon juice
4 portions strawberry ice cream,
   softened
few chopped nuts
few chopped glacé cherries

American
4 large firm bananas
little apricot jam
squeeze of lemon juice
4 portions strawberry ice cream,
   softened
few chopped nuts
few chopped candied cherries

Peel a strip from each banana, leaving a boat shape, and carefully remove
the bananas from the skins. Mash the bananas with the jam and lemon juice,
then return them to the banana skin boats. Top with the ice cream, nuts and
cherries. Freeze for 30 minutes.
Serves 4

Blackcurrant or Blackberry Flummery

Metric/Imperial
1 packet lemon jelly
300 ml/½ pint boiling water
2–3 tablespoons blackcurrant or
   blackberry syrup
300 ml/½ pint evaporated milk, or
   half evaporated milk and half
   natural yogurt

American
1 package lemon-flavored gelatin
1¼ cups boiling water
2–3 tablespoons blackcurrant or
   blackberry syrup
1¼ cups evaporated milk, or half
   evaporated milk and half
   unflavored yogurt

Dissolve the jelly (gelatin) in the boiling water. Stir in the blackcurrant or
blackberry syrup. Leave until on the point of setting, then gradually beat in
the evaporated milk (or milk and yogurt). Pile into four glasses and leave to
set.
Serves 4

Variation:
Use an orange-flavoured jelly (gelatin) and the juice of 1 orange instead of
the lemon jelly (gelatin) and blackcurrant or blackberry syrup.

Nutty Bananas

Metric/Imperial
4 bananas
apricot jam
chopped nuts

American
4 bananas
apricot jam
chopped nuts

Peel the bananas, then coat them in jam. Roll in chopped nuts to cover all over.
Serves 4

Butterscotch Raisin Pudding

Metric/Imperial
75 g/3 oz brown sugar
25 g/1 oz butter
450 ml/¾ pint milk
75 g/3 oz raisins
75 g/3 oz fresh breadcrumbs
2 eggs, beaten

American
½ cup brown sugar
2 tablespoons butter
2 cups milk
½ cup raisins
1½ cups fresh breadcrumbs
2 eggs, beaten

Put the sugar and butter in a saucepan and heat gently, stirring to dissolve the sugar. Add the milk and heat, still stirring, until well mixed. Remove from the heat and stir in the raisins and breadcrumbs. Leave for 20 minutes to soak.

Stir in the eggs and pour into a baking dish. Place the dish in a roasting pan containing hot water and bake in a preheated moderate oven (160°C/325°F, Gas Mark 3) for about 1 hour.
Serves 4

PUDDINGS

Strictly for Slimmers

DESSERTS

Fruit Snow

Metric/Imperial
500 g/1 lb fruit, such as cooking
*   apples, berry fruits, etc, peeled,*
*   cored and chopped if necessary*
sugar or sugar substitute to taste
2 egg whites

American
1 lb fruit, such as tart apples, berry
*   fruit, etc, peeled, cored and*
*   chopped if necessary*
sugar or sugar substitute to taste
2 egg whites

Put the fruit into a saucepan with just enough water to cover the bottom of the pan and poach gently until the fruit has pulped. Purée the fruit in a blender or sieve (strainer), or mash it to a purée, and sweeten to taste. Cool.

Beat the egg whites until stiff and fold into the fruit purée. Spoon into individual glasses and chill before serving.
Serves 4

Variation:
Minted Apple Snow: Poach 1 kg/2 lb cooking (tart) apples, peeled, cored and chopped, with the finely grated rind and juice of 1 orange, 3 tablespoons honey and 4 large mint sprigs. Discard the mint, then purée the apple pulp. Fold in 2 egg whites, stiffly beaten, and chill. Serve garnished with mint sprigs.

Stuffed Peaches

Metric/Imperial
4 ripe peaches, peeled, halved and
   stoned
juice of 1 lemon
175 g/6 oz raspberries
sugar or sugar substitute to taste
natural yogurt to serve

American
4 ripe peaches, peeled, halved and
   pitted
juice of 1 lemon
1½ cups raspberries
sugar or sugar substitute to taste
unflavored yogurt to serve

Sprinkle the cut surfaces of the peaches with the lemon juice to prevent discoloration.

Mash most of the raspberries with sugar to taste and spoon into the peach halves. Top with the rest of the raspberries and serve with yogurt.
Serves 4

Baked Yogurt Custard

Metric/Imperial
300 ml/½ pint natural yogurt
few drops of vanilla essence
few drops of liquid glucose
2 eggs, beaten
150 ml/¼ pint milk
¼ teaspoon grated nutmeg

American
1¼ cups unflavored yogurt
few drops of vanilla extract
few drops of liquid glucose
2 eggs, beaten
⅔ cup milk
¼ teaspoon grated nutmeg

Beat together the yogurt, vanilla, glucose, eggs and milk and pour into a baking dish. Sprinkle with the nutmeg.

Place the dish in a roasting pan containing hot water and bake in a preheated moderate oven (160°C/325°F, Gas Mark 3) for 40 minutes.
Serves 4

Slimmers' Syllabub

Metric/Imperial
300 ml/½ pint natural yogurt
pinch of grated lemon rind
juice of 1 lemon
2 tablespoons white wine
sugar or sugar substitute to taste

American
1¼ cups unflavored yogurt
pinch of grated lemon rind
juice of 1 lemon
2 tablespoons white wine
sugar or sugar substitute to taste

Beat together all the ingredients and spoon into serving glasses. Chill.
Serves 2

Orange Cheese Pots

Metric/Imperial
1½ teaspoons gelatine
3 tablespoons orange juice
1½ tablespoons lemon juice
350 g/12 oz cottage cheese
6 tablespoons buttermilk
sugar substitute to taste
orange slices to decorate

American
1 envelope unflavored gelatin
3 tablespoons orange juice
1½ tablespoons lemon juice
1½ cups cottage cheese
6 tablespoons buttermilk
sugar substitute to taste
orange slices to decorate

Dissolve the gelatine in the warmed orange and lemon juices. Blend the cottage cheese with the buttermilk to a smooth purée, or use a sieve (strainer). Stir in the gelatine mixture and sweeten to taste. Divide between six dessert glasses and chill until set.

Serve decorated with orange slices.

Serves 6

Apple Raisin Mould

Metric/Imperial
2 large cooking apples, peeled,
    cored and chopped
300 ml/½ pint water
finely grated rind and juice of 1
    orange
sugar or sugar substitute to taste
15 g/½ oz gelatine
3 tablespoons raisins
orange slices to decorate

American
2 large tart apples, peeled, cored
    and chopped
1¼ cups water
finely grated rind and juice of 1
    orange
sugar or sugar substitute to taste
2 envelopes unflavored gelatin
3 tablespoons raisins
orange slices to decorate

Put the apples in a saucepan with the water and orange rind. Poach gently until the apples have pulped. Beat until smooth, then sweeten to taste.

Dissolve the gelatine in the orange juice. Add to the apple purée and mix well.

Sprinkle the bottom of a dampened mould with the raisins and spoon over the apple mixture. Chill until set.

Turn out to serve, decorated with orange slices.

Serves 4

Peaches with Spiced Raspberry Sauce

Metric/Imperial	American
6 ripe peaches, peeled, stoned and sliced	6 ripe peaches, peeled, pitted and sliced
lemon juice	lemon juice
225 g/8 oz raspberries	½ lb raspberries
1 tablespoon clear honey	1 tablespoon clear honey
pinch of ground cinnamon	pinch of ground cinnamon
1 tablespoon orange juice	1 tablespoon orange juice

Put the peaches into a serving bowl, sprinkle with a little lemon juice to prevent discoloration and chill.

Rub the raspberries through a nylon sieve (strainer), then mix the honey, cinnamon and orange juice into the purée. Chill the sauce.

Pour the sauce over the peaches just before serving.

Serves 4

Prune Mould

Metric/Imperial	American
225 g/8 oz prunes	½ lb prunes
450 ml/¾ pint water	2 cups water
pared rind and juice of 1 lemon	pared rind and juice of 1 lemon
25 g/1 oz sugar	2 tablespoons sugar
15 g/½ oz gelatine	2 envelopes unflavored gelatin
blanched almonds to decorate	blanched almonds to decorate

Soak the prunes overnight in the water. The next day, tip the prunes and liquid into a saucepan. Add the lemon rind and simmer until tender.

Drain the prunes, reserving the strained liquid. Remove the stones (pits), then purée the prunes in a blender or sieve (strainer). Add the lemon juice and sugar to the prune purée. Stir in enough of the reserved prune liquid to make the mixture up to 750 ml/1 ¼ pints (3 cups).

Dissolve the gelatine in 2 tablespoons of the prune juice over heat and stir into the prune mixture. Pour into a mould and chill until set.

To serve, turn out and decorate with blanched almonds.

Serves 4

Rhubarb and Yogurt Fool

Metric/Imperial
500 g/1 lb rhubarb, chopped
2 tablespoons demerara sugar
1 tablespoon grated orange rind
1 tablespoon orange juice
pinch of ground ginger
600 ml/1 pint natural yogurt

American
1 lb rhubarb, chopped
2 tablespoons raw brown sugar
1 tablespoon grated orange rind
1 tablespoon orange juice
pinch of ground ginger
2½ cups unflavored yogurt

Put the rhubarb, sugar, orange rind and juice and ginger in a saucepan and cook gently until tender. Cool.

Stir in the yogurt, then taste and add more sugar to taste. Chill for at least 1 hour before serving.

Serves 4

Coffee Jelly (Gelatin)

Metric/Imperial
600 ml/1 pint strong black coffee
sugar or sugar substitute to taste
1 tablespoon gelatine

American
2 cups strong black coffee
sugar or sugar substitute to taste
1 envelope unflavored gelatin

Sweeten the coffee to taste. Dissolve the gelatine in a little of the coffee over heat, then add to the rest of the coffee. Divide between four dessert dishes and chill until set.

Serves 4

Mock Coeur à la Crème

Metric/Imperial
2 teaspoons gelatine
2 tablespoons water
350 g/12 oz cottage cheese, sieved
150 ml/¼ pint natural yogurt
juice of ½ lemon

American
1 envelope unflavored gelatin
2 tablespoons water
1½ cups strained cottage cheese
⅔ cup unflavored yogurt
juice of ½ lemon

Dissolve the gelatine in the warmed water. Cool, then mix with the remaining ingredients. Divide between four individual serving dishes and chill until set.

Turn out to serve, with fruit in season.

Serves 4

Yogurt California

Metric/Imperial
225 g/8 oz prunes
grated rind and juice of 1 orange
450 ml/¾ pint natural yogurt
honey (optional)

American
½ lb prunes
grated rind and juice of 1 orange
2 cups unflavored yogurt
honey (optional)

Put the prunes in a bowl and just cover with water. Add the orange rind and juice and leave to soak overnight.

The next day, tip the prunes and liquid into a saucepan. Simmer gently until tender. (If using tenderized prunes they will become quite soft with soaking alone.) Cool, then drain.

Sweeten the yogurt with a little honey, if you like, then fold in the prunes.
Serves 4

Greek Fruit Salad

Metric/Imperial
2 bananas, sliced
1 apple, cored and chopped
2 oranges, peeled and segmented
1 tablespoon dry sherry
2 tablespoons clear honey
250 ml/8 fl oz natural yogurt

American
2 bananas, sliced
1 apple, cored and chopped
2 oranges, peeled and segmented
1 tablespoon dry sherry
2 tablespoons clear honey
1 cup unflavored yogurt

Put the fruit in a serving bowl, sprinkle with the sherry and leave for 1 hour.

Beat together the honey and yogurt and fold lightly into the fruit. Chill for about 1 hour before serving.
Serves 4

Cottage Pears

Metric/Imperial
4 ripe pears, peeled if necessary,
   halved and cored
lemon juice
100 g/4 oz cottage cheese, sieved
¼ teaspoon grated nutmeg
8 strawberries

American
4 ripe pears, peeled if necessary,
   halved and cored
lemon juice
½ cup strained cottage cheese
¼ teaspoon grated nutmeg
8 strawberries

Sprinkle the pear halves with a little lemon juice to prevent discoloration. Arrange them, cut sides up, on four individual serving dishes.

Mix together the cottage cheese and nutmeg and use to fill the hollows in the pears. Top each half with a strawberry.

Serves 4

Rhubarb Meringue

Metric/Imperial
500 g/1 lb rhubarb, chopped
pinch of grated nutmeg
2 tablespoons sugar (or more to
   taste)
3 egg whites
2 tablespoons sifted icing
   sugar

American
1 lb rhubarb, chopped
pinch of grated nutmeg
2 tablespoons sugar (or more to
   taste)
3 egg whites
2 tablespoons sifted confectioners'
   sugar

Put the rhubarb in a baking dish and sprinkle with the nutmeg and sugar.

Beat the egg whites until stiff and fold in the icing (confectioners') sugar. Pile on top of the rhubarb.

Bake in a preheated moderate oven (180°C/350°F, Gas Mark 4) for 30 minutes.

Serves 4

Variations:
Use plums, apricots, gooseberries or a mixture of apples and blackberries instead of rhubarb.

Orange and Grape Salad

Metric/Imperial
6 oranges, peeled and thinly sliced
juice of 1 lemon
thinly pared rind of ½ lemon
1 tablespoon brown sugar
few drops of vanilla essence
225 g/8 oz black grapes, pipped

American
6 oranges, peeled and thinly sliced
juice of 1 lemon
thinly pared rind of ½ lemon
1 tablespoon brown sugar
few drops of vanilla extract
½ lb purple grapes, seeded

Put any juice from slicing the oranges into a saucepan with the lemon juice and rind, sugar and vanilla. Bring to the boil and simmer until syrupy. Cool.

Arrange the orange slices and grapes in a serving bowl. Discard the lemon rind from the syrup and pour over the fruit. Chill before serving.
Serves 4

Melon with Lemon Sauce

Metric/Imperial
1 ripe melon (honeydew, cantaloup
  or ogen)
grated rind and juice of 2 lemons
1 tablespoon sugar
lemon slices to decorate

American
1 ripe melon (honeydew,
  cantaloup)
grated rind and juice of 2 lemons
1 tablespoon sugar
lemon slices to decorate

Halve the melon and discard the seeds. Scoop out the flesh with a melon-baller. Chill the melon-balls.

Scrape out the flesh remaining in the melon halves and put into a saucepan with the lemon rind and juice and sugar. Bring to the boil and simmer for 5 minutes. Cool slightly, then pour the mixture into the blender goblet. Blend to a smooth sauce. Chill.

Pour the sauce into a glass bowl and add the melon balls. Decorate with lemon slices.
Serves 4

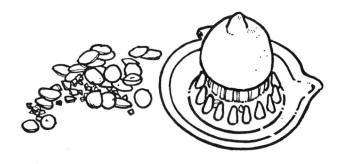

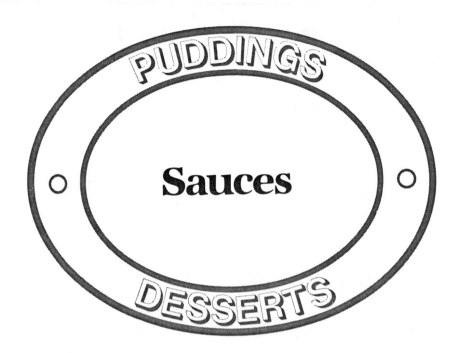

PUDDINGS

Sauces

DESSERTS

Coffee Nut Sauce

Metric/Imperial
2 tablespoons golden syrup
2 tablespoons brown sugar
15 g/½ oz butter
2 teaspoons arrowroot
2 tablespoons coffee essence
300 ml/½ pint milk
2 tablespoons coarsely crushed
    peanut brittle

American
2 tablespoons light corn syrup
2 tablespoons brown sugar
1 tablespoon butter
2 teaspoons arrowroot
2 tablespoons coffee flavoring
1¼ cups milk
2 tablespoons coarsely crushed
    peanut brittle

Put the syrup, sugar and butter in a saucepan and bring to the boil, stirring to dissolve the sugar. Simmer until the mixture turns golden, then remove from the heat.

Mix together the arrowroot, coffee essence (flavoring) and milk and slowly stir in the syrup mixture. Return to the pan and bring back to the boil, stirring. Simmer until thickened.

Stir in the peanut brittle and serve.
Serves 6

Crème Pâtissière (Confectioners' Custard)

Metric/Imperial
550 ml/18 fl oz milk
1 vanilla pod or a few drops of vanilla essence
115 g/4½ oz sugar
3 egg yolks
25 g/1 oz plain flour
25 g/1 oz cornflour

American
2¼ cups milk
1 vanilla bean or a few drops of vanilla extract
½ cup plus 1 tablespoon sugar
3 egg yolks
¼ cup all-purpose flour
¼ cup cornstarch

Put the milk, vanilla pod (bean) and 50 g/2 oz (¼ cup) of the sugar in a saucepan and bring to the boil, stirring to dissolve the sugar. Remove from the heat and set aside to infuse.

Put the remaining sugar and the egg yolks in a bowl and sift in the flour and cornflour (cornstarch). Beat until smooth, then gradually strain in the hot milk, beating constantly. Stir in the vanilla essence (extract), if used.

Return to the saucepan and bring to the boil, stirring. Cook gently for 1 minute. Use immediately, or cover with greaseproof (wax) paper to prevent a skin forming and allow to cool.
Makes about 600 ml/1 pint (2½ cups)

Caramel Coffee Sauce

Metric/Imperial
100 g/4 oz butter
100 g/4 oz soft brown sugar
1 tablespoon cornflour
150 ml/¼ pint milk
2 tablespoons coffee essence

American
8 tablespoons (1 stick) butter
⅔ cup light brown sugar
1 tablespoon cornstarch
⅔ cup milk
2 tablespoons coffee flavoring

Melt the butter in a saucepan and stir in the sugar and cornflour (cornstarch). Bring to the boil, stirring until the mixture begins to thicken, then remove from the heat and gradually stir in the milk. Add the coffee essence (flavoring). Return to the heat and cook, stirring, until thick again. Serve hot.
Serves 4–6

Apricot Sauce

Metric/Imperial
3 tablespoons apricot jam
250 ml/8 fl oz water
2 teaspoons arrowroot
lemon juice to taste
sugar to taste

American
3 tablespoons apricot jam
1 cup water
2 teaspoons arrowroot
lemon juice to taste
sugar to taste

Put the jam and water in a saucepan and bring to the boil, stirring. Dissolve the arrowroot in a little water and add to the pan. Simmer, stirring, until clear and thickened. Stir in lemon juice and sugar to taste.

Sieve (strain) the sauce before serving.
Serves 4

Sweet Lemon Sauce

Metric/Imperial
225 g/8 oz sugar
2 tablespoons cornflour or
 arrowroot
pinch of salt
120 ml/4 fl oz lemon juice
120 ml/4 fl oz water
50 g/2 oz butter
few drops of yellow food colouring
 (optional)

American
1 cup sugar
2 tablespoons cornstarch or
 arrowroot
pinch of salt
½ cup lemon juice
½ cup water
4 tablespoons butter
few drops of yellow food coloring
 (optional)

Put the sugar, cornflour (cornstarch) or arrowroot and salt in a saucepan and stir in the lemon juice and water. Bring to the boil, stirring to dissolve the sugar. Add the butter and simmer for 5 minutes or until the sauce becomes thickened and clear. Add a few drops of yellow food colouring, if liked. Serve hot.
Serves 4

Brandy Custard Sauce

Metric/Imperial
50 g/2 oz sugar
150 ml/¼ pint water
2 egg yolks
pinch of salt
2 tablespoons brandy
3 tablespoons whipped cream

American
¼ cup sugar
⅔ cup water
2 egg yolks
pinch of salt
2 tablespoons brandy
3 tablespoons whipped cream

Dissolve the sugar in the water, then bring to the boil. Simmer for 10 minutes.
    Beat together the egg yolks and salt, then gradually stir in the hot sugar syrup. Continue beating until thick and creamy. Fold in the brandy and whipped cream.
Serves 4

Custard Sauce

Metric/Imperial
2 eggs
300 ml/½ pint milk
1 tablespoon caster sugar
few drops of vanilla essence

American
2 eggs
1¼ cups milk
1 tablespoon sugar
few drops of vanilla extract

Beat the eggs in a bowl. Heat the milk to scalding point and pour onto the eggs. Strain the egg mixture into a heatproof bowl placed over a pan of simmering water or into a double boiler. Cook, stirring, until the sauce is thick and creamy. Stir in the sugar and vanilla. Serve hot or cold.
Serves 4

Melba Sauce

Metric/Imperial
225 g/8 oz raspberries
icing sugar to taste

American
½ lb raspberries
confectioners' sugar to taste

Rub the raspberries through a nylon sieve (strainer) to make a smooth sauce. Sweeten to taste.
    Fresh, canned or thawed frozen raspberries may be used.
Serves 4

Butterscotch Sauce

Metric/Imperial
25 g/1 oz butter
40 g/1½ oz soft brown sugar
4 tablespoons condensed milk
1 tablespoon golden syrup
150 ml/¼ pint hot milk

American
2 tablespoons butter
¼ cup light brown sugar
¼ cup condensed milk
1 tablespoon light corn syrup
⅔ cup hot milk

Put the butter, sugar, condensed milk and syrup in a saucepan and cook gently, stirring, until the mixture is a rich golden colour and pulls away from the side of the pan. Remove from the heat and gradually stir in the hot milk. Return to the heat and cook for 1 to 2 minutes.
Serves 4

Orange Sauce

Metric/Imperial
3½ teaspoons cornflour
pinch of salt
150 ml/¼ pint water
150 ml/¼ pint orange juice
1 teaspoon lemon juice
1 teaspoon grated orange rind
15 g/½ oz butter
1 tablespoon sugar (or more to taste)

American
3½ teaspoons cornstarch
pinch of salt
⅔ cup water
⅔ cup orange juice
1 teaspoon lemon juice
1 teaspoon grated orange rind
1 tablespoon butter
1 tablespoon sugar (or more to taste)

Mix together the cornflour (cornstarch), salt and 3 tablespoons of the water. Put the rest of the water in a saucepan with the orange and lemon juices, orange rind and butter. Bring to the boil. Stir a little of this hot liquid into the cornflour (cornstarch) mixture, then add to the pan. Simmer, stirring, until thickened. Add the sugar and stir until dissolved.
Serves 4

Chocolate Sauce 1

Metric/Imperial
50 g/2 oz plain dark chocolate,
    grated
2 tablespoons water
1 teaspoon cornflour
150 ml/¼ pint milk
1 teaspoon caster sugar
½ teaspoon vanilla essence
1 tablespoon single cream (optional)

American
⅓ cup semi-sweet chocolate
    chips
2 tablespoons water
1 teaspoon cornstarch
⅔ cup milk
1 teaspoon sugar
½ teaspoon vanilla extract
1 tablespoon light cream (optional)

Melt the chocolate gently with the water. Dissolve the cornflour (cornstarch) in the milk and add to the pan. Bring to the boil, stirring, and simmer for 5 minutes. Stir in the sugar and vanilla until dissolved, then add the cream if using.

If you prefer a thicker sauce, use only 5 tablespoons milk.
Serves 4

Chocolate Sauce 2

Metric/Imperial
75 g/3 oz caster sugar
75 g/3 oz soft brown sugar
75 g/3 oz cocoa powder
300 ml/½ pint milk
1 teaspoon vanilla essence
25 g/1 oz butter

American
6 tablespoons sugar
½ cup light brown sugar
¾ cup unsweetened cocoa
1¼ cups milk
1 teaspoon vanilla extract
2 tablespoons butter

Put all the ingredients in a saucepan and heat gently, stirring to dissolve the sugars. Bring to the boil and boil for 2 minutes. Serve hot or cold.
Serves 4–6

Apple and Raspberry Sauce

Metric/Imperial
500 g/1 lb cooking apples, peeled,
  cored and chopped
4 tablespoons raspberry jam
1 tablespoon water
sugar to taste

American
1 lb tart apples, peeled, cored and
  chopped
¼ cup raspberry jam
1 tablespoon water
sugar to taste

Put the apples, jam and water in a saucepan and cook gently until the apples
are pulpy. Strain the sauce and sweeten to taste. Serve hot.
Serves 4–6

Marshmallow Sauce

Metric/Imperial
100 g/4 oz marshmallows
2 tablespoons coffee essence
1 tablespoon sherry

American
¼ lb marshmallows
2 tablespoons coffee flavoring
1 tablespoon sherry

Put all the ingredients in a saucepan and heat gently, stirring, until the
marshmallows have melted and the sauce is smooth. Serve hot.
Serves 6

Vanilla Sauce

Metric/Imperial
2 tablespoons cornflour
300 ml/½ pint milk
2 tablespoons sugar
½–1 teaspoon vanilla essence

American
2 tablespoons cornstarch
1¼ cups milk
2 tablespoons sugar
½–1 teaspoon vanilla extract

Dissolve the cornflour (cornstarch) in the milk, then pour into a saucepan and
add the sugar. Heat, stirring, until the sauce has thickened. Stir in the vanilla
and serve.
Serves 4

Variation:
Rum Sauce: Substitute 1 to 2 tablespoons rum for the vanilla.

Honey Sauce

Metric/Imperial
1 teaspoon cornflour
150 ml/¼ pint water
2 tablespoons honey
1 teaspoon lemon juice

American
1 teaspoon cornstarch
⅔ cup water
2 tablespoons honey
1 teaspoon lemon juice

Dissolve the cornflour (cornstarch) in 1 tablespoon of the water. Put the rest of the water in a saucepan with the honey and lemon juice and bring to the boil. Stir in the cornflour (cornstarch) and simmer, stirring, until thickened.
Serves 4

Chocolate Rum Sauce

Metric/Imperial
175 g/6 oz plain chocolate, chopped
150 ml/¼ pint black coffee
1 tablespoon rum

American
1 cup semi-sweet chocolate chips
⅔ cup black coffee
1 tablespoon rum

Melt the chocolate gently with the coffee. When smooth, stir in the rum. Serve warm.
Serves 4

Syrup Cream Sauce

Metric/Imperial
50 g/2 oz butter
50 g/2 oz icing sugar, sifted
50 g/2 oz golden syrup
2 tablespoons milk
few drops of almond essence

American
4 tablespoons butter
½ cup confectioners' sugar, sifted
2½ tablespoons light corn syrup
2 tablespoons milk
few drops of almond extract

Cream together the butter and sugar until pale and fluffy. Beat in the syrup, milk and almond essence (extract). Chill until firm.
    Serve spoonfuls over hot baked or steamed puddings or baked apples.
Serves 4–6

Crème Chantilly

Metric/Imperial
6 tablespoons double cream
2 teaspoons caster sugar
½ teaspoon vanilla essence
1 egg white

American
6 tablespoons heavy cream
2 teaspoons sugar
½ teaspoon vanilla extract
1 egg white

Whip the cream with the sugar and vanilla until thick. Beat the egg white until stiff and fold into the cream.
Serves 4

Hard Sauce or Brandy Butter

Metric/Imperial
100 g/4 oz butter, preferably
  unsalted
350 g/12 oz icing sugar, sifted
1 tablespoon brandy (or more to
  taste)

American
8 tablespoons (1 stick) butter,
  preferably sweet
3 cups confectioners' sugar, sifted
1 tablespoon brandy (or more to
  taste)

Cream the butter until softened, then gradually beat in the sugar. Mix in the brandy. Chill until firm.
Serves 6–8

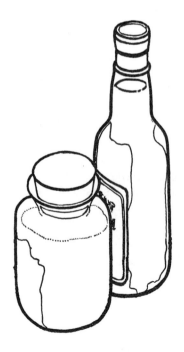

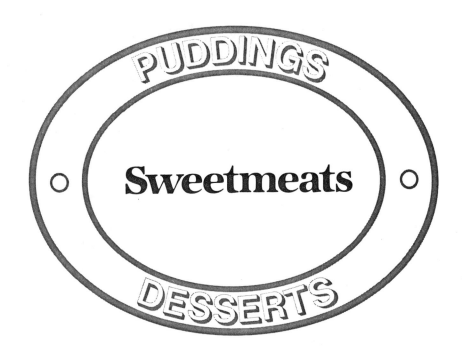

Fondants

Metric/Imperial	**American**
2 egg whites	*2 egg whites*
500 g/1 lb icing sugar, sifted	*4 cups confectioners' sugar, sifted*

Beat the egg whites lightly and gradually work in the sugar.

To make:
Peppermint Creams: Work a few drops of oil of peppermint or peppermint essence (mint flavoring) into some of the fondant. For a soft, creamy-like fondant, work in a little full cream evaporated milk. Knead the mixture well, then roll out and cut into small rounds. Leave to harden.

Assorted Fondants: Divide the fondant into three portions. Add a few drops of orange food colouring and orange juice to one portion; add raspberry essence (flavoring) and red food colouring to another portion; add almond essence (extract) and blue or purple food colouring to the third portion. Press into sweet (candy) moulds and leave to harden.

Cherry Fondants: Add chopped glacé (candied) cherries to the fondant and roll into small balls.

Continental Chocolate Squares

Metric/Imperial
75 g/3 oz butter
100 g/4 oz sugar
1 tablespoon cocoa powder
1 egg
½ teaspoon vanilla essence
225 g/8 oz digestive biscuits,
crushed
90 g/3½ oz desiccated coconut
50 g/2 oz walnuts, chopped
Icing:
100 g/4 oz butter
500 g/1 lb icing sugar, sifted
2 tablespoons custard powder
2 tablespoons hot water
1 tablespoon brandy (optional)
175 g/6 oz dark cooking chocolate

American
6 tablespoons butter
½ cup sugar
1 tablespoon unsweetened cocoa
1 egg
½ teaspoon vanilla extract
2 cups crushed graham crackers or
plain sweet cookies
1 cup shredded coconut
½ cup chopped walnuts
Frosting:
8 tablespoons (1 stick) butter
4 cups confectioners' sugar, sifted
2 tablespoons custard powder
2 tablespoons hot water
1 tablespoon brandy (optional)
1 cup semi-sweet chocolate chips

Melt the butter in a saucepan and stir in the sugar and cocoa. Remove from the heat and add the egg, vanilla, biscuit (cracker) crumbs, coconut and walnuts. Mix well.

Spread the mixture in a neat oblong about 1 cm/½ inch thick on a greased baking sheet and chill until set.

For the icing (frosting), melt the butter in a saucepan. Remove from the heat and add the sugar, custard powder, hot water and brandy, if using. Beat until smooth and creamy. Spread over the oblong and return to the refrigerator to set.

Melt the chocolate gently and spread over the icing (frosting). Chill until set.

About 20 minutes before serving, allow to soften at room temperature. Cut into 2.5 cm/1 inch squares.

Note: these will keep for 3 weeks in a covered container in the refrigerator.

Makes about 40–48

Stuffed Dates

Metric/Imperial
1 × 100 g/4 oz packet cream cheese
25 g/1 oz walnuts, chopped
75 g/3 oz ground almonds
75 g/3 oz sugar
1 egg yolk
few drops of vanilla essence
few drops of almond essence
1 teaspoon lemon juice
stoned dates
sifted icing sugar

American
½ cup cream cheese
¼ cup chopped walnuts
¾ cup ground almonds
6 tablespoons sugar
1 egg yolk
few drops of vanilla extract
few drops of almond extract
1 teaspoon lemon juice
pitted dates
sifted confectioners' sugar

Mix together the cream cheese, walnuts, almonds, sugar, egg yolk, flavourings and lemon juice. Use to stuff the dates, then roll them in icing (confectioners') sugar.

Cinnamon Balls

Metric/Imperial
2 egg whites
100 g/4 oz caster sugar
225 g/8 oz ground almonds
1 tablespoon ground cinnamon
sifted icing sugar

American
2 egg whites
½ cup sugar
2 cups ground almonds
1 tablespoon ground cinnamon
sifted confectioners' sugar

Beat the egg whites until stiff. Beat in half the sugar and continue beating for 1 minute, then fold in the rest of the sugar with the almonds and cinnamon.

Roll the mixture gently into small balls and arrange on greased baking sheets. Bake in a preheated moderately hot oven (200°C/400°F, Gas Mark 6) for 10 to 15 minutes. Coat the balls in icing (confectioners') sugar while still warm, then allow to cool.
Makes about 24

Almond Cherries

Metric/Imperial	American
100 g/4 oz ground almonds	1 cup ground almonds
50 g/2 oz caster sugar	¼ cup sugar
50 g/2 oz icing sugar, sifted	½ cup confectioners' sugar, sifted
½ teaspoon lemon juice	½ teaspoon lemon juice
1 egg yolk	1 egg yolk
fresh cherries, stoned	fresh cherries, pitted
To finish:	**To finish:**
sifted icing sugar	sifted confectioners' sugar
finely grated chocolate	finely grated chocolate

Mix together the almonds, sugars, lemon juice and egg yolk and knead well. Take a small piece of the mixture, about the size of a walnut, and roll it into a ball. Flatten it, then mould it around a cherry. Roll in icing (confectioners') sugar and grated chocolate.

Repeat with the remaining almond mixture.

Truffles

Metric/Imperial	American
100 g/4 oz plain or bitter eating chocolate, broken into pieces	⅔ cup semi-sweet chocolate chips
1 tablespoon milk	1 tablespoon milk
1 tablespoon golden syrup	1 tablespoon light corn syrup
100 g/4 oz unsalted butter	8 tablespoons (1 stick) sweet butter
100 g/4 oz icing sugar, sifted	1 cup confectioners' sugar, sifted
2 teaspoons instant coffee powder	2 teaspoons instant coffee powder
50 g/2 oz cocoa powder	½ cup unsweetened cocoa

Put the chocolate, milk and syrup in a saucepan and heat gently until the chocolate has melted. Remove from the heat.

Beat together the butter, sugar, coffee powder and 25 g/1 oz (¼ cup) of the cocoa powder. Gradually beat in the chocolate mixture and continue beating until the mixture is pale and fluffy. Chill for 1 hour.

Roll the chocolate mixture into walnut-sized balls and coat in the remaining cocoa powder.

Chocolate Nougat

Metric/Imperial
120 ml/4 fl oz honey
225 g/8 oz sugar
2 egg whites
175 g/6 oz cocoa powder
3–4 tablespoons water
500 g/1 lb hazelnuts, chopped and
  toasted

American
½ cup honey
1 cup sugar
2 egg whites
1½ cups unsweetened cocoa
3–4 tablespoons water
4 cups chopped toasted
  hazelnuts

Put the honey and sugar in a saucepan and stir to dissolve the sugar. Heat until the mixture begins to colour. Remove from the heat.

Beat the egg whites until stiff and add to the honey mixture. Mix the cocoa with the water until smooth, then add to the honey mixture with the nuts. Mix well together.

Pour into a 25 × 20 cm/10 × 8 inch tin lined with rice paper. Leave to set. Cut into pieces for serving.

Fruit Balls

Metric/Imperial
100 g/4 oz stoned dates
100 g/4 oz raisins
100 g/4 oz stoned prunes
1 pear, peeled and cored
100 g/4 oz mixed nuts, chopped
pinch of ground cinnamon
2 teaspoons orange juice
1 tablespoon lemon juice
To finish:
chopped nuts, desiccated coconut or
  grated chocolate
glacé cherries
candied angelica

American
⅔ cup pitted dates
⅔ cup raisins
⅔ cup pitted prunes
1 pear, peeled and cored
1 cup chopped mixed nuts
pinch of ground cinnamon
2 teaspoons orange juice
1 tablespoon lemon juice
To finish:
chopped nuts, shredded coconut or
  grated chocolate
candied cherries
candied angelica

Mince (grind) together the dates, raisins, prunes, pear and nuts. Mix in the cinnamon and fruit juices, then roll the mixture into small balls. Coat in chopped nuts, coconut or grated chocolate. Decorate with glacé (candied) cherries and angelica. Put into paper cases and leave to dry.

Liqueur Rum Truffles

Metric/Imperial	American
75 g/3 oz cake crumbs	1½ cups cake crumbs
75 g/3 oz caster sugar	6 tablespoons sugar
75 g/3 oz ground almonds	¾ cup ground almonds
1 teaspoon cocoa powder	1 teaspoon unsweetened cocoa
1 tablespoon grated dark chocolate	1 tablespoon grated dark chocolate
1 egg yolk	1 egg yolk
1 tablespoon liqueur	1 tablespoon liqueur
chocolate vermicelli	chocolate sprinkles

Mix together the cake crumbs, sugar, almonds, cocoa and chocolate. Add the egg yolk and liqueur and mix to a smooth paste. Divide into 18 to 24 portions and roll into balls. Coat in chocolate vermicelli (sprinkles) and place in paper cases. Chill until firm.
Makes 18–24

Tayglech

Metric/Imperial	American
50 g/2 oz plain flour	½ cup all-purpose flour
pinch of salt	pinch of salt
½ teaspoon ground ginger	½ teaspoon ground ginger
1 egg	1 egg
225 g/8 oz honey	⅔ cup honey
chopped nuts or desiccated coconut to finish	chopped nuts or shredded coconut to finish

Sift the flour, salt and ginger into a bowl. Add the egg and mix to a dough. Roll into pencil thin ropes with floured hands, then cut into 6 mm/¼ inch pieces.

Bring the honey to the boil in a saucepan. Drop in the dough pieces, a few at a time, and simmer for about 15 minutes or until they are a rich brown. Pour onto a dampened board and flatten the tayglech with a wet spoon. Sprinkle with the nuts or coconut and cut into squares when cool.

Marzipan and Raisin Truffles

Metric/Imperial
225 g/8 oz plain chocolate
175 g/6 oz raisins
1 tablespoon rum
225 g/8 oz bought marzipan
1 teaspoon coffee essence
chocolate vermicelli

American
1⅓ cups semi-sweet chocolate chips
1 cup raisins
1 tablespoon rum
½ lb bought marzipan
1 teaspoon coffee flavoring
chocolate sprinkles

Melt half the chocolate gently in a double boiler. Stir in the raisins and rum. Cool until firm enough to shape, then roll into small balls.

Knead the marzipan until pliable and work in the coffee essence (flavoring). Roll out the marzipan to about 5 mm/¼ inch thick and cut into rounds large enough to enclose the chocolate and raisin balls. Wrap the marzipan around the balls and round gently.

Melt the remaining chocolate in the double boiler. Dip in the balls to coat on all sides, then coat them with chocolate vermicelli (sprinkles). Leave to cool and set.

Makes about 24

Caramelled Grapes

Metric/Imperial
175 g/6 oz sugar
6 tablespoons water
small bunches of seedless grapes

American
¾ cup sugar
6 tablespoons water
small bunches of seedless grapes

Put the sugar and water in a saucepan and stir to dissolve the sugar. Bring to the boil and boil until the syrup is pale golden. Dip the grapes into the syrup, then allow them to harden. Eat the same day.

Index